Community Education
and Crime Prevention

Community Education and Crime Prevention

Confronting Foreground and Background Causes of Criminal Behavior

CAROLYN SIEMENS WARD

Bergin & Garvey
Westport, Connecticut • London

Library of Congress Cataloging-in-Publication Data

Ward, Carolyn Siemens, 1942–
    Community education and crime prevention : confronting foreground
and background causes of criminal behavior / Carolyn Siemens Ward.
      p.   cm.
    Includes bibliographical references and index.
    ISBN 0–89789–574–6 (alk. paper)
    1. Crime prevention—United States. 2. Crime prevention—United
States—Citizen participation. 3. Crime prevention—Missouri—Saint
Louis—Case studies. 4. Community education—United States.
5. Community education—Missouri—Saint Louis—Case studies.
6. Education and crime—United States. I. Title.
HV7431.W36   1998
364.4—dc21   98–9537

British Library Cataloguing in Publication Data is available.

Library of Congress Catalog Card Number: 98–9537
ISBN: 0–89789–574–6

First published in 1998

Bergin & Garvey, 88 Post Road West, Westport, CT 06881
An imprint of Greenwood Publishing Group, Inc.

Printed in the United States of America

The paper used in this book complies with the
Permanent Paper Standard issued by the National
Information Standards Organization (Z39.48–1984).

10 9 8 7 6 5 4 3 2 1

Each person, withdrawn into himself, behaves as though he is a stranger to the destiny of all the others. His children and his good friends constitute for him the whole of the human species. As for his transactions with his fellow citizens, he may mix among them, but he sees them not; he touches them, but does not feel them; he exists only in himself and for himself alone. And if on these terms there remains in his mind a sense of family, there no longer remains a sense of society.

Alexis deToqueville

Contents

x   **Contents**

Illustrations

Acknowledgments

Special thanks to the Hyde Park community—its members, its service providers, its residents—for sharing your wisdom, creativity, dreams, and frustrations with me. Your contributions have not only enriched my work but my life as well. Thanks to Kathy Schwab, Kathy Keeser, Frank Muehlheausler, and John Windom for reading sections of this work for accuracy. I would also like to acknowledge Lainie Smith for either designing or refining graphics for the following figures: "Crime and Punishment" in chapter 1, "Friedens Haus Model" in chapter 8, and "Community Education: Addressing Background and Foreground Causes of Criminal Behavior" in chapter 20; and Eric Baumer for his design of Figures 2–4, "Monthly Aggravated Assault Frequencies," "Monthly Burglary Frequencies," and "Monthly Robbery Frequencies" in chapter 5.

Appreciation also goes to Richard Wright for consistent support during the time of this study and for guidance in the field of criminology, to John Henschke for prompting me to define "community education" in precise terms, and to the National Community Education Association for reading my first drafts and encouraging my contributions to the discipline. To my husband—best friend, first editor, paste-up artist—who empathized with my anxieties, joys, and despairs and reassured and enheartened me through all, mere words are inadequate to express my gratitude and love. Finally, I thank Heather—you always bring a smile to my face.

Introduction

John Clark, a black St. Louis resident and owner of a building where a baby was killed during a suspected gang related feud remarked, "life is cheap . . . there's no more caring left" (Smith and Gillerman, 1992: 1A). These words express the feelings of many of our nation's citizens who, while recognizing progress in certain arenas such as race relations and while recognizing that we are no longer the society we once were, are also very much aware that we are not the society we had hoped to become. Our society remains the most violent yet the most punitive of western industrialized nations (Currie, 1985; Federal Bureau of Investigation, 1994).

While the population has increased 41 percent since 1960, the number of violent crimes (murders, rapes, robberies, and aggravated assaults) has increased more than 550 percent (Federal Bureau of Investigation, 1994). Even though killings by adults age twenty-five years or older have fallen steadily over the last fifteen years, the homicide rates for people twenty-four years old or younger have risen sharply since the 1960s until a recent, slight downturn. Among those aged fourteen to seventeen, the rate tripled between 1984 and 1993 (Office of Juvenile Justice and Delinquency Prevention, 1994). Between 1960 and 1992 the violent crime rate quintupled, the teen suicide rate tripled, the delinquency rate more than doubled (Meyers, 1992), and murder became the leading cause of death for young black males between the ages of fifteen and thirty (Federal Bureau of Investigation, 1994). All of this while our nation disproportionately spent more money to build prisons and improve the criminal justice system, and mandated longer prison terms in harsher surroundings than any other western, industrialized nation. As one author notes: "We have become a country in which it is possible to be sentenced to a year behind bars for stealing six dollars worth of meat from a supermarket, but we are still by far the most dangerous society in the developed world" (Currie, 1985: 12).

On a lighter note, the FBI offers encouraging reports about reduced crime rates across the United States, especially in larger cities. In St. Louis, for example, crime dropped in 1997 for the third straight year. As cited in the *Congressional Quarterly* (1997), the FBI's index of seven serious crimes more than doubled from 1960 to 1970 when today's middle-aged baby boomers were in their young crime-prone years. The rise slowed after the 1970s, and by 1992 the crime rate began dropping. Criminologists and sociologists cite various and complex reasons for this decline. Included among them are:

- A vigorous economy
- A greater number of police and more effective policing
- A decline in numbers of males in crime-prone years (now at the lowest point since 1980)
- Innovative gun control laws
- Tougher penalties, including increased incarceration of young criminals at a rate that has almost doubled over the last ten years
- High technology used for enhanced communication, pinpointing high crime areas, and tracking criminals

These reasons pertain to both background (social malaise and demographics) and foreground causes (opportunity) of criminal behavior. It must be noted, however, that the perception of the United States as a violent and dangerous society has not diminished (*Congressional Quarterly*, 1997). Some sociologists/criminologists believe that news coverage and politicians are major factors causing this perception. Nevertheless, James Alan Fox, professor at Northeastern University's College of Criminal Justice in Boston, cautions that when the United States is faced with the baby boomer "echo" (children of baby boomers), we are in for another upsurge in criminal behavior (*Congressional Quarterly*, 1997). Professor Fox's caution emphasizes that the search must be for effective, long-term approaches to solving our crime problem.

COMPREHENSIVE CRIME PREVENTION

Scholars in various disciplines are recommending comprehensive measures to solving multiple societal as well as individual problems. Since violent crime in the United States is correlated to multiple conditions of community destabilization and deterioration due to high unemployment and transitions to large black populations, large populations of low socioeconomic status, female-headed households, and youth (Wilson, 1987; Currie, 1985) criminologist are also looking for comprehensive measures. Lawrence Sherman, chairman of the criminology department at the University of Maryland-College Park maintains, "The argument that it's a matter of root causes and has nothing to do with policing is as silly as saying it's a matter of sanctions and has nothing to do with families and school and communities. We've got to work on both"

(*Congressional Quarterly*, 1997). The problem is that the philosophy of "community education" has been overlooked as a theory and process that offers a comprehensive as well as feasible approach to addressing criminal behavior in the United States.

The term "community education" as used in this book, is a philosophy, process, and program comprised of three overriding and interrelated elements: community empowerment, community problem-solving, and the effort to involve all community members in the pursuit of lifelong learning. These elements and their sub-elements have been modeled in Flint, Michigan, beginning in 1935 and are delineated in the goals of the National Community Education Association.

However, several questions need to be answered. Is community education working anywhere to help solve multiple societal problems? If not, why not? If so, why so? And if the problems of our cities lead to acts of violent criminal behavior (disproportionately, more violent crime is committed in urban areas), then is it reasonable to assume that potential solutions to social malaise that is magnified in urban settings are also potential solutions for crime prevention?

Criminology suffers from the same theory-practice disconnectedness as do other disciplines. Although criminologists know of the many variables correlated with criminal behavior, connecting these variables to crime prevention and deterrence policies remains elusive. Scott Decker and colleagues at the University of Missouri-St. Louis write: "Researchers are fond of saying that we need more information before we can act. In our view, we know enough about homicide to take meaningful and prudent first steps" (1991: xii and xiii). The authors of this homicide report go on to say that there needs to be a comprehensive and community-wide approach to homicide prevention. Many other criminologists support this view (Currie, 1985; Wilson, 1987; Hope and Shaw, 1988; Rosenbaum, 1988; Titus, 1984; and Sherman, 1997).

Although noted criminologists are embracing the idea of a comprehensive, community-wide approach to the prevention of violent crime, practitioners in other disciplines have not reinforced this concept. There needs to be research conducted in the fields of education that will merge with further research of comprehensive approaches to crime prevention called for by criminologists.

Specifically, practitioners in the field of community education have not contributed significantly to this research; therefore, the community education philosophy that offers a comprehensive approach to crime prevention is not recognized as a workable and effective means to address the comparatively high rate of crime in the United States. Community education programs already in place across the nation can be expanded, refined, and custom fit to meet the calls coming from the White House, businesses, and communities. National leaders do not have to start from scratch; therefore, money can be saved.

The United States is a nation of cities in that 83 percent of its people live on 2 percent of the land. Yet the political leadership of our nation has failed to institute effective public policies to address ever expanding and intensifying urban problems. Many inner-city neighborhoods have deteriorated aesthetically, socially, educationally, and economically to the point where a substantial number of residents see no hope for a better life. Their life savings have been invested in property that has little resale value, and/or resources are lacking for mobility to healthier environments. They feel trapped.

The Hyde Park neighborhood in St. Louis is comprised of many such residents. The community lays claim to several crime inducing variables such as population loss resulting in a high number of boarded-up housing units, population shift resulting in a higher percentage of black population, a high rate of unemployment, a very low per capita income and a high percentage of citizens living below the poverty line, and a high percentage of female-headed households (United States Department of the Census, 1990). The St. Louis Police Information Service (1993) reports that the Hyde Park area has one of the highest rates of reported drug sales and high rates of homicide, robbery, aggravated assault, arson, and burglary.

Conversely, as the narrative and data explain in Part II of this book, a comprehensive, multi-systems model of community education was found to be present in the Hyde Park neighborhood. The Friedens Haus (House of Peace) coalition comprised of a school, church, private social service agency, and the Hyde Park community and its many linkages to external services was determined to be the core of a comprehensive approach to alleviating criminal behavior. The plan exhibited high levels of all elements and sub-elements of a viable community education program. These elements and sub-elements are:

Community empowerment
 Political awareness and action
 Inclusiveness
 Citizen councils
 Leadership development
Community problem-solving
 Community organization
 Interagency cooperation
 Assessing, planning, and evaluating
 Volunteerism
The effort to involve everyone in the pursuit of lifelong learning
 Use of community resources and the community as a classroom
 Maximum use of school facilities
 Accessibility (facilities, programs, and services)
 Programs for all
 Parent and community involvement in school governance

These indices as well as the required leadership-style for effective community education programs are explained, discussed, and then assessed in terms of their presence and extent of presence within the Hyde Park neighborhood. Housing and economic problems and the community's efforts to solve them are examined at length.

Part I of the book covers preventive measures for the *foreground* causes of criminal behavior such as opportunity while Part II covers preventive measures for the *background* causes of criminal behavior such as social malaise. First, chapter 1 explores the possible underlying causes of criminal behavior, especially pertaining to the United States, and makes a good case for a comprehensive approach to crime prevention. It is the author's contention that a fully and successfully implemented community education program offers such a comprehensive approach—a thesis explored in the following chapter, which focuses on "block watch" and other community crime prevention measures. Chapters 3, 4, and 5 are devoted to the crime problem in Hyde Park and how community members attempted to solve this problem, including mobile patrol efforts and improving police/community relations. The community oriented problem-solving (COPS) philosophy of policing is examined, and a comparison is made between and among demographically similar neighborhoods concerning criminal behavior. It was found that Hyde Park crime prevention efforts made a positive difference in at least one crime category—robbery.

METHODOLOGY

Most information and data included in this book were gathered over a one year period. Research was conducted implementing a case study approach by immersion into the Hyde Park community while using multiple methods to collect and analyze data. This involved participating in and observing Hyde Park activities and community and organizational meetings (approximately 132); becoming a member of the Hyde Park Safety Committee; riding biweekly in the Hyde Park Mobile Patrol; and becoming a member of a community education endeavor involving the local elementary school, a local church, a private social service agency, and additional Hyde Park neighborhood organizations. Quantitative data were collected from the St. Louis Metropolitan Police Information Service (1993) and St. Louis Public School System records concerning Clay Elementary located in Hyde Park; public archival records such as meeting minutes, city and Hyde Park organizational records and reports, and articles written by *St. Louis Post-Dispatch* reporters; private archival records such as letters, video tapes, and photographs; physical traces; artifacts; and direct-response data garnered from six focus group sessions, sixteen formal interviews, and multiple informal interviews conducted on an almost daily basis. Sharon Merriam (1988) maintains that the use of triangulation in case studies alleviates the problem of maintaining external and internal validity and reliability. This type of analysis (participant-observation, direct response data, and document examination), buttressed by the investigator's lifetime participation in and observation of St. Louis community life, provides high levels of validity and reliability.

Quantitative monthly indicators of crime spanning a six-year period (1988 through 1993) in the categories of robbery, aggravated assault, and burglary were collected from the St. Louis Police Information Service for the Hyde Park area and seven demographically similar neighborhoods. General population indicators of social and economic factors were collected from 1990 National Census Bureau data (United States Department of the Census, 1990). Average monthly reported crimes per 10,000 were compared among the eight neighborhoods. These numbers were then compared to St. Louis and U.S. crime rates in the same categories. A descriptive analysis was made of demographic variables and their possible impact on criminal behavior in the eight selected neighborhoods.

Crime data in the same categories and for the same years were also observed via trend analyses, comparing four north side St. Louis neighborhoods (including Hyde Park) taken from the eight neighborhoods previously examined. Monthly (seventy-two months) reported crime frequencies were charted before and during crime prevention initiatives in the Hyde Park neighborhood. Finally, differences between yearly mean crime rates of Hyde Park and an adjacent neighborhood (Old North St. Louis) were determined for each of the three crime categories during the same time period. *t-tests* for independent samples were performed to determine if there were positive effects of Hyde Park comprehensive crime prevention efforts on numbers of reported crimes in the Hyde Park neighborhood and possible displacement of crime to a contiguous neighborhood. The three methods of analyses—demographically descriptive and crime rate comparisons of eight neighborhoods, crime-frequency trend analyses of four of these neighborhoods that are proximately located (including Hyde Park), and *t-tests* performed of yearly mean crime rates between Hyde Park and a bordering neighborhood—provide gradually intensifying and mutually supportive observations and analyses to determine possible effects of Hyde Park community crime prevention activities. Finally, immersion into community life and a multi-methods approach to data collection and analyses, as described earlier, provide affirmation that there were no additional contributing crime prevention variables present in the Hyde Park neighborhood during the six-year period of concern.

Limitations of correlating community education practices with crime deterrence are acknowledged. Possible effects of implemented community education principles on crime in the Hyde Park neighborhood can only be examined with the intent of encouraging longitudinal studies of such a relationship. This will be a task to accomplish after such problem-solving processes that address entrenched deteriorating social conditions have been in place over time. Also, this work relies on crime data reported by the St. Louis Metropolitan Police Department rather than on more valid victimization or self-report crime data because the latter were not available before the initiation of the community problem-solving collaborations of concern. Additionally, it must be noted that reported crimes may increase as a "result of" rather than "in spite of" block watch programs implemented within communities because of heightened awareness of criminal acts and an organized effort to report criminal behavior.

These are added reasons for the necessity of future longitudinal study-approaches to the concerns of this work.

The book gives the reader an in-depth look at a slice of community life within one city (St. Louis) and one inner-city neighborhood (Hyde Park) during a one-year period. The number and make-up of Hyde Park's organizations, organizational members, service providers, and residents may have altered since that time. Where appropriate, the reader is provided with updated information.

Finally, it is my intent to share with the reader the wisdom emanating from Hyde Park community members. This wisdom was derived from numerous informal and formal, tape recorded conversations and by observing and participating in Hyde Park community life. Although analytical comments are included here and there, the reader is often required to analyze the conversations while, at the same time, enjoying the spontaneity of the "give and take." Much of the knowledge is cleverly stated and "to-the-point" by Hyde Park residents and service providers; there is not much room for improvement or elaboration. In short, you will find that the most effective teachers of inner-city community life and those who are experts in knowing what can be done to solve neighborhood problems as well as how to go about solving them, are those who live and work in the neighborhood.

Part I

Confronting Foreground
Causes of Criminal Behavior

Chapter 1

A Theory of Crime Causation

INTRODUCTION

While one may assume that practice is connected to theory, educators, for example, know this is not always the case and may, in fact, more often than not be an aberration. U. S. crime prevention policies suffer from the same theory-practice disconnectedness. James Q. Wilson (1985) asserts that this was especially true during the liberal, Great Society years when social scientists reached conclusions concerning social theories of crime causation but were not able to develop concrete, implementable policies connected to these theories. The result tended to be disjointed, hit and miss, and expensive policies. Conversely, some criminologists maintain that there *were* effective social programs emerging from this era that addressed criminal behavior, but they were not kept in place long enough to evaluate properly (Wilson, 1987; Currie, 1985).

Conservative governmental policies, on the other hand, were very much connected to the conservative perspective of crime causation. This conservative perspective viewed criminals as, for the most part, making rational decisions as to the cost and benefit of their criminal behavior. If there were underlying causes of poor family conditions, genetics, human nature, and the American cultural influence of the market place, decaying moral values, the "do your own thing" mentality, and the desire for self-expression, there was little that could be done about these issues. The conservative answer, therefore, was to address the cost and benefit theory by strengthening the punishment component of crime prevention, because this was easier to do and would, at least, marginally alleviate the crime problem through deterrence and incapacitation (Currie, 1985; Wilson, 1985). The following discussion attempts to connect policy to both liberal and conservative views of crime causation and to determine if there are theories of crime causation that are unique to the United States.

CRIME CAUSATION AS GENETICS AND HUMAN NATURE

It is reasonable to assume that one's view of humans as basically "evil" or basically "good" would affect one's practices in dealing with human beings. Furthermore, it would make a difference if one thought that little could be done environmentally to help or hinder an individual or that one's environment had a great deal to do with individual behavior. The first perspective would call for an after-the-fact punishment and incapacitation policy for crime prevention, while the latter would call for the earliest possible intervening measures to alleviate negative environmental influences, influences that could contribute to one's susceptibility to criminal behavior.

Relatively recent research in the field of behavioral studies focused on identifying protective factors as well as risk factors in predictions of psychopathology based on a child's at-risk status (Bernard, 1987). Researchers in this field have found that babies with a "sunny" disposition are more likely to be resilient individuals even when they have experienced abuse and stress (Werner and Smith, 1982). However, researchers at Washington University in St. Louis have found that the entire picture is very complex and that behavioral disorders are probably caused by interacting genes that are, in turn, affected by the environment (O'Connor, 1997).

There is also recent interest among multiple disciplines to reexamine the role that genetics play in criminal behavior. A three-day conference organized by the University of Maryland was held at the private Aspen Institute in Queenstown, Maryland in September 1995 to discuss ethical implications of research seeking a genetic basis for violence, and to examine screening possibilities for genetic markers indicating criminal tendencies. Since more crime is disproportionately committed by the black population in our nation, the implications of such genetic research may indeed be very worrisome. One of the conference participants, Dr. Alvin F. Poussaint, a Harvard professor of psychiatry and a black civil rights activist states, "There's a history going way back to slavery of white Americans and Europeans saying that blacks are in some way inferior genetically. . . . There's such a strong chance of misuse that we have to be extremely cautious" (*St. Louis Post-Dispatch*, 1995: 13B).

Added to this concern, what are the implications of resiliency, risk factors, and genetic research except for screenings and intensive therapy for those children who possess less than a "sunny" disposition or a less than desirable genetic make-up? Another University of Maryland conference participant, Garland Allen, a historian of science at Washington University in St. Louis, asserts, "There's no technology for doing gene therapy—that is, replacing the defective gene. That's pie in the sky. So right now, the only thing you can do is say, 'Well, we'll drug people. We'll give them drugs' " (*St. Louis Post-Dispatch*, 1995: 13B). Disagreeing somewhat, Alan Templeton maintains that the complex causes of disorder development probably mean treatment by some combination of drugs, psychotherapy, and social interventions. "What it means," says Templeton, "is that we have to treat disorders much more individually" (O'Connor, 1997: 14). Richard Todd, a professor of psychiatry at Washington University, concurs, "Knowing the genetic elements will help us to identify environmental elements and improve both medical and nonmedical interventions" (O'Connor, 1997: 11 and 12). Garland Allen comes back with the point that even if genes can be shown to contribute something to behavioral traits, they are so *entangled* with environmental factors that there is no way to separate the threads (O'Connor, 1997).

Governmental advisors during the Reagan and Bush administrations concluded that the underlying genetic and social problems that may be contributing factors to criminal behavior were too difficult to alleviate by governmental policies. The Reagan administration's Task Force on Violent Crime wrote, "We are not convinced that a government, by the invention of new programs or the management of existing institutions, can by itself recreate those familial and neighborhood conditions, those social opportunities, and those personal values that in all likelihood are the prerequisites of tranquil communities" (as cited in Currie, 1985: 10). Although containing merit, this line of thought was used as an *excuse* to lessen governmental responsibility for supportive social systems.

On the other hand, many behavioral scientists and sociologists would encourage governmental intervention to aid in developing supportive social systems for the family, schools, and community. Researchers such as Rutter, Garmezy, Werner, and the aforementioned from Washington University assert that human development is a dynamic process with personality factors and environmental factors interacting. Finally, James S. Coleman advocates the necessity of building linkages between individuals, families, schools, and communities (Bernard, 1987).

Whatever conclusion is reached in the debate concerning genetics and human nature, it would be presumptuous to assume that the human nature of Americans is different, or criminal-prone genes of Americans are more prevalent than of other populations. No matter what one thinks about genetic makeup and human nature linkages to criminal behavior, these issues do not present unique problems for the United States.

CRIME CAUSATION AS RATIONALIZATION
OF COST AND BENEFIT

The idea that criminals weigh the costs and benefits of criminal acts before committing crimes is based on the assumption that most criminals exercise rational judgment concerning their criminal activities. Will the prize be worth the risk?

Policy implications for this theory of crime causation could be of two types—increase the costs or lessen the benefits. If the benefits are lessened, one could argue that if more and better jobs are available, there would be less incentive for people to turn to crime. Also, if fewer goods are available to steal, the lure would not be so great. The first idea demands long-term solutions and changes of economic and social policy. The second idea would seem to indicate educating the public to lessen its display of wealth.

If the costs are raised to deter crime, the results would be the same crime prevention policies that have recently been advocated and supported by our government: longer prison terms, additional prisons, harsher imprisonment, expansion of the death penalty, improved policing capabilities, additional patrol officers, expanded court capabilities and other components of the criminal justice system, and "block watch" programs to enhance crime detection and protection of property. As indicated earlier, an emphasis on these reactive measures has not worked even though these policies have been implemented with more determination and money than any other social program dealing with crime prevention. Based on data from the United States Department of Justice, the National Criminal Justice Commission in *The Real War on Crime* reports that from 1980 through 1994, prison and jail populations have increased 212.7 percent. The Commission reports: "The increase in the prison population did not reduce crime, nor did it make Americans feel safer. . . . Compared to other countries, this is by far the highest rate of incarceration relative to population in the Western world" (1996: 33). (See Figure 1.1.)

The cost and benefit theory also overlooks research findings that show most criminals are not very rational (Katz, 1988; Cromwell et al., 1991). Many criminal acts are committed because of the thrill experienced; because of the "group" phenomena, especially among adolescents; because of humiliation which has turned into rage (Katz, 1988); and because of a sense of alienation as well as other reasons.

For example, Richard Wright and Scott Decker (1994) concede that the rationale exhibited by burglars is "bounded"—not taking into account all available information before acting. Burglars exhibit some rational choice, but there is more of a "general flow of action emanating from and shaped by their involvement with street culture" (205). Interviews with 105 active burglars revealed the following reasons for their criminal activities: boredom; frustration and failure at legitimate activities like work or school; a way to demonstrate personal competence; the spontaneity of the activity; the ability to be his/her own boss; to keep the party going (street life); and securing money to purchase clothes, drugs, and cars. Overall, the burglaries were not planned except for target selection, and this was done most often on a casual, ad hoc basis.

Finally, one could argue that rational choice as a cause of criminal behavior may be unique to the United States if one believes that criminals have less chance of being apprehended and punished than in other nations or that the United States is less wealthy. This is not the case. In fact, the United States is the most punitive and boasts the highest standard of living of all industrialized societies. We do display our material wealth, and many would say in a most flamboyant manner, and we do tend to accept domestic violence and punitive

Figure 1.1

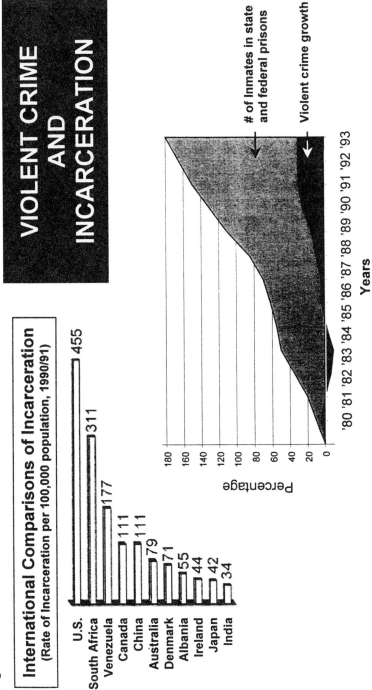

VIOLENT CRIME AND INCARCERATION

International Comparisons of Incarceration
(Rate of Incarceration per 100,000 population, 1990/91)

U.S.	455
South Africa	311
Venezuela	177
Canada	111
China	111
Australia	79
Denmark	71
Albania	55
Ireland	44
Japan	42
India	34

# of Inmates in state and federal prisons

Violent crime growth

Percentage: 180 160 140 120 100 80 60 40 20 0

'80 '81 '82 '83 '84 '85 '86 '87 '88 '89 '90 '91 '92 '93

Years

Source: FBI (1994.) Bureau of Justice Statistics, *The Sentencing Project.*
Graphic by Lainie Smith

discipline practices in raising our children. These last factors may be unique to the United States in their prevalence as compared to other industrialized nations (Currie, 1985).

CRIME CAUSATION AS DETERIORATING FAMILY CONDITIONS

James Q. Wilson (1985) concedes that deteriorating family conditions probably *do* have an influence on criminal behavior, but that there is no governmental policy that could effectively deal with the problems of families other than removing a child from the family environment and/or intensive counseling. These would not be acceptable to our society as long-term and general governmental policies.

It is worth noting that only 10 percent of American families conform to the traditional, nuclear model of a bread-winning father, stay-at-home mother, and their children. The percent is lower for the black family in the United States (United States Department of the Census, 1990). Moreover, many children are left unsupervised for long periods of time on a daily basis. Recent studies found that the time periods most teens get into trouble (pregnancy, criminal activity) are during workdays in the mid-afternoon. "There are at least five million children whose parents admit they are in the euphemism of euphemisms—self-care" (Goodman, 1997).

Moreover, the data reveal that family problems are worse for America's black population. In *The Negro Family* (1965), Daniel Patrick Moynihan wrote of the breakdown of the American black family, "A community that allows a large number of young men to grow up in broken families, dominated by women, never acquiring any stable relationship to male authority, never acquiring any set of rational expectations about the future—that community asks for and gets chaos." This report was decried by conservatives, liberals, and many black leaders. The latter disputed the report's unflattering depiction of the black family by asserting the strengths of the black experience and the extended family from which to draw positive black male role models. They emphasized the resilience of the black family in the face of poor economic opportunities and racial inequality (Wilson, 1987). Additionally, many liberals were afraid of being labeled "racist" if they continued to support the views expressed by Moynihan that the conditions of many underclass black families of female-headed households, children born out of wedlock, joblessness, and dependency upon welfare bode ill for America's future, even though Moynihan laid the blame at the feet of racial and economic inequality (Wilson, 1987).

The circumstances that we find ourselves in today support Daniel Moynihan's prognosis. The data for black families have continuously worsened. Almost 68 percent of black babies are born out of wedlock as compared to 20 percent of white babies; the black unemployment rate is double that of whites; while the U.S. black population is now 13 percent, blacks account for 61.2 percent of all arrests for robbery and over 50 percent of all violent crime; and blacks make up

45.3 percent of the prison population compared to 23 percent in 1930 (Litonjua and Hacker, 1992). Finally, female-headed households in the black population were 18 percent in 1940 and are now above 50 percent, and 40 percent of black children live in poverty (Wilson, 1987).

St. Louis, ranking second among U.S. cities for the rate of violent crime in 1994 and claiming the distinction of being the tenth most segregated city in the nation, is an intensified example of the same deteriorating statistics. Blacks comprise 47.5 percent of the population but represent 88 percent of murder victims and homeless families. The unemployment rate for blacks is 17 percent compared to less than 5 percent for whites, the infant mortality rate is 16.7 percent as compared to 5 percent for whites, and 84.4 percent of black children are born out of wedlock as compared to 28.8 percent of white children (United States Department of the Census, 1990). (See Figures 1.2 and 1.3.)

William Wilson (1987) makes the connection between the disintegration of the black family to the declining economic status of black men. Because the availability of marriageable black men is declining due to incarceration, mortality, and joblessness more black women stay single longer, never marry, or divorce and remain single than do white women. This accounts for more female-headed households, more children born out of wedlock, and more welfare dependency in the black population. He maintains that the problem of joblessness should be a top priority in solving the plight of the "truly disadvantaged" in our inner cities.

Other solutions would include more support for families, such as child care for working mothers, pre-school programs such as Head Start, flexible leave policies and work hours in the workplace, and programs designed to keep teen mothers in school. The industrialized nations that have the lowest dependency on public assistance are those nations with the greatest social support programs for *all* families. This removes the stigma of public assistance programs aimed to serve the poor and, therefore, these services receive wide public support (Wilson, 1987). (It must be noted that the nation's new "family leave" law has been enacted without causing the hardships for businesses that critics had feared [as reported to Congress by the bipartisan Commission on Family and Medical Leave; May 1996].)

As discussed later, the severity of poor family conditions is the worst in the United States when compared to all other industrialized societies. As sociologist Marc Miringoff, director of the Fordham Institute for Innovation in Social Policy reports: in the United States since 1970, the rate of reported child abuse is four times greater; one in four children lives in poverty, ranking the United States first, a rate four times greater than our closest competitor; and the number of teen-agers committing suicide or attempting to kill themselves has doubled. Fewer infants are dying at birth, but the United States still ranks twentieth out of twenty-three developed countries in infant mortality (Centers for Disease Control and Prevention, 1994).

Although the Census Bureau's mid-decade review of socioeconomic data

Figure 1.2

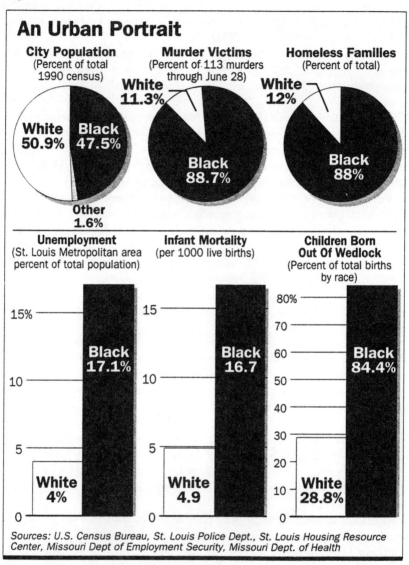

An Urban Portrait

City Population
(Percent of total
1990 census)

White
50.9%

Black
47.5%

Other
1.6%

Murder Victims
(Percent of 113 murders
through June 28)

White
11.3%

Black
88.7%

Homeless Families
(Percent of total)

White
12%

Black
88%

Unemployment
(St. Louis Metropolitan area
percent of total population)

Black
17.1%

White
4%

Infant Mortality
(per 1000 live births)

Black
16.7

White
4.9

**Children Born
Out Of Wedlock**
(Percent of total births
by race)

Black
84.4%

White
28.8%

Sources: U.S. Census Bureau, St. Louis Police Dept., St. Louis Housing Resource Center, Missouri Dept of Employment Security, Missouri Dept. of Health

Source: St. Louis Post-Dispatch, June 30, 1991, 8A

indicates that Americans living in poverty dropped to 13.8 percent from 14.5 percent, recent welfare reform legislation could again raise this figure. The rate of child poverty continues to rise (now at 25 percent), as do the number of children living in single-parent households (United States Department of the Census, 1995). Finally, a recent study prepared by researchers at the Urban Institute, a Washington think tank, found that 42 million people in the United

Figure 1.3

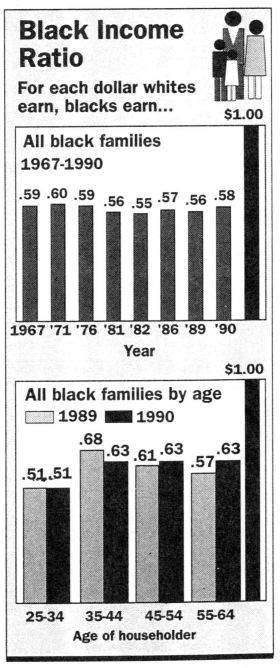

Source: Associated Press, *St. Louis Post-Dispatch,* April 2, 1992, 9A

States lack health coverage and another 29 million are under insured.

Reminiscing on the positive side, Peter Edelman, a Georgetown University law professor, and Beryl Radin, who teaches public administration at the University of Southern California, assert that many of the programs in the 1960s War on Poverty did, in fact, work to help families. They point out that a proper analysis of both the successes and failures of these programs could help us find new approaches for the 1990s. They write:

We seem to have lost the idea that a significant social policy aim is embodied in the notion of community, of a social infrastructure that embodies stability and security and shared values. For many today, individual opportunity is nullified because there is no community around them. . . . Surely one role of government is to help rediscover and rebuild the sense of community that we have lost in too many places. (1991)

CRIME CAUSATION AS AMERICAN CULTURE

By definition, "American culture" is unique to the United States if "American" is taken to mean the United States exclusively rather than the inclusion of Central and South America. There are certain beliefs and practices, when taken together, that make our culture different from that of other nations.

James Q. Wilson (1985) writes about the deterioration of religious influences and the importance of self expression as two cultural factors that contribute to criminal behavior. Elliott Currie adds America's bent toward individualism, the accumulation rather than utilization of wealth, possible remnants of a frontier mentality, and the lack of patience for long-term results: "In a society that values its people for what they can acquire rather than what they can contribute and that encourages predatory and manipulative behavior in the service of immediate gain as the guiding principle of economic life, we should not be altogether surprised if more explosive forms of the same ethos are expressed among the most deprived" (1985: 277).

Bruce Ledewitz, a professor of law at Duquesne University in Pittsburgh, writes that the values of the market dominate American culture instead of the values of church, civic leaders, or parents. He asserts that there is no truth in the market; there are just products. This perpetuates the idea that all values are of equal worth. "Pleasing yourself is what market advertising tells us to do twenty-four hours a day" (1992: 3C).

Messner and Rosenfeld (1993) agree. They maintain that the "American Dream" fosters a commitment to material success, it creates a selfish society in which one-fifth of the people control 45 percent of the country's wealth, and it encourages illegal or unethical means to an end. Additionally, it must be noted that the American media and other entertainment avenues constantly bombard us with the values of conspicuous consumption; self-gratification; violence; degradation of women; "the tough guy image;" "go for the gusto;" and the glorification of athletic, entertainment, and corporate "stars." Finally, it is revealing that, as Ralph Nader reports in *The Monitor* (1996), the fastest growing industries in the United States are temporary services, prison construction, gambling casinos, and amusement parks.

Benjamin Barber adds to the discussion and makes the case that our children learn what our society teaches, not what they read in books:

Are our kids stupid or smart for ignoring what we preach and copying what we practice? . . . The very first lesson smart kids learn is that it is much more important to heed what society teaches implicitly by its deeds and reward structures than what school teaches explicitly in its lesson plans and civic sermons. . . . The illiteracy of the young turns out to be our own reflected back to us with embarrassing force. We honor ambition, cherish success, and we commercialize the classroom—and then we bark at the young about the gentle arts of the spirit. . . . TV sends the same messages to everyone, and the success of Donald Trump, Pete Rose, Henry Kravis, or George Steinbrenner makes them potent role models, whatever their values. . . . Although we can hardly be proud of ourselves for what we are teaching them [kids], we should at least be proud of them for how well they've learned our lessons. (1993: 40)

Barber then provides a real-world cultural literacy test that is partially reprinted here. (For each question, all responses are correct except the last one.)

1. According to television, having fun in America means
   a) going blond
   b) drinking Pepsi
   c) playing Nintendo
   d) wearing Air Jordans
   e) reading Mark Twain
2. A good way to prepare for a high-income career and to acquire status in our society is to
   a) win a slam-dunk contest
   b) take over a company and sell off its assets
   c) start a successful rock band
   d) earn a professional degree
   e) become a kindergarten teacher
3. Book publishers are financially rewarded today for publishing
   a) mega-cookbooks
   b) mega-cat books
   c) megabooks by Michael Crichton
   d) megabooks by John Grisham
   e) mini-books by Voltaire

. . .

5. Colleges and universities are financially rewarded today for
   a) supporting bowl-quality football teams
   b) forging research relationships with large corporations

c) sustaining professional programs in law and business
d) stroking wealthy alumna
e) fostering outstanding philosophy departments

In view of what most American youth have learned about what is deemed "success," it is not difficult to understand why many young black males, in particular, would take pride in nonconformity or being "bad" when there is little chance they will fit into the previously described materialistic structure. Their gangs are exhibiting a group phenomena of what Albert Cohen calls "sectarian solidarity" (1962: 387), a pride in nonconformity in line with the American cultural advocacy of "do your own thing." As an example, Nathan McCall describes his "homies" as "streetwise pseudo baad-asses who were really frightened boys, trying to mask their fear of the world behind muscular frames" (1994: 63).

Policy implications of the "American culture" theory of crime causation are, indeed, difficult to imagine. External control or semi-control of the media is an alien idea to our First Amendment rights of free speech and the concept of free enterprise. Furthermore, to change the hearts and minds of individuals seems an insurmountable task. Education as to the influence of cultural factors on the lives of our children may be a beginning. Also, education as to the values placed upon the various elements that make up our society and how these values compare to those of other societies may be the next step. If our society values "this" over "this and that," what may be the consequences? Who are the heroes of our society? Problem-solving and critical-thinking skills may prove to be the most important learning objectives for our educational programs in terms of rethinking out nation's exhibited values and priorities

David Glidden, a professor of philosophy at the University of California at Riverside, writes in the *Los Angeles Times* (as cited in the *St. Louis Post-Dispatch,* 1990: 3B) that Aristotle viewed the community as reinforcing the habits of the good and setting visible standards of good character: "What is central to morality, as Aristotle conceived it, is the presence of a genuine community—a place where people of good character can visualize their lives. Morality is social."

CRIME CAUSATION AS ALIENATION AND FRUSTRATION DUE TO RELATIVE DEPRIVATION

Elliott Currie, noted criminologist, sociologist, and scholar, (1985) makes a strong case for economic and social inequalities as the underlying causes of the crime problem in the United States, especially violent crime. He recognizes the roles racism plays. He also notes that low crime rates in some poor Third World countries are usually because of strong community life with meaningful work and family roles.

Giving credence to Currie's description of U.S. economic disparity, Robert Christenson (1990) decries an emerging economic plutocracy. He points out that there are twenty-six billionaires averaging between four and five billion dollars and two million millionaires. The average chief executive officer of a major U.S. corporation earns ninety-three times as much as the average factory worker and forty-four times as much as the average engineer (up from forty-one and nineteen times as much in 1960). The top 1 percent of households owns 34 percent of the national wealth (up from 28% in 1973), and the same 1 percent owns as much wealth as the bottom 90 percent of households. The Census Bureau (1995) reports that the disparity between rich and poor has reached its highest level since the end of World War II.

The supply-side economic policies of past federal administrations have not bode well for the "have-nots." In fact, the wealthy have become wealthier while the poor have become poorer. Wealth generated by supply-side economic theories has not trickled all the way to the bottom (Cross, 1987; Currie, 1985; Wilson, 1987). While many large corporations have been helped and inflation is under control (usually at the expense of higher unemployment [Bowles, Gorden, and Weisskopf, 1983]), many social programs have been cut and more fiscal responsibility has been laid at the doors of states and municipalities that are already overburdened.

A 1991 study sponsored by the Joint Center for Political and Economic Studies, a Washington-based research organization primarily concerned with issues affecting black Americans, found that the United States has more poverty and is less able to cope with it than any of the other major industrialized Western democracies. The study found that poverty in the United States is more widespread and more severe, poor families stay poor longer, and government programs in the United States are the least able to lift families with children out of poverty.

Adding race to the mix, the U.N. Human Development Index, which ranks the quality of life among nations, reported in 1993 that white Americans enjoy the world's highest quality of living. However, if black Americans were viewed as a separate nation, they would rank 31st on the index, behind Trinidad and Tobago. A 1991 study by the same organization found that although the United States has the highest standard of living, it ranks thirteenth in terms of freedom. The practice of execution and inequities are the two factors that lowered the rating.

Moreover, the unemployment rate in the United States is more than doubled for minority youth, and the rate is multiplied by seven for black youth who reside in some of our inner cities (United States Department of the Census, 1990). Holly Sklar (1996) reports that black per capita income is three-fifths that of whites, and white males hold 95 percent of senior corporate management positions. Finally, the Milton S. Eisenhower Foundation's 1997 report on the status of American cities found the same or worse conditions than the Kerner Report found in the 1960s. The Kerner report warned of two emerging societies in our nation—one black, the other white. Added to this racial division, the Eisenhower report asserts that there is a greater economic division as well. If there has been political progress for blacks in America, it is a hollow victory without substantial economic progress.

Racism does remain in our nation, permeates our society—its people and institutions, has yet to be dealt with openly and fully, and will remain a festering sore for generations to come. The desire to maintain power and the resistance of a status-quo mentality will make positive change in this arena a continuing glacial movement.

Although in a state of flux, St. Louis, for example, is a racially polarized city: the north side is heavily populated by blacks and the south side is heavily populated by whites. Racism in the form of redlining, political maneuverings, and outright scare tactics has prevented a more racially integrated community. Recent letters to a black *St. Louis Post-Dispatch* columnist bear this out. One reads. "I'm enclosing copies of news stories where black people have been involved in crimes. Is it any wonder that no one wants to live near you people?" And another: "I am so sick and tired of you people whining about how you're treated. We white people treat you badly because you don't deserve any better. If you people would stop robbing and killing everybody, maybe we would treat you with respect. But until you can learn to take care of your own 'brothers,' none of you deserve to be treated like anything but dirt" (Freeman, 1993: 9D).

Added to the economic and social inequalities in the United States, there is a feeling of powerlessness and, therefore, apathy and alienation among citizens in the political arena, especially among the black population (Grier and Cobbs, 1968; Hutchinson, 1990; Josephson and Josephson, 1962; Cross, 1987). As an example, the decision-making process in the St. Louis area is, for the most part, an elitist process. Within the last few years, the public has been made privy to the fact that many of the major decisions affecting the St. Louis metropolitan area have been made by a group that calls itself Civic Progress. This group is made up of heads of major corporations; no blacks or women were members until the "glass ceiling" for women, at least, was broken in May 1997. Civic Progress has oftentimes operated without public knowledge, with impunity, without community input, and with the approval of the city and county governments. It is well known that Civic Progress makes things happen and has a great deal to say about who gets what and how much.

This elitist decision-making process was also mentioned in the *Peirce Report* that analyzed the city's obstructions to economic and cultural growth. The report quotes a head of a local nonprofit as saying, "people hate Civic Progress and defer to it in the same sentence. Groups like mine show up because we need the money." A public affairs specialist is quoted as saying, "Sometimes Civic Progress types are just too important to get things done" (Peirce and Johnson, 1997: 36). Civic Progress probably has "sister" organizations in most other metropolitan areas in the United States, re-enforcing the perception that the "haves" make the important decisions.

It is no wonder that there is a feeling of alienation in an increasingly complex and unequal nation. Worse than that, for the least powerful, this feeling of alienation may turn into humiliation. The dehumanization of the individual in a society of social, economic, and political inequality may contribute to humiliation that turns into rage that Jack Katz talks about in his book, *Seductions of Crime* (1988). (He does not talk about the social issue of inequality as a causal factor, but is referring to situational causes.) Nathan McCall (1994) and the authors of *Black Rage* (Grier and Cobbs, 1968), however, *do* refer to institutionalized racism and other social conditions as reasons for humiliation that may manifest itself in rage within the black population.

As alluded to previously, young black males in our cities have felt the greatest impact of a socially, economically, and politically unequal society. Our nation is not competing for these youngsters who often join pseudo-families (gangs) as Reginald Wilkson, director of the Ohio Department of Rehabilitation and Corrections, refers to them, and exhibit their frustrations, alienation, and distorted sense of power in violent criminal activities, often resulting in homicide (Grier and Cobbs, 1968). Nathan McCall writes, "Sometimes when I sit back and think about the crazy things the fellas and I did and remember the hate and violence that we unleashed, it's hard to believe I was once part of all that—I feel so removed from it now that I've left the streets. . . . Yet when I consider white America and the way it's treated blacks, our random rage in the old days makes perfect sense to me. Looking back, it's easy to understand how it all got started" (1994: 4). He goes on to say, "There's nothing more dangerous and destructive in a household than a frustrated, oppressed black man" (1994: 83).

In his book, *Race, Crime, and the Law* (1997), Randall Kennedy, Harvard professor, describes black Americans as having an invisible question mark over their heads. He asserts that black Americans are forced to pay a "racial tax." For example, the police see black skin as a signal to increased drug trafficking. Nathan McCall relates, "I shot and nearly killed a black man and got a thirty-day sentence; I robbed a white business, and didn't lay a finger on anybody, and got twelve years. I got the message" (1994: 144).

Although many young black males may not be respected and powerful among our nation's dominant culture, they *are* respected and powerful with guns in their hands. If a young black male feels like his life does not mean anything, what worth does he imbue to the lives of others? On the other hand, if he sees opportunity and feels good about himself, he will not take the risk of death. William Grier and Price Cobbs (1968) forewarned white America of black rage expressing itself in one way or another, and Martin Luther King (1968) wrote, "The job of arousing manhood within a people that have been taught for so many centuries that they are nobody is not easy" (197).

Senator Bill Bradley (1992) speaks to the issue of inequality manifesting itself in a crisis of meaning for our nation's inner-city youths:

Without meaning there can be no hope; without hope there can be no struggle; without struggle there can be no personal betterment. Absence of meaning, influenced by overt and subtle attacks from racist quarters over many years, as well as an increasing pessimism about the possibility of justice, fosters a context for chaos and irresponsibility. . . . For kids who have no family outside a gang . . . government is at best incompetent and at worst corrupt. Instead of being rooted in values such as commitment and community service, their desires, like commodities, become rooted in the shallow ground of immediate gratification. (1992: 11)

The founding of our country in a climate of racism and beliefs in the innate inferiority of African people, hundreds of years of slavery, decades of Jim Crow legislation, and racial bias within the criminal justice system must be acknowledged and reflected upon. The Roper Center for Public Opinion Research reports that 71 percent of blacks believe the criminal justice system to be biased against blacks. This finding was recently supported via discussions emanating from the opposite reactions between black and white Americans to the O. J. Simpson trials.

These factors juxtaposed to the *espoused* American values of freedom, democracy, equality, opportunity, and "justice for all" must insult and enrage many black Americans who are at the low end of the socio-economic, political, and justice scales. It is no wonder that race (due to institutionalized racism) is correlated to crime. As Senator Bradley asserts, "Conversion requires listening to the disaffected as well as the powerful." We must recognize "that all of us advance together or each of us is diminished . . . involve the community in its own salvation" (1992: 10).

SUMMARY

As with most cause and effect analysis, it is usually a combination of theories that explain specific outcomes. Like the correlates, there are multiple causes of criminal behavior that may include: multiple and complex inter-related genes (some children seem to be more resilient than others to unfavorable environmental conditions [Werner and Smith, 1982; Bernard, 1987; O'Connor, 1997]); cost and benefit of an act (Cromwell, Olson, and Avery, 1991); deteriorating family conditions (Wilson, 1987); cultural influences (Messner and Rosenfeld, 1993; Wilson, 1985); alienation and frustration (Katz, 1988; Grier and Cobbs, 1968; McCall, 1994); relative deprivation (Cross, 1987; Currie, 1985); and institutionalized racism (Cross, 1987; McCall, 1994; Wilson, 1987). One of these causal factors may be classified as foreground or situational (cost and benefit) whereas the remaining factors may be classified as background or underlying causes.

The underlying causes of criminal behavior that may be peculiar to the United States when compared to other democratized, industrialized nations are explained by the cultural and institutionalized racism theories that are then related to relative deprivation (there is a wider gap between the "haves" and "have-nots" in the United States [Currie, 1985]). Also, as Theodore Cross (1987) so thoroughly and eloquently explains, there are disproportionately more blacks living below the poverty line and there are disproportionately less accumulation of wealth and those holding positions of economic and political power within the black population.

Although institutionalized racism may be considered an integral *part* of our American culture, I believe this factor must be considered separately. When crime data reveal that, disproportionately, more violent crime is committed by blacks and more *victims* of violent crime are blacks, it draws attention to institutionalized racism as a specific cancer within our society that we must attend to.

Multiple correlates to and multiple causes of criminal behavior demand multiple solutions or a solution that encompasses multiple factors. The following chapter discusses community crime prevention efforts and compares their effectiveness. This and following chapters find that some crime prevention efforts address only foreground causes of criminal behavior such as opportunity, others address only background causes such as deteriorating social conditions, and at least one addresses both background and foreground causes through a community problem-solving approach.

Chapter 2

Community Crime Prevention

INTRODUCTION

A study of imprisoned burglars in 1978 by Peter Palmer found, "the majority of inmates said that merely being noticed by a neighbor was enough to deter them. All of them indicated that they would leave the area if challenged by a neighbor" (cited in Podelefsky, 1983: 122). Although this quote seems to support the idea of "neighborhood" or "block watch" programs, research findings have been inconclusive as to their success.

This chapter looks at the evolution of community crime prevention programs such as "block watch," addresses the inconclusive research findings of these programs, discusses possible reasons for these findings, and examines several types of community crime prevention programs and their possibilities for success in various types of communities.

EVOLUTION OF COMMUNITY CRIME PREVENTION PROGRAMS

Although one could say community crime prevention has existed as long as communities and crime have existed, organized community crime prevention in the United States may be traced to the industrialization and urbanization of the nation. With these economic and social movements, our communities became more diversified, less intra-active, and seemingly less caring. High rise apartment buildings took the place of many individual family dwellings with the consequence of condensed groups of citizens who no longer knew each other, watched out for each other, or cared for one another.

As crime and juvenile delinquency increased in such environments, the federal government became increasingly involved with the passing of various laws and the implementation of social programs. In reaction to this, the Chicago Area Projects (CAP) was incorporated in 1934 under the leadership of Clifford

Shaw as a community effort to address the problems of crime and juvenile delinquency where, in CAP's view, government solutions had failed. The organization used the tools of indigenous leadership, influence, and persuasion to change city policies affecting the community (Coates, 1987).

A former employee of the Chicago Area Projects, Saul Alinsky, took this idea even further through his Back of the Yard's Project in 1940. This project differed from the CAP endeavor in that it often included political confrontation and conflict (Coates, 1987).

By the 1950s and 1960s crime and delinquency prevention had become a national issue. During the 1950s, the Mobilization for Youth Projects was initiated in fifteen U.S. cities in cooperation with the Ford Foundation. This program involved local governments but failed to obtain grass-roots support. The success of the projects differed across the fifteen cities depending on the organization and commitment of the various local governments. Overall, the program was deemed to be a failure because of "outside people trying to identify local power influentials, roadblocks of various kinds by city officials who guarded their perogatives for distribution of spoils on a patronage basis, and the unwillingness of individuals and groups who had seen themselves as natural enemies to coalesce and coordinate merely because of the existence of federal dollars" (Coates, 1987: 227).

The present phenomenon of "block watch" programs in many communities across the nation may have been spurred by incidents such as the infamous 1964 Kitty Genovese murder in New York City. The crime was notorious in that the police were not notified of the victim's screams and cries for help for over thirty minutes. Although the area was comprised of numerous apartment dwellings and the screams were heard by many, no one came to help. After one man yelled to leave the girl alone, the perpetrator, having stabbed the girl four times, left and sat in his car. When he saw that no one was coming to her aid, he returned to the scene, sexually assaulted the girl, and stabbed her repeatedly. She died on the way to the hospital (Castleman, 1984). This outrageous set of circumstances appalled the nation, engendered questions about our increasingly uncaring communities, and set many gears into motion concerning community crime prevention.

Increased interest in community crime prevention encouraged federal and state funding for block watch programs in the 1970s. In 1977 seventeen states established community crime prevention programs most often called, "Crime Watch" (Doleschal, 1984). The programs usually comprised the following components:

- Reducing the opportunity for crime through such projects as environmental design, security surveys, elderly escorts, proper identification of possessions, citizen car patrols, and so on;
- Improving the responsiveness of the criminal justice system through strategies such as citizen monitoring of police action; and

- Providing assistance to local citizens who might otherwise turn to crime, or what one may call alternative activities and/or social programs. (DeJong and Goolkasian, 1982)

Today, "block watch" is a popular title for community crime prevention programs; however, this title claims multiple meanings depending on the degree of community involvement. Also, these programs have exhibited varying levels of success.

A SAMPLE OF COMMUNITY CRIME PREVENTION PROGRAMS

Michael Castleman (1984) cites the Detroit community crime prevention program as a success. During the 1970s Detroit was deemed to be one of the worst cities in the nation. Because of the declining automobile industry, the unemployment rate was high and in some neighborhoods, the black teenage unemployment rate reached 80 percent. Also, the Detroit police claimed the highest national per capita rate of civilian killings in 1971 while Detroit's poor economic situation led to a reduction in the police force by 25 percent (Castleman, 1984). Finally, Detroit was still recovering from a 1967 riot that left forty-three dead. The white population was leaving in droves, the crime rate soared, and Detroit's nickname became "Murder City, USA."

Circumstances began to change in 1974 when the first black mayor, Coleman Young, was elected, and the police force began to be integrated. In 1976 a black police chief was appointed who had earned a Ph.D. in education, and a community crime prevention program was initiated (Castleman, 1984).

One requirement of the police department for a community to be designated as a crime watch community and to merit police support was at least 50 percent citizen participation. The police would then provide training and signs designating the neighborhood as a "crime watch" community. They were operating under the idea that the police alone could not cut the crime rate. Saturation police patrolling had been shown to make no difference (Castleman, 1984).

Castleman writes that the Crime Analysis Section of the police department reported the following results. One hundred forty block groups cut crime rates by 57 percent. Between 1977 and 1979 rape declined 67 percent; robbery, 56 percent; home burglary, 62 percent; automobile theft, 51 percent; larceny, 47 percent; and purse snatching, 61 percent. This was done while police patrols remained unchanged. Furthermore, not one of the successful burglaries took place in a home whose occupants participated in the neighborhood watch program. Finally, there was no displacement of crime to adjoining neighborhoods (1984).

Castleman (1984) asserts that a 50 percent crime rate reduction is common through the implementation of community crime prevention programs. He maintains that although program maintenance is difficult, this type of proactive policing can break the cycle of crime whereas reactive policing cannot. In Detroit, where the police force had actually been reduced and gun availability had increased, the crime rate had been reduced and/or had stabilized in most of the communities as of 1984.

Other cited successes are Seattle's Community Crime Prevention Program, a comprehensive plan, and a community crime prevention program in Hartford, Connecticut. Of the latter initiative Doleschal states, "Increased resident involvement in and responsibility for the neighborhood was identified as the most important reason for the success in crime reduction" (1984: 68). Three years later, however, the same program was not found to be as effective. A possible reason was that the police force was reduced because the crime rate had dropped so dramatically (1984).

On the other hand, many evaluators and researchers have found community crime prevention programs to have little or no beneficial effect. Trevor Bennett (1987) found two neighborhood watch schemes in London to be not very successful because of their general design and administration. Geason and Wilson (1989) maintain that if a program is successful, program implementers need to ensure that local police have information and details of the plan and that there are regular meetings concerning crime prevention procedures in order to update and reinforce this type of knowledge. Stickers and looking out for suspicious behavior are not enough.

Also, the police cannot be too busy to respond to calls, residents need sufficient equipment to mark their property, police need to be available to carry out security surveys, and the programs need to be constantly monitored and evaluated for effectiveness (Geason and Wilson, 1989). Elmer Johnson (1987) adds that part of the problem with community crime prevention programs is that they reflect America's reactionary society and its aversion to long-term planning. This results in disjointed crime prevention activities.

Adding to the discussion, Rosenbaum (1988) asserts that crime prevention programs are initiated under some often held assumptions about neighborhood watch: (1) a program can be implemented easily on a large scale; (2) people will become involved regardless of social and demographic characteristics; (3) interaction at meetings will produce immediate effects like reduction in the fear of crime and an increase in crime prevention behaviors; (4) crime prevention activities will endure; and (5) crime will be reduced. He cites several studies where the fear of crime actually increased because of consciousness raising and knowing the extent of crime victimization. Finally, Rosenbaum suggests multiple approaches to community crime prevention because multiple approaches may more effectively support the aforementioned hypotheses.

PROGRAM EVALUATIONS

Whether or not a crime prevention program is deemed to be successful often depends on the method of program evaluation. Data can be derived from crime statistics, surveys, and/or observation and archival records (DeJong and Goolkasian, 1982), but the method of data collection and analysis must also be considered. Is the study correlational? Does it intend to show cause and effect? Are control groups used, and is there randomization of the samples? All of these factors and more need to be considered before assigning validity and reliability to results of crime prevention program evaluations.

Also, there are limits to the validity of reported crime data as a measure of the "real" crime rate in that the number of reports could rise with increased sensitization to crime through crime prevention programs. Finally, the police sometimes do not file citizens' complaints depending on the perceived seriousness of the crime, the victim's social class, whether or not the victim knows the perpetrator, and the victim's wishes in the matter (DeJong and Goolkasian, 1982).

Castleman (1984) reports that the FBI's compilation of the national crime index from the Uniform Crime Reports (UCR) depends on voluntary reporting by police departments. Even though the majority of police departments *do* report, census victimization surveys reveal that only 45 percent of violent crimes and 25 percent of theft crimes are reported. It is interesting to note that nonreporting counties in rural areas are increasing in numbers. The most recent FBI figures (1994) show that law enforcement agencies representing only 55.8 percent of Missouri's and 22.7 percent of Mississippi's rural populations submitted crime statistics.

Rosenbaum (1988) identifies another problem: often community crime prevention programs are evaluated by a pre-test/post-test design that shows no comparison to control groups. The change in the crime rate may, therefore, be due to statistical regression toward the mean. He also maintains that there is an "under-use of statistical significance tests, a poor conceptualization and definition of treatments, the absence of a valid and reliable measurement of programme implementation and outcomes, and a consistent failure to address competing explanations for observed effects" (Lurigio and Rosenbaum, 1986: 2).

Rosenbaum (1988) sees the Seattle crime prevention evaluation as a good study showing reduction in residential burglary in target areas compared to control areas. Cirel and coauthors (1977) reports that the evaluations showed that rates of burglary for participants in the program fell 48 percent to 61 percent. On the other hand, they found methodological problems with most community crime prevention program evaluations citing uncontrollable variables and programs initiated at peak crime rate periods that would probably normalize even without a crime prevention program.

PROGRAM ANALYSIS

Strategies implemented in community crime prevention programs derive from underlying theories and general principles (Johnson, 1987). It follows that the underlying assumptions of human behavior will make a difference as to the type of implemented crime prevention program.   This can be seen in the victimization prevention approach as compared to the social problems approach to crime prevention. The first approach assumes that criminal behavior cannot be altered by addressing social needs of lawbreakers, while the latter approach negates this assumption.   "Block watch" programs would emerge from a victimization prevention approach (Podolefsky, 1983).

Elliot Currie maintains that this latter defensive approach ignores the more "hidden" crimes such as child abuse, violence against women, racial harassment, and drug misuse. The author asserts that "block watch" works best in areas with few social problems and in communities that have already established networks for crime prevention. Moreover, these programs often ignore the police and they seem to be quick-fix rather than long-term approaches (Currie in Hope and Shaw, 1988).

James Gillham (1992) states that block watch programs work best where there are economic interests such as home ownership, where people already talk to each other, where residents are able to watch each other's homes, where people have not already lost hope, and where the population is somewhat homogeneous. Podolefsky (1983) points out that ethnic populations are less likely to cooperate with block watch and police programs. Many of these types of communities may, in fact, watch out for police abuses. Also, they are more inclined to address broader issues and support a social problems approach to crime prevention.

Elliott Currie (1988) asserts the social problems approach or reformist model seeks to change conditions that breed crime. This approach views offenders and victims as part of the same community. He maintains that this method is superior in reducing serious crime and looks at the community in more structural or institutional terms. He admits that there are little hard data to support this view and that there may need to be more ethnographic research in this area.

Robert Weiss (1987) views community crime prevention approaches on a continuum from "place" to "solidarity" and from programs based on sentiment to programs based on integrative processes. He maintains that there are three types of crime prevention programs: (1) Situational—the term "community" is viewed as a locale. The crime prevention measures are threat processes such as walling, wariness, and watching. Deterrence measures used are based on an "us" and "them" type of mentality. (2) Stake in conformity—the term "community" is viewed as a social service delivery system and as a socioeconomic opportunity structure depending on exchange processes—"if services are supplied, there will develop a sense of usefulness that will translate into great allegiance to the established order" (112). (3) Informal control—the term "community" is viewed as an integrative process that promotes solidarity through moral suasion.

Weiss goes on to say that, first, the situational crime prevention approach may displace crime, tends to benefit middle and upper social classes at the expense of poor people, and may increase the fear of crime. It also may create a siege mentality, isolating individuals and families. Second, the stake in conformity approach may develop citizen empowerment through mediation for social services and privatizing social welfare; however, the crime problem is also cultural. Finally, the informal control approach is based on communal sentiment (the unit of thinking becomes community or even global rather than individual) and there is common concern. Weiss notes and believes that during the Civil Rights movement, crime dropped in many cities and communities because of a perceived sense of common purpose.

The second and third approaches that Weiss addresses would seem to require a comprehensive approach to community crime prevention, addressing both foreground (situational) and background causes of criminal behavior. Richard Titus (1984) cites authors who view this approach as superior because crime is related to economics, community racial change, and disorder (Skogan and Maxfield, 1981; Taub and Taylor, 1982; Wilson and Kelling, 1982). He documents several evaluations of successful comprehensive community crime prevention programs with place, time period, treatment, process measures, and impact measures. Many of these studies included control groups but none included randomized samples. The pattern, however, is rather consistent in showing resulting crime reduction. Finally, another criminologist, Eugene Doleschal (1984), agrees that a comprehensive approach to crime prevention produces more favorable results and a feeling of control by members of the community.

SUMMARY

Multiple causes of criminal behavior demand multiple solutions, confronting crime from both foreground (situational) and background (underlying social malaise) perspectives. To state it another way, solutions must involve more than "block watch" and the criminal justice system—it must involve the entire community implementing a comprehensive solution. The philosophy of community education as described in this book and implemented in the Hyde Park neighborhood offers such a solution.

Community education as a potential avenue to the alleviation of criminal behavior is a stand taken by several criminologists. For instance, Tim Hope and Margaret Shaw (1988) see a movement toward a community education approach to crime prevention. It is not clear if Hope and Shaw are referring to the community education philosophy that was modeled in Flint, Michigan and adopted by the National Community Education Association, but it is clear that they are referring to a comprehensive approach. A comprehensive approach could address social problems within the community as well as situational or foreground problems such as opportunity for criminal behavior via community problem-solving processes that implement solutions such as block watch and mobile patrol-type activities.

Finally, if we take criminologist, Jack Katz (1988), seriously and turn our attention to the foreground causes of criminal behavior such as opportunity and availability of guns rather than focusing exclusively on the background causes, the "watch" and criminal justice system parts of community crime prevention must not be thrown overboard in favor of a social programs approach. An integrative, comprehensive approach, acknowledging both foreground and background causes of criminal behavior, may yield the best results.

The inner-city neighborhood of Hyde Park in St. Louis is implementing such a comprehensive approach to address its crime problem. The next few chapters provide the reader with a look at this community, its crime problem, and community efforts to solve it. Most of the descriptions are derived from Hyde Park community members—residents, service providers, business owners, and those who work in the neighborhood. The community typifies many inner-city neighborhoods in that it exhibits an environment comprising demographic characteristics that correlate to high levels of criminal activity.

Chapter 3

The Hyde Park Neighborhood

INTRODUCTION

The Hyde Park neighborhood is a five minute drive from the Arch and downtown St. Louis on the near north side of the city. The boundaries (forming a distorted map-triangle) are Interstate 70 on the east, separating the neighborhood from river front industries; Palm Street and Natural Bridge Avenue on the south and west; and Glasgow Avenue and Ferry Street on the west and north (ConServ, 1992). The neighborhood is entered from Illinois across the Mississippi River by way of the McKinley Bridge onto Salisbury Street (Map 3.1).

The area is easily recognized when traveling Interstate 70 by the national historic landmark water towers (the white Corinthian column structure on Grand Avenue and the red brick Moorish Minaret structure on Bissell and Blair—two of only seven remaining in the United States), the pale orange brick Bissell Mansion situated on a hill overlooking Interstate 70 and the Mississippi River, Clay Elementary school, the old Divoll Library next to Clay, and the twin steeples of Holy Trinity Catholic Church. It must be noted that, until 1995, one of the more recent landmarks noticed from the highway was a dilapidated, burned-out building surrounded by a wooden fence. In many ways, the neighborhood typifies the general perception of inner-city communities: population loss; change of population composition to higher percentages of black, lower socio-economic status, female-headed families, and youth; loss of industries and small businesses; vacant lots; and boarded-up buildings. In short, Hyde Park lays claim to many variables correlated to criminal behavior.

Map 3.1

Source: Operation ConServ (1992)

A BRIEF HISTORY

Hyde Park was once known as the small town of Bremen, a German settlement on the Mississippi river front founded in 1844. Emil Mallinckrodt was one of the town's founders who enticed many German immigrants to

Map 3.1 (Cont'd)

1. Holy Trinity Church
2. Holy Trinity School
3. Bethlehem School
4. Turnverein Hall
5. Bethlehem Lutheran
6. William Shands House
7. School Admin. Bldg.
8. Fire Station
9. Gazebo
10. Irving School
11. Living God Church
12. Piekutowski's Shop
13. Eliot School
14. Friedens Church
15. Shiloh Missionary
16. Clay School
17. Old Police Station
18. Bissell Mansion
19. Bissell Water Tower
20. Grand Water Tower
21. Community Center
22. Krey Meat Packing Plant
23. Divoll Library
24. St. John's Church

Source: Operation ConServ (1992)

establish their homes in the area. In addition to Emil Mallinckrodt, landowners in Bremen included E. C. Angelrodt, George Buchanan, N. Destrehan, Bernard Farrar, John O'Fallon, Clement B. Penrose, and Captain Lewis Bissell. Several Hyde Park streets bear the names of these historical figures, and the home of

Captain Bissell is now a neighborhood landmark, restaurant, and dinner theater (ConServ, 1992).

Interaction between St. Louis and Bremen was then by way of the "Great Trail," which is now known as Broadway within St. Louis and Bellefontaine Road in St. Louis County. In 1855 Bremen was annexed by St. Louis and the name of the community was changed to Hyde Park, taking the name of a twelve acre park created as the focal point of the neighborhood. With annexation, the river front industries of sawmills and lumber yards flourished (ConServ, 1992).

The Union Stockyards, Hyde Park Brewery, and Mallinckrodt Chemical Works added to the area's industrial base during the decade following the Civil War. At one point, the Union Stockyards covered twenty-four acres, and cattle were herded down Broadway and up Bremen Avenue to the Krey Packing Company. The community park (Hyde Park) was fenced along Bremen to keep the cattle out. Krey Packing Company then covered one and a half city blocks with red brick buildings and tall smokestacks. Finally, coming much later, uranium was purified at Mallinckrodt Chemical for use in the Chicago's Manhattan Project in 1942 (ConServ, 1992).

Added to this industrial base, Hyde Park residents were able to conduct most of their daily business activities within the neighborhood. Various entrepreneurs lined Salisbury Street to service residents' needs such as butchers, grocers, doctors, tailors, shoe salesmen, and midwives who generally lived above their shops and places of business (Young, 1983).

Besides three parks (Hyde Park, Strodtman, and Windsor) and several churches (Holy Trinity, Bethlehem Lutheran, and Friedens United Church of Christ), the social needs of the community were serviced by the North St. Louis Turnverein organization housed in a large building erected in 1879 (now vacant). The German owners furnished gymnastic activities for the community as well as advocating social and political reform, including the restriction of child labor. In the 1880s they worked to establish physical education as part of the St. Louis public school curriculum (Young, 1983).

In short, Hyde Park was a self-contained community with industry, commercial enterprises, recreational and educational activities, community parks, and beautiful churches. How would the neighborhood look to someone who left the area in the early 1950s and returned for a visit in the early 1990s?

THE PRESENT COMMUNITY

Hyde Park is designated by the City of St. Louis as a historic neighborhood. Years ago residential properties were predominantly red brick structures with a few frame structures, the latter (for the most part) lost to fire. Approximately 70 percent of the streets and alleys were brick but are now covered with a thin layer of asphalt (ConServ, 1992).

As the older Hyde Park residents died or moved out to the suburbs, a majority of the housing became rentals, some became dilapidated and were razed, and others were boarded up.   The Land Reutilization Authority (LRA—the City) now owns many of the properties.   The abundance of side yards, empty lots, and vacant land where buildings once stood, as well as numerous boarded-up buildings are very noticeable to the first time visitor. (Some of the boards have been artistically painted by Clay Elementary and Holy Trinity students.)

Several of the vacant lots in certain sections of Hyde Park are littered with used tires, furniture, cardboard boxes, building materials, paper, and broken glass.   When the sunlight hit the broken glass just right, one vacant lot looked as though it was covered with snow.   As the former mayor stated, "We are living in a community where you can stand on one block and see two blocks down because of all the vacant lots."   (The former mayor resides just outside Hyde Park boundaries.)

Another factor contributing to the gradual deterioration of the community was the construction of Interstate 70 in the late 1950s, which severed the residential and small business neighborhood from the industrial complexes along the river.   Several hundred houses were demolished with the Bissell Mansion, the area's most historic home, also listed for destruction.   That landmark was spared only after a group of concerned citizens intervened, convincing officials to reroute the highway (Young, 1983).

Overall, the Hyde Park community experienced a population decrease of approximately 18 percent since 1980 whereas the population loss for the City of St. Louis was 12.4 percent.   One of the area's elementary schools closed in the Fall of 1993.   Presently, Hyde Park's population is approximately 4,900 with 68 percent black and 32 percent white residents.   This represents a 50 percent decrease in the white population and a 19 percent increase in the black population since 1980.   Approximately 45 percent of households are headed by females (United States Department of the Census, 1990).

Less than 50 percent of residents twenty-five and older have a high school education or better and approximately 28 percent of sixteen- to nineteen-year-olds are not enrolled in school, have no high school diploma, and are not in the labor force.   The unemployment rate is approximately 21 percent with male unemployment at 22.7 percent, and the median family income at $14,417. Approximately 33 percent of households earn less than $10,000 per year and 46 percent of the population live below the poverty line while 28 percent live 50 percent below this line (United States Department of the Census, 1990).

Only 23 percent of housing is owner-occupied.   Twenty-two percent of the land parcels are vacant, approximately 35.7 percent of the buildings are vacant, and the median resale value is $18,000 while the median rent is approximately $283 (United States Department of the Census, 1990).

Most of the housing was built before 1900.   The four family flats are three-room "shot gun" configurations with the living room in front and the kitchen in back.   The single-family and two-family units have the same configuration but with bedrooms on the second floor.   All have small or no front yards with backyards opening to an alley.

"Project Respond" (1993) reports the following findings for children living in the zip code area that includes Hyde Park: 83 percent receive AFDC, 90 percent experience poverty and the related problems of hunger, and 60 percent lack adequate skill levels for kindergarten entrance. The area has an excessive school dropout rate of 52 percent.

Also, the Hyde Park area is one of the areas in St. Louis with a high percentage of births to teen mothers, a high percentage of infants born at low birth weight, a high infant mortality rate, a high percentage of infants born to women with inadequate pre-natal care, and a large number of children per thousand who are reported to be abused and/or neglected. The area has the highest level of lead poisoning in St. Louis and the lowest number of social programs serving "at risk" youth (Project Respond, 1993).

There are approximately seventy small businesses remaining in Hyde Park—some are unregulated and should be improved or shut down. Approximately forty businesses and industries are located east of Interstate 70 along the river front, including Mallinckrodt Chemical.

A small percentage of the population would be considered "middle class" in terms of socio-economic status. A few residents moved to the area in the hopes of renovating, rebuilding the community, or making a profit. Some residents may have felt trapped by deteriorating values of their properties, while others have chosen to remain or have felt trapped and eventually chose to remain.

One former Hyde Park resident expressed it this way:

I was like a lot of other people before and since me who became overwhelmed with the problems of the neighborhood and left. I lived over on Newhouse. When I first moved up there in about 1983, it was kind of right at the height of the development that HYPRE (Hyde Park Renovation Effort) was doing. There was a lot of activity and I bought a house. At the time I moved in, there were some folks who had just rehabbed a building across the street and were living there, I had homeowners living on both sides, and it was pretty much all homeowners on at least half the block.

The four family flats on the block were being rehabbed, and the first group of tenants were fine. After that, they were steadily worse. My neighbors and I used to take charge on Saturday literally shoveling up the alleys. As soon as the four family flats were rehabbed, the alleys were just full of trash with mostly diapers. It was a real mess—the dogs would get into the diapers.

First, the people across the street moved. The neighbor on the west had a teenage daughter who was molested by one of the tenants in the four family flats, and he immediately sold his house and left. Then the guy to the east of me stayed until about a year later—this was all in a three-year period.

By the time that we left in three years, the street had gone from a pretty nice, quiet street to a bad situation. It was almost as bad as it is now. There were people fighting with 2x4s in the middle of the street, there were people exchanging gunfire up and down the street, and the last week we were there, somebody threw a brick through the window of my wife's car.

My wife broke down and was crying one day and said, "I'm leaving—go with me if you want." We were planning to be long-term residents in the neighborhood. That's a picture of a building I started rehabbing on 20th street which was approved by a design company back in 1985. I put $30,000 into that building—I was doing a real state-of-the-art rehab and I was planning to spend the rest of my life in Hyde Park. Really, the reason why I left was because I felt powerless. I felt powerless to do anything about the trend.

Several community members had rather bleak perceptions of the Hyde Park neighborhood, while others viewed the community from a more positive perspective. Consequently, some pessimistically described the neighborhood, others somewhat optimistically described the community, and yet others were waiting for the neighborhood to "turn around." A current resident and former member of HYPRE (1970s and 1980s) had this to say:

It's just been so frustrating and depressing. We had so many promises and dreams, and part of that is transition from youth to middle age, just a sense of not being fulfilled and not accomplishing what we dreamed of. In our vision we had just a neat neighborhood where all the people got along, where all the houses were done, all the kids played together and went to the neighborhood school, you had shops, and you just had a nice little nuclear community. I guess that was naive. It was the idealism of youth and inexperience, and I hadn't had a chance to be cynical yet. . . .

I grew up in the suburbs where all the white middle class kids had dads who worked at McDonnell-Douglas, and it was such a fucking bore. Everybody was in their own little house, and if you were lucky, you knew the neighbor on each side because you saw them when you cut the grass. There was no social interaction, and it was such a sterile community. . . .

This whole experience has really affected me. I'll not try this again. My social experimentation and dreams of doing something like this are gone. I can't. I've got fifteen years of my life and probably $100,000 invested in my house and the buildings I have bought, and I'll walk away with nothing.

I always thought down the road this will pay off—I'll have these nice people to sell or rent to, and I'll do OK. But I'll end up with nothing. My wife and I have always worked; our money is all tied up in this neighborhood, and I have to walk away from it. Now we're going to look for a piece of ground with a house in the middle—but we have no money. I'll be lucky to get what I owe on the house I'm in now. I think Hyde Park will, someday, turn around; but I no longer have the ambition, the motivation, or the money to stick around and see it happen.

Describe the Hyde Park community and the people who live here.

A neighborhood in transition—continuing migration of white and black middle class—deterioration of city services. There are some efforts to improve social services. Generally, the neighborhood is still on the way down.

The people are still quite a mix. It runs the gamut of extremely low income people on public assistance to all the way up to college-educated professionals. There are still a good amount of those types around, but not near the extent that we had in the 80s. There is not much of a black middle class right now.

During the last ten years we've had a large influx of nonworking males, and theft and property crimes have increased quite a bit. Some large public housing in St. Louis had to be cleared out, and those people had to go somewhere, and to a large extent they came up this way. . . . The marginal people (the unemployed, the unemployable, the drug-pins, basically the ones you can't do anything with) ended up here because of the housing stock. No responsible management company is going to rent to that type of person, so where do they go? . . .

There have been a number of programs like ConServ officers, neighborhood liaison officers, police-community relations—they've all been largely ineffective in my opinion. Drive around. It's all the little things that pile up. You look at derelict cars, people parking cars on unpaved lots, building violations, trash piles—nothing is done. . . .

I'm very supportive of what Friedens does, but I hope they try to get that mix you've got to have. You don't want to develop another ghetto. It's not going to help to develop another community of low income people. You're not going to create a dynamic, living community with all one type or another. Ladue [an affluent St. Louis neighborhood] is one type of ghetto, Hyde Park is another, and they're not either one healthy communities. You don't get the diversity and the interaction that you want with the diversity of all types of people. That's always been one of the neat things about Hyde Park—the diversity—but it has also been one of the things that's made it tough to bring people together. . . .

I don't think you're going to get the white middle class to come back in here. I'm comfortable with a half and half racial mix. Anything beyond that, [higher percentage black] I start to get uncomfortable. You had a good shot in the late 1970s, now the racial makeup [more blacks] has gone too far.

Other residents expressed a more optimistic view:

People don't feel that they're trapped here for the most part, although a lot of people need to go where certain types of housing are like Section 8 housing. People who could do something don't really seem to want to—they're burnt out, they have been vandalized and feel, "What's the use?" They don't feel that they can make a difference or have control over what kind of people come into the neighborhood. . . .

Hyde Park is not as depressed as some people say it is. There are a lot of professional people who live here, but they don't make themselves visible. Most of them are white, they're afraid of crime, and, also, the black professionals don't come out. We're all basically human beings. I don't feel trapped here.

The former priest in the Hyde Park community (southeast section) described the neighborhood and the people who live there this way:

I love the city. The neat thing about this neighborhood is the integration of black and white people, especially in Sunday worship—each population brings their special gifts. I really feel lucky that black and white people are coming together in this church [recently merged congregations]. I can't think of any other place that I'd like to be than right here. Next year will be my sixth year and I could ask to be moved, but I would definitely choose to stay. . . .

These people are what I would call "real" people—they don't put on airs—they are a very caring people. I don't feel that I have to impress anyone here—I can just be myself. I just really do like the people here. There's a real warm, loving spirit in our church community here as well as in the neighborhood. There are a lot of people willing to work and help.

I wish we had more leadership types. We don't have people who have been trained to take charge of something and get it done compared to like the Shaw neighborhood [south St. Louis]. Those people are more used to being professional leaders in their careers, so it flows over into their neighborhood concerns. There is willingness here to help, but there is lack of experience and knowledge of what to do next.

(Several months after this interview, a shot was fired through the priest's bedroom window. He subsequently was reassigned to a parish in south St. Louis.)

The pastor of another church in the Hyde Park neighborhood (southwest section) described the community this way:

I like Hyde Park because it's a place where there are more needs for the church to meet. I think this community is more reachable than others. When you cross Grand you get into a more difficult world—gang and crime-wise. I think there's just some good people in Hyde Park from what I've known. There's more housing here also—not as many vacant units as in other neighborhoods. . . .

The Hyde Park neighborhood is economically very impoverished. There are a lot of people who are just making it, who work very hard to take care of their families—there are a lot of children in this neighborhood.

The children who live here have many needs. They have educational needs, and they need help with things. The families at home are not always strong about helping the children—not necessarily that the kids are neglected. In some cases the parents just don't want to and they are irresponsible—but not all. In other cases, it's a case where resources are not there. Mothers are out really working hard to try to take care of their families, and the time necessary just to rear the family isn't there, so brothers and sisters help rear the family.

There are a few different Hyde Park neighborhoods. There's a neighborhood around Holy Trinity and then there's a neighborhood around the Water Tower, and then there's a neighborhood from let's say 20th Street and west. So there are neighborhoods within a neighborhood.

It goes back to the educational problem and the holistic need that's here. Problems mount up on each other. A lot of the young mothers are overwhelmed and don't know where to turn. . . .

Most of the development that the community organizations have done has really never reached "our" neighborhood per se. One housing director about five years ago said the phases of housing development weren't going to make it to this area of the neighborhood for five years. Well that's been five years ago, and the phases they were trying to start down there really didn't even start. I know some of the people in that community, but we've just kind of stayed on this side of the neighborhood because there are so many people and so much work to do on this side. . . .

There's crime in the neighborhood like in any other neighborhood. While the crime is bad and the streets can be very dangerous, it's not what the media describes. The media sometimes wants to label the entire north St. Louis area as being south-central LA with drive-bys and all that. It isn't all that. There are some areas like that, but it's not all like that.

SUMMARY

One city service provider expressed a rather dichotomous view and gave a succinct descriptive summary of the Hyde Park neighborhood:

The community is a very diverse, complex, and intellectually stimulating group of people on one hand; on the other hand they're needy, very depressed, and very oppressed financially and economically. You've got two different groups in there—it's like a generation gap, but between those in the know and those in the need. I don't know if they're coming together. . . .

Hyde Park is rich in history, rich in architecture, and rich in tradition. But this tradition, architecture, and all the economics are not translating into the 90s and to those who are coming in. When you look at it aesthetically, it's not pleasing. But if you are an artist, if you are well versed in these areas, you can look and think, "Oh my, that's a beautiful structure!" You can begin to see the beauty as it once was and you want to preserve it. But if you're just poor, you look at the dilapidation, degradation, drugs, and there has been a careless attitude. On one hand you see one thing, on the other hand you see another thing—it's just according to which direction you look and who you are!

Chapter 4

Policing in the Hyde Park Neighborhood: Racial Bias, Political Pressures, and Community Policing

INTRODUCTION

St. Louis is considered to be one of the ten most crime-ridden major cities in the country. While crime rates declined throughout the nation in 1993, they increased in St. Louis. Serious crime was up 8 percent in the city while it was down 3 percent in the nation, and St. Louis murders increased 15.6 percent while robberies increased 26.1 percent. St. Louis ranked second for violent crime rates in 1994 (Federal Bureau of Investigation, 1995).

In 1970 the population of St. Louis was more than 622,000 so that the 1970 record of 266 murders represented a rate of forty-three per 100,000. With the city's 1990 population at 396,000, the 174 killings for that year represented a rate of more than sixty-nine murders per 100,000, a 60 percent increase over the 1970 rate (Federal Bureau of Investigation, 1990). St. Louis's decreasing population, losing more than 28,000 residents between 1990 and 1994 (ranking St. Louis *43d* in the nation in terms of population [United States Department of the Census, 1995]), and the failure to incorporate surrounding suburban communities are two of several determinants for higher than average major-city crime rates. (The St. Louis metropolitan area's population is approximately 2.5 million, ranking the area *17th* in the nation [United States Department of the Census, 1995]).[1] It must be noted, however, that crime rates in St. Louis have decreased over the past two years as they have across the nation.

As explained previously in "A Theory of Crime Causation" chapter, St. Louis is a racially polarized city. Needless to say, this racial polarization is reflected within city government and the St. Louis Metropolitan Police Department (SLMPD) and serves as a backdrop for policing practices within the city. Supporting this cultural view of St. Louis, the following information was reported in the *St. Louis Post-Dispatch* and electronic media over the course of five years. None of the information was refuted (ascertained via careful monitoring by the author of local news stories from various sources).

THE BACKDROP

St. Louis elected its first black mayor in 1992 and the Police Board selected St. Louis's second black police chief in 1995—the first was hired in 1991. The SLMPD is presently under Missouri state control (St. Louis is one of very few cities whose Police Board members are appointed by the governor). The former mayor of St. Louis attempted to gain city control. Many fear that if the city gains control, there will be even more political pressure emanating from both black and white politicians and business groups than what is already exerted on the SLMPD.

At the time of this study, the city's Police Board was comprised of four members plus the mayor of St. Louis, resulting in a factionalized body—one faction was comprised of three black members (including the mayor) and the other faction was comprised of two white members. Many board decisions were controversially reached after members voted along racial lines.

The selection of the former police chief was unusual in that he was not backed by an influential "ace" (corroborated by informal conversations with police officers and news media reports). The former president of the St. Louis Police Board stated, "I think the promotion of [the former chief] was a big defeat for the 'ace' system. He did not come with political backing, he came with performance." (It was reported that the former chief was considered a "safe" choice rather than one of two other candidates who were backed by opposing "aces"—one black and the other white.)

Many in the St. Louis metropolitan area believe the resignation of this chief was prompted by political pressures having much to do with his refusal to do the bidding of "aces" and his attempt to "buck" politicians from both black and white groups in terms of hiring and promotion practices. Also, the chief claimed that many of his personnel decisions were overridden by the Police Board, and some board decisions that should have required his input were made while he was out of town. In fact, the chief stated that the Police Board was, at times, "micro-managing" the SLMPD.

Also, there were complaints about the chief coming from several in the city's black community who claimed that the chief was not assertive enough in supporting black officers—some even complained about the fact that his wife was white. Additionally, the former mayor's father, a St. Louis alderman, complained that killings of whites were treated more seriously than killings of blacks and that policing was carried out more thoroughly and effectively in white communities. Finally, a black police officer who admitted that the *mayor* was responsible for his hiring by the SLMPD, alleged that the officer-to-sergeant promotion exam was mailed to him. He claimed that whites had outperformed blacks on the test because they may have had copies before the test was given.

White officers threatened to sue if the Police Board threw out the test results.

It was subsequently learned, via an internal police investigation, that this same officer was, in fact, the one who had the test stolen. The former chief had recommended that the officer be terminated; however, the new chief recommended a suspension of thirty days.

Conversely, a group of white officers complained that less qualified black officers were unfairly promoted. The federal Equal Employment Opportunity Commission upheld the officers' complaint, accusing the Police Board of discrimination. The board reached a settlement with the officers who received compensation with adjusted back pay and security and retirement benefits.

With the former mayor as an additional outspoken critic coupled with the lack of assurance by the Missouri's governor that he, the governor, would not be politically pressured concerning a forthcoming Police Board appointment, the chief decided that it was time to alter careers, ending twenty-seven years of policing in St. Louis. It is reported that the chief (the first black chief hired in St. Louis) was well liked by an overwhelming majority of city residents and was believed to have done a good job. He became nationally known for championing community-oriented problem-solving policing (COPS) and was popular with black and white community groups as well as with the majority of rank-and-file-officers. Proof of this was his recent election as the city's second black mayor.

As the selection of a new police chief was being considered, the leader of the black officers group stated, "It's important to have a black chief." He claimed that race had polarized the police department: "We were sitting on a powder keg." He asserted that it would be difficult for a white chief to bring the department together (Bryan, 1995). Adding to the turmoil concerning the upcoming chief-selection, a *Post-Dispatch* columnist reported that one of his sources claimed the selection of the new chief, and those to be promoted into subsequent vacant slots caused by his selection, had been determined through a bargaining process among members of the Police Board several weeks before the candidates were administered tests and interviewed (McClellan, 1995a). (It is required that the chief be selected from the SLMPD.) The selection and promotion results were exactly as the source predicted (McClellan, 1995b). The newly appointed black chief had been supported by an influential black state legislator. The fact that most police chiefs are supported by influential "aces" is nothing new, but the fact that the community was led to believe that the chief's selection would be implemented in a fair and unbiased manner through testing and interviewing procedures, and then to learn of political "gamesmanship," strengthened citizens' perceptions of government illegitimacy.

The newly selected chief was immediately and practically tested after his "swearing in" ceremony. A black youth living in one of the city's housing projects was shot twice in the back by a white police officer. Conflicting reports were made by the police department concerning the sequence of events, the location of bullet wounds on the victim's body, and whether or not the victim possessed a gun. Several unissued guns were found in the officer's car trunk. Many believed these were "throw down guns" used for planting evidence around a victim's body. The officer was suspended without pay, and the investigation was transferred to the city's circuit attorney.

Nevertheless, an extended investigation by the SLMPD into the matter with refusal to divulge pertinent information, prompted an outcry from the black community. The funeral procession for the victim circled police headquarters in protest. One friend of the youth's family expressed her frustration this way, "This is the only way we can show how we feel. The police are preying on kids in our area. A lot of them are being harassed, and we just want some justice" (Yaquib, 1996). (A recent study had shown that shootings by St. Louis police officers were at a higher rate than the nine other major cities studied [Bryan, 1991].)

Also, it should be noted that background checks of police applicants had been lax for several years in the 1980s during the tenure of the second to last chief and the tenure of a former mayor. The SLMPD implemented a corruption investigation involving twenty officers who were hired during this period. Three officers were arrested for dealing drugs, several were under investigation for the same offense, others were under investigation for accepting pay for unperformed work as security guards, and two were arrested for "shaking down" a citizen. The former chief claimed that several investigations were hampered and/or delayed by city and state politicians. One investigation involved an officer who was hired as the former mayor's bodyguard and who was supported by the aforementioned black state legislator.

Conversely, several white officers brought under investigation were previously supported by white politicians and business leaders. For example, one white officer who was supported by a former chief (white), a former mayor (white), and a city alderman (white) had an arrest record that indicated excessive drinking and fighting problems. He was hired anyway. The officer subsequently resigned from the force after pleading guilty to first-degree assault resulting from shooting a man three times just outside a tavern. A recent revealing statement was made by this former officer, "I still drink, but not to the excess I [did] when I was a police officer" (Sorkin, 1994).

Turning now to the Hyde Park neighborhood and with the previously described city's racial polarization and political pressures from both black and white power-holders concerning the SLMPD serving as background, descriptions and discussions follow concerning prevalent complaints voiced by residents in the Hyde Park neighborhood about policing, police responses to these complaints, the community-oriented problem-solving (COPS) policing philosophy and how several Hyde Park police officers view this philosophy, and the neighborhood's attempt to make the police accountable. A summary of a focus group session conducted with rank-and-file police officers who patrolled the Hyde Park neighborhood and portions of interviews with the former police captain who headed the 5th Police District and one sergeant who also worked in the neighborhood support the legitimacy of many resident complaints and reveal questionable motives of police action and even racial bias. City problems of racial polarization, unethical practices, and political pressures on city government and the SLMPD are shown to have seeped through to the neighborhood level, affecting the lives of individual residents and hampering community-oriented problem-solving policing efforts. The common link between and among these issues concerning effective policing center around little or no locus-of-control at the following levels: the city of St. Louis; the SLMPD; rank-and-file police officers; and community members, especially neighborhood residents.

Following are results of observations, informal conversations, interviews, and focus group sessions that focused on policing in the Hyde Park neighborhood. Only the most salient results of numerous interviews and informal conversations are included.

RESIDENT COMPLAINTS ABOUT POLICING

Hyde Park lies within the Police 5th District known as the "Bloody Fifth." (See Map 4.1). Most complaints about policing in Hyde Park centered around poor police response. This pertained to the amount of response-time, rude and unresponsive dispatchers, negative attitudes toward residents on the part of police officers, lack of filing reports, lack of follow-up to responses, and "no shows." Also, residents asserted that some crime and juvenile problems were ignored by the police. Finally, a recurring complaint was that several officers put the "crime-blame" on residents for choosing to live in Hyde Park. Residents felt that officers were telling them there really was nothing that could be done to rid the neighborhood of crime; therefore, it was incumbent upon residents to move out.

Poor police response was exemplified in various ways. One resident related that she called 911 repeatedly one evening and told the dispatcher about a woman wielding a knife and beating her husband in the alley. After waiting an extended period of time, the resident called again and told the dispatcher, "Come and get the corpse!" Another resident heard the shattering of windshields. When she called 911 she was told that nothing could be done and she should call another number. When she called the second number, the dispatcher said nothing could be done and "hung up" on the woman three different times. The resident gave up.

Another resident's car was run into and shoved onto the sidewalk. When she called, the dispatcher asked, "Are you sure you're right about this?" The police arrived thirty minutes after the call. One property owner called 911 about gang activity and was told to call the "gang hot line"—he got a recording. A resident called about the same gang, and a police car stopped directly in front of her house and knocked on the door. (She now uses the back door when going and coming—she feels she is considered a nag by police and city agencies as well as being a "marked" woman.)

One resident stated that kids were stealing possessions from her elderly father, and when she reported this to the police, there was no response. Other residents were asked by officers, "What can we do about it?" When one resident

Map 4.1

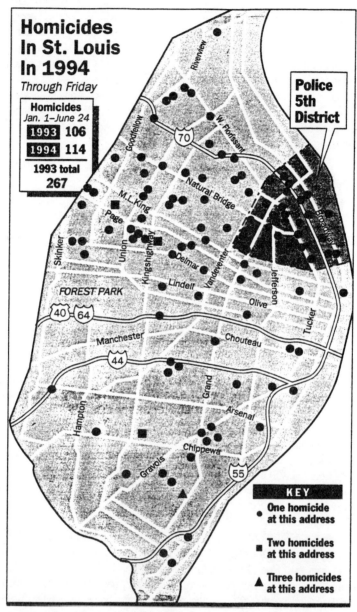

The 5th Policing District is known as "The Bloody Fifth." The Hyde Park
neighborhood is a smaller area located in the center of the district. Hyde
Park's boundaries are I70, Palm and Natural Bridge, and Glasgow and
Ferry streets which are several blocks south of Grand Avenue.

Source: St. Louis Post-Dispatch, June 26, 1994, 6A

was burglarized, there was no dusting for fingerprints. Even when shootings occurred it was reported that police response-time was thirty to forty minutes. In short, reports about crime were sometimes not made by residents because they felt it did no good.

THE SLMPD RESPONDS

Police response to complaints about policing in Hyde Park centered around understaffing, lack of detailed information, poor communication between residents and police, and some uncooperative residents. Furthermore, instead of directly responding to citizen complaints at numerous police/community meetings, police reports were made in terms of numbers of guns confiscated, drug busts, arrests made, and similar information. The following summary of results obtained from a focus group session with four rank-and-file St. Louis police officers and excerpts from interviews with a sergeant and the former captain of the 5th Police District shed further light on the ongoing problems between community residents and police.

The Rank-and-File

The former captain of the 5th Police District was asked to provide a representative sample of Hyde Park rank-and-file officers to participate in a focus group session. The focus group was comprised of four males (two black and two white) with from four to nine years policing experience. They were nonvoluntary participants called to the area station for the session, although they seemed to welcome the opportunity for socialization and a break. Three of the participants were talkative while the other was less talkative, quite fidgety, and had the least favorable views about the Hyde Park community. There may have been an element of providing the investigator with the most favorable responses at the beginning of the session; however, the conversation among participants quickly turned to a relaxed exchange of personal views. Results from this focus group session are revealing, especially when recognizing that participants were "selected" by the captain.

Most participants expressed dichotomous opinions regarding the role and/or duties of an effective rank-and-file police officer. This dichotomy was a desire to get closer to the public and to help residents solve their problems on the one hand, and the desire for a "kick-ass" police department on the other. In short, they felt that using their own judgment to handle various situations was essential to effective policing.

The officers seemed to be somewhat knowledgeable of the COPS program in the St. Louis Police Department. Their general feeling was that it was an ineffective program in St. Louis because there was insufficient time and not enough police officers to implement the program effectively. It was described as an "ill-attempt" for police to interact with the community. Finally, one officer stated that the program was headed by "some guy" who was a cop for only two years, had a law degree from Harvard, and was a civilian telling them how to do police work.

The list of blockages to effective policing was very long and consumed most of the session's time. The greatest blockage to effective policing was seen as "lack of time" because of inadequate manpower and time spent doing trivial and unimportant work such as writing reports and "counting buildings and ducks." It was felt that officers spent all their time shagging radio calls and were evaluated favorably if all calls were answered (not if they showed up on a call) and if they "kept up" with report-writing. The implication was that all calls were answered, but they were not necessarily followed up with a "show" at the designated location.

Additionally, the officers expressed feeling handcuffed by rules, regulations, and mandates coming from the "command ranks." Locus-of-control was definitely not perceived to be with themselves: "We're used as tools!" They desired to see results from their police work and see a problem through to the end. As one officer expressed, "We need a passion for our job; the passion is slowly and methodically being taken away from us!" Another expressed it this way, "I'm going to do my eight hours and go home!"

The participants expressed fear of being "written up" for a range of things from uniform violations to abuse of a person's civil rights. It was the consensus that effective policing was impossible "nowadays." Some wished for a "kick-ass" kind of police department where the "shit-heads" could be "taken down" and the troublemakers could be "weeded out" no matter where they were sent. In general, participants desired the leeway to be "aggressive on the streets."

Only one officer indicated that he would "go in a minute" if offered an assignment to an easier policing district. The others liked the 5th District and the Hyde Park neighborhood because they knew the people and liked the fast pace, action, and excitement: "You may have a couple different homicides going on at one time, a couple different car chases, a couple different robberies." One participant stated he felt "hurt" when he was assigned to the district because he thought "nothing was going on here."

This information begged the question, "Why did you become a police officer?" Responses included excitement, an outdoor job, fast pace, authority, respect, and the desire to be loved by the community. They all wanted to make a difference. One black officer stated that as a young black man, he wanted people to look up to him and wanted to prove that, "I could do more than be a stick-up man or steal cars."

(Some indication of the "excitement" appeal to officers was noted when seven two-man police cars arrived for one call in response to a Hyde Park business robbery. When it was reported that the suspect may have been seen driving towards Interstate 70, the officers jumped in their cars and gave chase. No one was caught. Meanwhile, someone reported he/she saw the robber walking another direction in the neighborhood. One wonders how well Hyde Park and even the entire 5th District was protected during this time. When asked about this, the captain said some of the police cars may have just happened to be driving by at the time, and some cars were probably from the Mobile Reserve and/or Canine Units. He seemed to resent the question.)

When describing the people who lived in Hyde Park, the officers' responses were generally favorable including people who talked to each other, called when they saw something happen, supported the police, congregated, and were really trying to take care of the neighborhood: "I wouldn't say they are winning, but they're not losing any ground." When it was mentioned that the Hyde Park Mobile Patrol (a community effort to patrol the neighborhood as extended "eyes" of the police) would soon be in operation again, most of the participants said they would "start hiding." Previously, they had been reported by the patrol when parked in order to write reports, take a break, and talk to girls (to obtain information).

One officer described the community as a ghetto similar to the one in which he grew up in East St. Louis with only a handful (about 20%) of real "shit-heads" that should be weeded out. Although another officer talked about the friendliness of the business owners in Hyde Park, he described the community this way: "To effectively police a community is impossible with the way a community is this day and age! . . . Maybe I'm just getting burned out working up in this area. . . . They're uneducated, they don't want to work—I mean—what is going on?—and the government just sits back and supports them!" (This was the officer who would have willingly gone to an easier policing district.)

The causes of criminal behavior were viewed by the officers as social issues in terms of lack of education, jobs, and responsible parents; children born out of wedlock; female-headed households; and disintegrating families. Surprisingly, foreground causes such as opportunity, lack of quick and effective punishment, and the availability of guns were not mentioned. (Lack of effective punishment was seen as a blockage to effective policing.) After probing for underlying causes, past and present racial discrimination was mentioned by the black officers. The lure of easy money was also seen by a white officer as an underlying cause (alluding to American culture?).

Paradoxically, even though social issues were perceived to be the main causes of criminal behavior, suggestions to remedy the crime problem in the United States focused on addressing foreground causes. These suggestions included speedier implementation of penalties, stiffer jail sentences, and additional and larger prisons. Education and decreasing the economic gap were mentioned only after the author reminded the participants that the United States has the highest incarceration rate and yet has the highest violent crime rate of all western, industrialized nations.

When asked if there was anything else they wanted to say before ending the session, a couple participants did not want the impression left that they were bitter. Another officer quickly added that he *was* bitter because when they *did* get additional police officers in the department, they would probably be detached to specialized units instead of being assigned to street patrol. One black officer mentioned a possible conspiracy on the part of the federal government desiring that certain neighborhoods fall. Another black officer agreed and added, "I believe if a dope house moved out next to [the St. Louis County commissioner], it wouldn't be there no time!"

The Captain

The captain's views are important for understanding policing practices in the Hyde Park neighborhood during his tenure (he has since been promoted to major). He was the "leader" of the 5th Police District and, therefore, his perceptions of resident-types living in the district and, therefore, living in Hyde Park, were reflected in the practices of his subordinates. The captain also led most of the police/community meetings in Hyde Park and his rapport/lack of rapport with community residents influenced their feelings about policing in the neighborhood and their level of cooperation with police officers.

The captain of the 5th District was viewed by Hyde Park residents as exemplifying an officer from the "old guard," a believer in punishment rather than prevention, and as non-community-oriented. When first assigned to the neighborhood, he informed residents during one community meeting that officers would not have time to talk to residents and discuss problems. When it was suggested that officers needed to respond to calls and follow through, the captain retorted that there were more officers assigned to north side neighborhoods than south side neighborhoods. He went on to say that residents see a lot and wonder why the police don't see the same—"They're not always there!" He ended his statement by advising that there were only twelve police officers on duty at one time for the entire 5th District.

During the course of the meeting, he expressed regret that some police officers were "let go" because of the Rodney King incident even though lines may have been crossed—"This makes it hard on police everywhere." For every resident complaint, he provided excuses rather than indicating complaints would be investigated or considered. He generally blamed the crime problem on "eroding family values."

Additional remarks made by the captain during subsequent meetings with residents included, "It's like putting a building back together block by block after it's been taken apart. . . . These are things we're doing for you, making the streets safe so you can live in a safe society. . . . You can't keep pushing all the problems on the police!"

Following are views the captain expressed during a formal interview just before being transferred out of the 5th District, revealing racial prejudice and bias:

What causes criminal behavior in your opinion?

A lot of it—what I see nowadays—is just a lot of lack of parenting. There is no strict family life in a lot of these groups where the kids are involved in criminal activity. There is no supervision. They see a one-parent family; they see how the boyfriends come over and treat mom, and they think that's the way life should be lived. They don't have it where you have a father who treats the mother with any type of respect. In a lot of these groups, that's how they grow up—a woman doesn't receive any respect.

You have to bring the values back and make these people understand that this is the way a family is supposed to be. On different talk shows black men are saying that in the black culture (and I'm not picking on blacks) women are just looked down upon so badly, and that's why the kids have no respect for them. The way you turn that around is maybe take people off welfare where the father is still around, and make them more responsible. "This is your responsibility!" Trying to collect child support from somebody that doesn't work and just bed-hops is a tough thing to do.

Are there any underlying causes for this?

Whenever it began that way, it's just continued on. Reflecting on my upbringing, you just knew that you paid the consequences if you stepped across the line. Without the father figure there, there's nobody to discipline them. There *are* some strong black females who can keep a family in line.

Because of the standards in the United States, we've become somewhat liberal with them and accepted some things more. Other countries have rules (Japan)—you're in their country, you break the rules, you have to face the consequences. It may sound severe to us, but the severity of their punishments eliminates some of the crime problems. . . .

An example that happened in another country, which is a little severe, a guy was caught stealing a large item on a Saturday, was tried on a Sunday, and was publicly hung on a Monday. That's quick! It's immediate to these people—"Hey, this is what's going to happen!"

What are the most effective measures to prevent and/or deter this behavior?

I'm a firm believer that there are some people that no matter what you do, you're still going to have a problem. A two-parent family can do everything in the world and everything right and question what could we have done differently, and the answer is "nothing." I don't know how to explain it other than the "genes" as they say or just somebody that doesn't want to adhere to the societal rules, and they're going to be their own person no matter what. I wish I had the resolution because I could make some money! . . .

We need more prisons because of the amount of people being locked up today. The way prisons are now, one goes in and one has to come out. They let people out who are involved in nonviolent crimes. Well, selling drugs is considered nonviolent, a burglar is considered nonviolent—they all have an effect on society. I don't want them coming into my house. Now that he's back out, he's not going to change. They say a leopard never changes his spots.

The Sergeant

An interview with a police sergeant who worked in the Hyde Park neighborhood revealed a more community-oriented philosophy and a greater understanding for the need of preventive crime measures, yet he supported the rank-and-file officers' expressions of excitement-lures to police work:

If I had a choice, I would opt for this area. It's where I started out working, and I've always been here. I'm used to a faster track than the south areas. Some would consider these [south] to be the "better" districts because they're not as hard working, but I like the faster track, so I would much rather be here. If you're going to be a policeman, be a policeman and not be a watchman somewhere. If you want to work with crime, criminals, and victims, work with crime, criminals, and victims—otherwise, go guard a warehouse!

What are the most effective measures to prevent and/or deter criminal behavior?

The best thing to do—you're going to have to go on the long-range effect. A lot of the people out there now—the criminal element—aren't going to be saved no matter what you do with them. I think you have to work on the younger kids right now—try to make something out of them before you lose them too—as far as the formative years. Any type of youth program you can get would help. Programs to direct youth in any constructive way instead of the destructive ways they learn on the street. Any kind of controlled environment where you're telling these kids what's expected of them in later life, what's expected of them now, respect for each other, respect for the community and property. You can't get enough of these type programs. . . .

You have to have street patrol. More time to patrol would be great; however, we don't have it and it's going to get worse during the summer. All the officers are on call somewhere. It's good any time you can spend talking to people—find out what they think. They know what's wrong more than we do 'cause they live there—we don't. We spend eight hours here and then go home. You have to talk to the people who live there if you want to find out what's wrong, what's going on, who's doing it, and why they're doing it.

COMMUNITY-ORIENTED PROBLEM-SOLVING POLICING (COPS)

The sergeant's expressed philosophy of policing was not uncommon to that of the struggling community-oriented problem-solving policing effort in St. Louis that was advocated and supported by the former chief. As of 1993 a little more than half of St. Louis police officers had participated in a two-day in-service training that consisted of addressing the basic concept of problem-oriented policing, the need for change, the problem-solving process, and implications for organizational change. There was no manual or substantial printed materials dispersed. Revamping the "basic training" curriculum to include the COPS concept had been considered (telephone interview with the director of the SLMPD COPS program, 1993).

The director of the COPS program distinguished community-oriented problem-solving policing from community policing. He asserted the two concepts had emerged from two different perspectives and felt the philosophy of community policing was flawed in that it had been vaguely defined in the literature. The director defined problem-solving policing as a problem-solving approach that had to do with quality of communication with citizens and the ability to work with them. He believed it was a coming together of police officers and community members to address problems, and maintained that officers often harbored misconceptions about the COPS program as community policing defined as "warmed over public relations."

Robert Trojanowicz and colleagues in their book *Community Based Crime Prevention* (1975), define "community policing" when recommending that police develop methods to communicate effectively with various ethnicities, align themselves with a wide variety of community agencies and individuals, and communicate with schools. They *approach* the problem-solving method of policing when they suggest that officers work with community leaders. They also assert that police evaluations should be based on the way situations are handled rather than the number of arrests made. Finally, the authors maintain that in communities where there is a great deal of serious crime, this type of law enforcement orientation may carry over into situations that could be handled best by maintenance-of-order with discretionary use of power.

Herman Goldstein (1990) expands on these ideas in his description of "problem-oriented policing." He broadly defines problem-oriented policing as a better balance between reactive and proactive policing, making more effective use of the community, and making more effective use of rank-and-file officers in carrying out policing efforts. Goldstein delineates the fundamental elements of problem-oriented policing that suggest "action research" on the practitioner's part. Action research is advocated in diverse disciplines when practitioners reflect, study, research, and document their methods, data-use, and effectiveness in order to improve practice, develop professionally, and contribute to reform. In my view, this is what Goldstein is promoting along with advocating several elements of the "community policing" philosophy (developing improved relationships with the community). Goldstein's recommendations for effective problem-oriented policing are:

- Group incidents as specific types of problems
- Focus on substantive problems as the heart of policing and define them not as police problems (lack of sufficient manpower), but as community problems
- View the ultimate goal as policing "effectiveness"
- Systematically inquire (collection and analysis) into all problem characteristics and their contributing factors
- Disaggregate and accurately label problems as opposed to imposing overly broad or inaccurate labels such as "street crime" and "delinquency"
- Analyze various systems included in problems such as social and economic systems
- Document and analyze current police responses
- Search for alternative and multiple ways of responding to recurring problems and mobilize the community in this effort
- Adopt a proactive stance and share police knowledge with the community
- Strengthen the decision-making processes and increase accountability within the community
- Evaluate results—relationships could be established with universities for evaluation purposes

Goldstein laments that police officers are usually awarded publicly for traditional policing such as number of arrests, number of traffic tickets, and/or heroic actions instead of problem-solving efforts that are more difficult to evaluate. Moreover, although one part of effective problem-oriented policing is facilitation, militaristic labels designating positions of police management are anathema to this (sergeant, lieutenant, captain, and major).

Additionally, Goldstein suggests that recruitment of police officers should be subjective as well as objective, based on the idea that personality traits are important.   Also, training of recruits should encompass working through problems that may be encountered on the job, and management must reward problem-solving and provide officers with necessary time to practice this method. Finally, there should be opportunities for officers to remain in the same community and maintain the same work shift for an adequate length of time in order to gain familiarity with the community and its residents.

An example of problem-oriented policing in an urban setting that seemed to be working was the policing in New Haven, Connecticut, a city of approximately 130,000. The former police chief, Nick Pastore (interviewed on *60 Minutes*, 1994), received both praise and criticism for the change he initiated in New Haven's police force beginning seven years ago. The chief began the transition to problem-oriented policing by purging senior ranks and reassigning lower level officers to the streets. He also cruised the city to observe how officers were implementing their duties. Over 20 percent of the police force resigned; Pastore replaced them with predominantly minorities and women.

Praise for Pastore's efforts emanated from the New Haven community and outsiders who noticed that homicide decreased by one third and other serious crime substantially decreased. Condemnation came from many members of the New Haven police force, especially from the police union. In fact, five years ago, the union voted to get rid of the chief; his response was, "I wore that as a badge of honor."

During his interview, Chief Pastore asserted, "Mean-spirited policing leads to mean streets." He found that the usual hard-nosed policing was not effective in New Haven—crime had escalated. He felt that the problem was the marine mentality-type of policing and the past recruitment for "adventure-type" policing that turned citizens against the department.

Pastore indicated that he was out almost every night cruising the neighborhoods but almost never made an arrest. Likewise, he did not want his officers making many arrests; he viewed arrests as responses of last resort: "You have to understand what prevention of crime is. Officers are in the position to be role models and mentors and to connect people to resources." Pastore expected his officers to mediate conflicts, get people into counseling if needed, and to be problem-solvers. Finally, he expressed belief that having a basic understanding of the causes of criminal behavior was important for good policing practices.

In St. Louis, whether or not problem-oriented policing was effective within a police district depended on the district's captain (telephone interview with the COPS' program director, 1994). The application of the philosophy was, therefore, very uneven across the city. The following excerpt from an interview with the aforementioned 5th District captain gives some idea of the amount and kind of problem-oriented policing taking place in the Hyde Park neighborhood during 1994 and future implementation of this philosophy in a large portion of St. Louis (the captain is now a major, supervising several police districts).

Describe the COPS philosophy.

Well, this is where I get myself into trouble in this department. [The following was related in a rote, sarcastic fashion.] The COPS philosophy is to get involved in neighborhoods—you almost have your own personal policeman within your block. He knows everything and if someone needs something, he has a beeper and he gives his beeper number out to the people so they can call at any time. The policeman responds and takes care of *everything*.

It's a hard philosophy to sell to me because a lot of it gets away from some of the basics. Where we get into a problem with some of the COPS projects is we're doing the work of City Hall. We're finding the buildings and having to get the building inspectors out. Lots—we get ahold of Weed Control and a lot of things like this that makes me ask, "What's City Hall doing?". . . At times, the COPS philosophy, in my opinion, wants to make you more of a social worker rather than a law enforcer.

If you had adequate manpower, would the COPS philosophy work?

Even if you had adequate manpower, you'd give the people a more secure feeling that mere presence alone makes people happy to see that there's policemen. But, is it really? See, my bottom line is this. Even if you have that, is it going to resolve the crime problem by the different functions they want done with the COPS philosophy? In reality—no!

DISCUSSION

Considering the crime problems of Hyde Park residents and their feelings that police officers were not responding properly to these problems, the COPS program, if implemented fully and effectively, would seem to be a step in the right direction. The principal of the elementary school located in the neighborhood challenged the excuse that more manpower was needed in order to implement the COPS philosophy:

If the cops would come and interact with these kids, when they saw something go down, and they looked and saw the kids, they would already know who they are. They would know where they lived—they could run, but they couldn't hide! If a cop comes up in a car and sees a group of kids and doesn't know any of them, the kids take off running—how do you solve the problem? The cops don't know where to get them—they're gone—it's over—the cop leaves—the kids come back—they do the same damn thing they were doing before. If the cop could go to the kid's house and tell the parents what the kid was doing and threaten to fine them if the behavior is not stopped, that would be more powerful. They wouldn't *need* as much manpower if there was more proactive policing rather than just reactive policing!

Added to police complaints about inadequate manpower to effectively implement the COPS philosophy, the former police captain of the 5th District made racial allusions to "those people" and "that group" in his interview. As the "leader" of the 5th District, the captain's biased views understandably influenced policing practices in the Hyde Park neighborhood.

Moreover, with only two days of in-service training in the COPS philosophy and program, and a large portion of the police force yet to undergo even this minimal amount of training at the time of this study, it is difficult to imagine that this philosophy could have been fully understood, accepted, and then implemented effectively within the SLMPD. Focus group, interview, and informal conversation results along with observations of police response to efforts by the Hyde Park community to make police accountable, indicate that officers' understanding of the COPS program was "community relations" rather than "community problem-solving."

Additionally, Chief Pastore's experience in New Haven, Connecticut, may foreshadow what should yet transpire in St. Louis—a paradigm shift may require a *personnel* shift. It must be noted, however, that with the already documented political pressures on the former chief coming from both white and black St. Louis communities in terms of personnel decisions within the SLMPD, a significant personnel shift is not likely to take place in the foreseeable future as indicated by the promotion of the 5th District captain. With entrenched mind-sets of racial bias, militaristic policing styles, and "do what is necessary to get the job done" as results of focus group sessions and formal and informal interviews indicate, the COPS philosophy was not and could not be a catalyst for imminent or significant change concerning SLMPD policing practices. Rank-and-file officers expressed desires to see problems through to the end and the necessity of autonomy to implement effective policing practices. These views are compatible with the problem-oriented policing philosophy; however, there was not a consistent and determined effort at all levels to implement the COPS program within the SLMPD.

Furthermore, the "adventure" phenomenon revealed by the sergeant and rank-and-file when they expressed desires to remain in the 5th District because of the "fast pace" and "excitement" is anathema to a problem-solving approach. The thoughts and words of Herman Goldstein and Chief Pastore dismiss the adventure and excitement incentives to becoming a police officer. They see these lures feeding a "marine-type" mentality harmful to community and police relationships. These factors could even be deterrents to the "take-them-down" policing that some officers in the focus group desired. An example would be the seven two-man car response to one call, that probably meant all 5th District on-duty patrol officers were in one place at the same time.

Rank-and-file officers also expressed feelings that they needed the freedom "to do what you have to do" to get rid of the "undesirables" in the neighborhood. Addressing these views, Tobias Winright (1995) discusses the "just war theory" concerning harm and restraint (unacceptable actions by citizens justify the same-type actions and even accelerated actions by police). Winright asserts that the "just war theory" serves as a rationalization for reactive policing measures that may lead to police abuse of the citizenry.

Finally, all interviewed police personnel expressed little understanding of possible underlying causes of criminal behavior as outlined and discussed by criminologists, sociologists, and scholars from multiple disciplines (American culture based on competition, individualism, material gain, and conspicuous consumption [Messner and Rosenfeld, 1993; Bradley, 1992; Barber, 1993], institutionalized racism [Wilson, 1987; Cross, 1987], and relative deprivation promoting alienation and frustration [Currie, 1985; Grier and Cobbs, 1968; Hutchinson, 1990; McCall, 1994]). It is logical to assume that practitioners in all disciplines should base their actions on theories resulting from underlying philosophies. Although a philosophy (in this case based on social indices and human behavior) does not furnish solutions, it may define difficulties and suggest methods for dealing with them or clarifying them. Without prompting, only the sergeant expressed the need for preventive measures in deterring social and human behavioral correlates to crime. Exposure to and understanding possible underlying causes of criminal behavior would seem to be essential for effective proactive and ethical policing. This understanding linked with Goldstein's view of community problem-solving policing and eclectic methods to recruit and train police officers as well as confronting racial and ethnic biases offers at least a beginning for more effective policing in our communities.

All indicators point to a "bumpy" road ahead for Hyde Park resident and police relations. Admission by the rank-and-file that they answered all calls but did not necessarily "show up" in response to calls and were evaluated on this basis, gives credence to resident complaints of poor police response and may have provided incentive to initiate the Hyde Park Mobile Patrol. It must be noted that the above *admission* by the rank-and-file was the only "surprise" derived from the focus group session. Other views expressed in the session were repeated views (to a more or less degree) of those expressed by officers engaged in informal conversations at various community meetings and in several community establishments. It will take a determined and unwavering community focus to keep the police accountable.

Moreover, the city's racial problems as exemplified by the wide gap of general welfare data between the two races (black and white), racial separation in housing patterns, and the fighting between and among black and white politicians for control and influence have not bode well for effective and ethical policing at the neighborhood level. When those in leadership positions within the SLMPD have attempted to lessen political influence on hiring and promotion practices, implementation of disciplinary measures, and even efforts to initiate proactive policing policies embodied in the COPS program, these leaders have been blocked at all levels by state, city, and neighborhood politicians and business leaders (black and white). Described incidents of political pressure in St. Louis indicated that whatever racial group held power at a given time, members of that particular group were the beneficiaries in government and government-connected appointments/hiring—each group demonstrating unethical practices in exerting power and influence. Tobias Winright's discussion of "just war theory" is also relevant to "making up" for past injustices in the political arena by implementing equally unjust and unethical practices.

Finally, it would be safe to assume that policing practices within the city of St. Louis and the Hyde Park neighborhood are not unique among major cities in the United States as supported by national news media reports. The Hyde Park neighborhood serves as one microscopic example in terms of reactionary and unethical policing practices rooted in racial polarization and then compounded by pressures emanating from political and business communities. Little or complete absence of informed locus-of-control—within the city of St. Louis, the SLMPD, among rank-and-file police officers, and among community residents concerning policing efforts—is a common theme contributing to the aforementioned indices. The city lacks control of police board membership (state controlled), the chief lacks control of hiring and discipline practices (often controlled by a racially polarized police board, politicians, and business community), the rank-and-file have little control of their day to day operations because of police departmental bureaucracy, and Hyde Park community members exert great amounts of time and effort attempting to gain control of their neighborhood by making the police accountable. The lack of extensive and intensive community problem-solving policing makes the task of gaining factual and pertinent information an almost impossible task on the part of Hyde Park community members.

The COPS philosophy promotes policing methods that would positively affect both background (social malaise) and foreground (situational) contributions to criminal behavior via a proactive and analytical approach while providing an avenue for locus-of-control to remain with those closest to the problem—rank-and-file police officers and community residents. Conversely, inadequate, little, or no informed control at all levels concerning policing activities has blocked full implementation of the COPS initiative. In St. Louis the problem is circular and complex, demanding proactive problem-solving attacks from all sides in order to positively affect the quality of inner-city living.

NOTES

1. William Julius Wilson maintains that population loss may affect a city's crime rate by increasing social dislocation and economic disadvantage in the central city, thereby increasing the number of crimes committed by a shrinking population (W. Wilson, *The Truly Disadvantaged* [1987]). Rosenfeld in *St. Louis Homicide Project: Local Responses to a National Problem*, 1-4 (1989), reminds us:

A crime rate is a fraction that divides the number of actual crimes by the number of potential crimes, which is conventionally defined as the number of residents of the city. Thus potential crimes are limited by the size of the city's population, while number of actual crimes may reach a theoretical maximum equal to the number of offenders times the number of crimes they commit during a specified time interval. Contributions to actual crimes can be made regardless of residence; to contribute to potential crimes, you must live in the city. Cities that have experienced rapid population loss may well have upward pressure exerted on their crime rates, especially if those who leave the city do not leave the metropolitan area and therefore remain potential offenders or targets of crime within the city. Persons who move out of the city and return on a frequent basis to work, shop, attend sporting and cultural events, or commit crimes can make a potentially very significant contribution to the crime rate by withdrawing from the potential crime number while continuing to make regular deposits to the actual crime number.

Chapter 5

Hyde Park Crime: Prevention Efforts and Their Effects

The problem in St. Louis, as in other major U.S. cities, is finding and then implementing crime prevention approaches that offer the best chances to alleviate criminal behavior. The hypothesis offered is that *comprehensive* crime prevention programs implemented at the neighborhood level in partnership with police, the city, and other outside entities offer the best solution.

CRIME IN HYDE PARK

Many informal conversations with Hyde Park residents were interspersed with stories of criminal acts perpetrated on themselves, relatives, neighbors, and friends. Almost all interviewed residents and business owners owned guns and kept them nearby, ready for use. Here is what one resident had to say about her gradually growing fear of crime in the neighborhood:

I've lived in Hyde Park for about eight years. When I first moved here, it was a very quiet place. I never had any problems until last year in 1993. I had three break-ins—one break-in happened at 3:30 in the morning, and it was really frightening. Someone tried to break into my bathroom—when I heard glass break, I just jumped up. What scared me the most was that he told the police officer that if he had gotten in, he was going to kill me!

I don't jog around the park any more, and I don't go out and walk any more. When I come home late at night, I always blow my horn before I get out of the car, so I make sure that a neighbor is looking out. When I sleep at night, there are at least three lights on—I won't turn my TV off at all. I ended up getting bars on some of my windows, I ended up getting an alarm installed, and I ended up getting extra protection for my doors in the house.

I have dead bolts, and I rigged up a 2x4 that goes from my door to the wall so my door can't be kicked in. I want to be able to have time to get up and prepare myself if I hear something—to sound my alarm and to be able to get my gun ready. I have a .38 and I have a .25. The .38 is a revolver and the .25 is an automatic. It's loaded with the safety off. I live alone, so I don't have the problem of worrying about kids. It stays by my bed.

During a previous telephone conversation and after relating neighborhood incidents of two car jackings, a homicide, and hearing gun shots coming from the house behind her apartment (she called the gunfire "hot line"—it was disconnected), the same resident complained: "I'm tired of the violence! Residents have adjusted to the fact that we're living around crime. Why should we have to adjust to living like this? The police think that we're use to it, so why bother as much about us? That's the way it's suppose to be!"

A business owner had this to say when asked the question, "What would you say are the biggest concerns of business and industry in and around Hyde Park other than making a profit?" "Crime. Businesses have to have security and safety for their employees. Several employers and business owners have been mugged."

Gun shots were heard frequently in the Hyde Park neighborhood. One Saturday afternoon I heard shots from what was described as a semi-automatic. Only a few people from one house came out to see what was happening. I wondered if the other residents were not surprised—it must have been a common occurrence in the neighborhood.

Without asking community members to talk about crime, informal conversations very often centered around that topic. One resident related that she heard gun shots "all the time"—her children are not allowed out of the backyard to play. She told about her neighbor who now carries a gun because his wife was recently mugged. She related that the street lights are constantly being "shot out" as was one window of her home. Another resident revealed that he would be moving upon receiving his doctorate. Hearing a semi-automatic late at night was the "straw that broke the camel's back."

At least half the meetings I attended in the neighborhood included related incidents and/or discussions about recent criminal acts in the community. One business owner was burglarized, robbed, and threatened at knife point on three separate occasions during a one-year period. The owner slept in her shop until the doors could be replaced after the two most recent incidents. Her home was also burglarized three times. She now keeps a gas gun and a small pistol either on top of the store's counter or in her pocket. The adjacent store was also burglarized on several occasions. One time bricks were removed, and another time a wooden panel was removed in order to gain entry (the store has an alarm system).

Surprisingly, incidents of crime took place when police cars were visible. On the other hand, this served as an indicator that the on-duty officers were occupied and where they were occupied. For example, during one of the Safety

Committee meetings with police in attendance, the committee chair's truck was broken into and her coat was stolen. During another community meeting, a service provider's car was vandalized. There were many related incidents such as these. An elderly Hyde Park resident lamented, "The older men can't even go to the park to fish where there's no fish, because they get beat up and their poles are taken away!"

The most recent crime "fads" during the course of my study included stealing televisions; air conditioners; wrought iron fences, gates, and window decorations; and buildings (brick by brick). It was related at one community meeting that criminals had been targeting boarded-up buildings owned by the Land Reutilization Authority (the city) and tearing them down. One woman saw a building intact at 7:00 a.m., and then the two top floors down and the bricks loaded onto a dolly by 1:00 p.m.

Drug trafficking was prolific in Hyde Park. Many residents knew who some of the neighborhood drug dealers were, but were afraid to say or do anything about it. One of the dealers threatened his own wife and neighborhood residents—it was rumored that he threatened to have people "taken out." At least one policeman in the community was believed to be "on the take." One resident spoke to a former drug user who related about having to wonder why drug dealers know five minutes ahead of time when the police are coming: "There are police on the take!"

The growing crime problem and the fear of crime in Hyde Park spurred somewhat extreme views of possible solutions. Many residents viewed the justice system as being "soft" on criminals: "They have more rights than the victims!" One business owner felt that physical punishment could be an answer. She cited the criminal justice system in Iran where there is very little crime because punishment is carried out in public. "When a girl was raped, the citizens castrated and hung the rapist in public!" The "caning" solution for graffitists recently proposed by a St. Louis alderperson was not seen as a bad idea.

One alderperson representing the Hyde Park area wanted to propose a six-member strike force to be under the direction of a former police officer. "There is a lost generation—you can't do anything with them. . . . I'm for killing them. I want to put the fear of God in 'em. It's cruel, it's not fair, but that's what they do. Principles need to be applied that match the circumstances!"

THE HYDE PARK SAFETY COMMITTEE AND MOBILE PATROL

The Hyde Park Mobile Patrol was initiated in 1991 by a couple living in the community and out of a felt need to address the growing problem of crime in the neighborhood. Subsequently, a crime prevention committee was organized in 1991 by a resident, the Friedens Church pastor's wife, and a Hyde Park property owner. It was then decided to have the Mobile Patrol function as part of the crime prevention organization, later renamed the Hyde Park Safety Committee. For a time, the committee met in the Friedens Haus facility.

The mobile patrol was very organized and worked closely with the police captain of the 5th District. Weekly reports were made to the captain, and the police were to "follow-up." The cars patrolled every Friday and Saturday from 7:00 p.m. to 1:00 a.m., two cars at a time, each with two riders. All cars carried cellular phones, and there was a "pick-up" station with someone manning another phone—phone numbers were written down for all participants. Each car was equipped with a flashlight, log sheet, a list of "dos and don'ts" (Figure 5.1), and riders possessed an ID card identifying him/her as a Hyde Park Mobile Patrol rider.

The patrol operated from March 1991 to October 1991 and from March 1992 to October 1992 and then was reestablished in 1994. At its peak the patrol enlisted approximately sixty riders. Some reported that the patrol was responsible for fifty-five to seventy arrests and believed that crime was reduced between 30 to 50 percent. Crime data for this period do not support the latter claim for most crime categories, although burglary was down 40 percent in 1992. Reported incidents of burglary were up in 1991 as they were in seven demographically similar neighborhoods and the city. As will be seen later, the patrol may have had a deterring effect on incidents of robbery.

As part of participant-observation for research purposes, the author assisted the safety committee in reestablishing the mobile patrol in 1992. This proved to be time consuming for all involved because of scheduling, maintaining participant interest and enthusiasm, and some hindrances from neighborhood organizations. Police contacts were important, and the transfer of the police captain out of the 5th Police District and the orientation of a new captain were also hurdles to overcome. Although the new captain was initially leery of neighborhood mobile patrols, he was eventually convinced that the Hyde Park patrol was well organized and attempting to help the neighborhood become a safer community. He suggested all participants sign waivers, that copy-resistant ID cards be available, and police background checks be made for patrol participants. He emphasized that he wanted to be kept abreast of mobile patrol activities, including times and dates of patrols.

The patrol proved to be difficult to maintain, especially with volunteer leaders. It was a roll-up-your-sleeves and pick-up-the-phone-and-call type job. Maintaining workable car phones and pairing no-car and have-car riders were additional ongoing efforts. The goal was to eventually maintain a twenty-four hour patrol similar to a mobile patrol operation in one south side St. Louis neighborhood (Shaw). Hyde Park community members saw the mobile patrol as an attempt to not only assist in making the neighborhood safer, but also as an avenue for community-wide involvement and improving police accountability.

EFFECTS OF HYDE PARK CRIME PREVENTION EFFORTS

In order to determine if there were any positive effects of Hyde Park crime prevention efforts, a comparison concerning crime rates in the categories of

Figure 5.1

```
          HYDE PARK MOBILE PATROL - The Dos and Don'ts

   The Dos

     1.  Always ride with another person and with another Mobile
         Patrol vehicle in service.  Two cars always out
         together.

     2.  Ride with car doors locked.

     3.  Ride with mobile phone, log book, small flashlight,
         watch, and mobile patrol I.D.

     4.  Drive slowly, but unobtrusively, if possible.

     5.  Only use mobile phone to call police (311), other Mobile
         Patrol vehicle, and coordinator.

     6.  When calling police, identify yourself as a member of
         the Hyde Park Mobile Patrol.

     7.  Call police for felonies and misdemeanors in progress.
         (Includes tampering with autos and properties).

     8.  After calling police, wait at your location until police
         arrive.  If the location of the problem moves, notify
         police about the change.

     9.  Record the time when police were called and the time
         when they arrived.

    10.  Use log book to record suspicious activity.  (Log books
         will be given to police on a regular basis).

    11.  Record times, locations, and give descriptions of
         suspicious activity in the log book.

    12.  For vehicles, record license plate, year, body style,
         color, and make.

    13.  For persons, record information about clothing and
         shoes, height, weight, build, age, hair, facial hair,
         direction of travels, etc.

    14.  Make contact with other Mobile Patrol vehicle every half
         hour.

    15.  Your personal safety is the priority.

    16.  Be patient.  This project may take some time to achieve
         significant and observable results.
```

Source: Hyde Park Mobile Patrol

robbery, aggravated assault, and burglary was made among Hyde Park on the north side of St. Louis and contiguous and noncontiguous St. Louis neighborhoods comprised of similar demographic characteristics. The eight neighborhoods selected for demographic and crime rate comparisons in

Figure 5.1 (Cont'd)

```
The Don'ts

 1.  Never ride alone, without another vehicle on patrol, and
     without a coordinator knowing you are on patrol.

 2.  Do not get out of your car while on patrol.

 3.  Do not patrol on foot, bicycle, motorcycle, or
     horseback.

 4.  Do not drink before or during patrol.

 5.  Do not carry any weapons or liquor in the patrol
     vehicle.

 6.  Do not chase any cars.

 7.  Do not trail cars or pedestrians.

 8.  Do not confront anyone:  e.g., stop people and ask them
     what they are doing.

 9.  Do not shine flashlights on people or property.

10.  Once the police arrive at the crime scene or problem
     area, do not get out of the car.  Do not interfere with
     the police or get involved in the situation.

11.  Do not use police scanners while on patrol.

12.  Do not use the mobile phones to make personal calls.

13.  Do not travel particular streets or blocks if you feel
     unusually uncomfortable or in danger by doing so.

14.  Do not recklessly endanger yourself or other patrol
     members.

15.  We should not think of ourselves as police officers or
     law enforcement officials.
```

Source: Hyde Park Mobile Patrol

alphabetical order were Covenant Blu-Grand Center (middle-north side), Forest Park Southeast (middle-south side), Fox Park (south side), Hyde Park (north side), McKinley Fox (south side), Old North St. Louis (contiguous to Hyde Park), Shaw (south side), and St. Louis Place (contiguous to Hyde Park). Demographic data based on the 1990 Census for the eight neighborhoods were obtained from the Community Development Agency (1993).

Demographic Descriptions of Eight St. Louis Neighborhoods

Demographic characteristics of race, female-headed households, unemployment, education, and income were selected because of their correlation to criminal behavior. Race (African-American) in the United States is correlated to lower socio-economic status (Cross, 1987; Grier and Cobbs, 1968; Hutchinson, 1990); and socio-economic status, especially the gap between the haves and have-nots (which includes family composition, education, income, and housing), is correlated to crime (Wilson, 1987; Currie, 1985; Moynihan, 1965).

The demographic characteristics included in Table 5.1 indicate that the south side neighborhoods fared better than the north side neighborhoods. The south side Shaw neighborhood qualifies as an outlier. Almost all demographic characteristics of this neighborhood are the most favorable when compared to the other seven neighborhoods, especially the median house value ($73,138), percent unemployed (11.3), and percent of vacant units (17.9). The population is also significantly larger (7,579). Two additional south side neighborhoods, McKinley Fox and Fox Park, follow with favorable demographic characteristics, although these neighborhoods are in rapid transition and demographic data may be less accurate than for other neighborhoods. The population for McKinley Fox is the least at 1989.

The neighborhoods with the least favorable demographic characteristics are Covenant Blu-Grand Center, Hyde Park, and Hyde Park's neighbor, St. Louis Place, all north side neighborhoods. Table 5.1 gives indication of this by the number of asterisks placed next to data indicating highest or lowest, second highest or lowest, and third highest or lowest. Covenant Blu-Grand Center has the least favorable data in the categories of median family income ($11,659), percent living below the poverty line (51), and percent of owner-occupied homes (9). St. Louis Place has the least favorable data for percent unemployed (22.4) and percent males unemployed (34). Hyde Park has the least favorable data concerning percent of female-headed households (44.6). Each of these neighborhoods has eight categories with highest or lowest, second highest or lowest, or third highest or lowest indicators. Old North St. Louis, another Hyde Park neighbor, has the least favorable data concerning housing—median house value ($14,999), median rent ($223), and percent of vacant units (35.7).

Crime Comparisons of Eight Demographically Similar St. Louis Neighborhoods

For the crime category of robbery, Covenant Blu-Grand Center qualifies as the outlier for reported incidents per 10,000 monthly average. For the years 1988 through 1990 and 1992, Covenant Blu-Grand Center's rate for robbery was at least double that of the next highest rated neighborhood—Old North St. Louis. Other neighborhoods had approximately the same rate as the city (Table 5.2).

Covenant Blu-Grand Center's uniqueness concerning reported incidents of robbery may be because the neighborhood includes several centers of entertainment frequented during evening hours by people of wealth—Powell Symphony Hall, the Fox Theater, Sheldon Concert Hall, the Grandel Square

Table 5.1
Demographic Data for Eight St. Louis Neighborhoods (1990 Census)

	North Side				South Side			
	HydP	ONSL	StLP	CBGC	FPSE	FoxP	McKF	Shaw
Population	4,917	2,221	3,799	4,175	4,087	5,092	1,989	*7,579*
% Afr. Am	68[c]	48	*85*[a]	73[b]	66	42	35	38
% Fem. hd. households	*44.6*[a]	20.3	36.7[b]	32.6	32.9[c]	21.9	24.2	22.9
Med. fam. income	14,417[c]	15,850	15,173	11,659[a]	15,737	12,901[b]	20,386	22,367
% Below pov. line	46[b]	25	39[c]	51[a]	32	25	46[b]	24
% Unemployed	21[b]	19.5	22.4[a]	20.4[c]	16.3	14.6	16.1	11.3
% Males unemployed	22.7	33.2[b]	34[a]	32.2[c]	24.8	18.3	14.4	9.9
% no HS dip. or GED	56.5[b]	62.5[a]	50.1[c]	49.7	44.6	41.4	36.6	25.3
Med house value	26,725[b]	*14,999*[a]	26,770[c]	45,383	28,700	40,600	49,600	73,138
% Owner occupied	34	23[b]	38	9[a]	34	31	28[c]	36
Median rent	283[b]	223[a]	351	296[c]	329	377	354	374
% Vacant units	26.8	35.7[a]	30.3[b]	29.3[c]	22.8	25.4	24.6	17.9

Italics and bold indicate outliers. HydP = Hyde Park; ONSL = Old North St. Louis; StLP = St. Louis Place; CBGC = Covenant Blu-Grand Center; FPSE = Forest Park Southeast; FoxP = Fox Park; McKF = McKinley Fox; Shaw = Shaw

[a]Highest or lowest
[b]Second highest or lowest
[c]Third highest or lowest

Source: United States Department of the Census. (1990). *Country and City Data Book.*

Table 5.2
Neighborhood Crime Data Number of Offenses Per 10,000—Monthly Average

	North Side				South Side					
	HP	ONSL	StP	CBGC	FPSE	FoxP	McKF	Shaw	City	United States
1988										
Robbery	6	10^b	8	*20^a*	8	6	8	7	7	2
Aggravated assault	26^b	27^a	20	25^c	21	15	20	10	14	3
Burglary	40	47^c	34	29	53^b	37	62^a	30	26	11
1989										
Robbery	8	11^b	8	*25^a*	9	9	8	7	9	2
Aggravated assault	25	34^b	27	37^a	32^c	18	21	8	17	3
Burglary	45	66^c	41	39	70^b	55	80^a	43	29	11
1990										
Robbery	16^b	14^c	16^b	*28^a*	12	8	11	8	10	2
Aggravated assault	38^b	35	36^c	42^a	23	12	21	11	18	4
Burglary	48^c	58^a	31	38	50^b	26	36	32	24	10
1991										
Robbery	12	23^b	18	30^a	19^c	14	11	8	11	2
Aggravated assault	36^b	39^a	31	33^c	22	16	26	13	17	4
Burglary	68^a	65^b	39	40	53^c	35	44	25	28	10
1992										
Robbery	11	18^b	17^c	*40^a*	16	12	12	8	10	2
Aggravated assault	35^b	35^b	28^c	36^a	24	19	26	10	16	4
Burglary	40^c	56^a	29	36	39	37	55^b	32	26	10
1993										
Robbery	14	24^b	16	40^a	16	17	18^c	10	13	2
Aggravated assault	33^b	35^a	26^c	35^a	22	19	21	13	17	4
Burglary	57^a	47	28	38	53^c	26	56^b	30	26	10

Italics and bold indicate outliers. HP = Hyde Park; ONSL = Old North St. Louis; StP = St. Louis
Place; CBGC = Covenant Blu-Grand Center, FPSE = Forest Park Southeast; FP = Fox Park;
McKF = McKinley Fox; Shaw = Shaw
^{a}Highest or lowest
^{b}Second highest or lowest
^{c}Third highest or lowest

Source: St. Louis Metropolitan Police Department: Information Service, 1993

Theater, and the St. Louis University complex. The neighborhood also includes several commercial enterprises; consequently, there is more opportunity and incentive for robbery.

Hyde Park's and St. Louis Place's (contiguous to Hyde Park) 1990 rate for robbery doubled from the previous year (eight to sixteen) while the rate for robbery in another contiguous neighborhood to Hyde Park (Old North St. Louis) also increased. Hyde Park's rate declined for the following year (twelve) when Hyde Park's mobile patrol was in operation while St. Louis Place's again went up (eighteen) and Old North St. Louis' increased by more than 50 percent. In 1992 all three neighborhoods had lower rates for robbery, although Hyde Park had the lowest (another year of Hyde Park Mobile Patrol operation). By 1993 all eight neighborhoods, with the exception of Shaw, had higher rates for robbery than the city (thirteen). Hyde Park's rate increased from the previous year (post-mobile patrol operation).

For the category of aggravated assault, Covenant Blu-Grand Center again had the highest rate for most years, although not significantly so. Old North St. Louis had the highest rate for two years (1988 at twenty-seven and 1991 at thirty-nine) while Hyde Park had the second or third highest rate most years. For the year 1990 the rate for aggravated assault rose substantially for Covenant Blu-

Grand Center (thirty-seven to forty-two), Hyde Park (twenty-five to thirty-eight), and St. Louis Place (twenty-seven to thirty-six). The Shaw neighborhood was the only neighborhood that had rates for aggravated assault below that of the city.

For the category of burglary, McKinley Fox, Hyde Park, and Old North St. Louis each had the highest rates for two years. Forest Park Southeast had the second or third highest rates most years. This was the only crime category for which Shaw had higher rates than the city most years. Hyde Park had the highest rates in 1991 (sixty-eight) and 1993 (fifty-seven).

Burglary, compared to the crime categories of robbery and aggravated assault, seems to be more concern for neighborhoods that have several blocks of more expensive housing stock (Shaw, McKinley Fox, Forest Park Southeast, and Fox Park). Because only 9 percent of Covenant Blu-Grand Center's population live in their own homes, this neighborhood is not included although the median house value is $45,383.

The exception to the burglary problem and expensive housing stock correlational possibility among the eight neighborhoods is Old North St. Louis. This neighborhood has a substantial problem with burglary; however, the housing stock is the worst of the eight neighborhoods in the categories of median house value ($14,999), median rent ($223), and percent of vacant units (35.7). Burglary is also a substantial problem in Hyde Park, which has only one block of more expensive housing and then scattered expensive homes on some additional blocks. Criminologists, Wright and Decker (1994), explain that, for the most part, burglars will steal what they see as better than what they have. The victims usually live near the perpetrators.

As expected, the Shaw neighborhood, which has the most favorable demographic characteristics of the eight neighborhoods, has the lowest rates of crime and is the only neighborhood with lower rates for two crime categories than city-wide rates. Old North St. Louis which borders Hyde Park on the south, is the neighborhood where the demographic data does not seem to "fit" the crime data when compared to the other seven neighborhoods. Although selected demographic characteristics for Old North St. Louis are not favorable, they are more favorable than those found in Covenant Blu-Grand Center, St. Louis Place, and Hyde Park. Demographic data concerning housing stock are the only least favorable characteristics for Old North St. Louis. On the other hand, this neighborhood claims only two years where rates of robbery, aggravated assault, and burglary are not the highest, second highest, or third highest between 1988 and 1993. Years of exception are 1990 for the category of aggravated assault and 1993 for the category of burglary. One explanation for incongruities between demographic factors and crime rates for Old North St. Louis may be the possible displacement of crime from Hyde Park.

Finally, each of the eight selected neighborhoods as well as the City of St. Louis exhibits higher rates (1988 through 1993) for the three selected crime categories than the nation. For the category of robbery, the city's rate most years is five times that of the United States; for aggravated assault it is four or five times that of the United States most years; and for burglary it is two or almost three times that of the United States all years. As previously mentioned, the selected neighborhoods, with the exception of Shaw in the categories of robbery and aggravated assault, has even higher rates than the city for the three selected crime categories. Overall, crime rates in the three categories are highest in north side neighborhoods, the same neighborhoods having the least favorable demographic characteristics. This finding supports the belief of criminologists, sociologists, political scientists, historians, and educators that there are background (social malaise) contributors to criminal behavior (Currie, 1985; Wilson; 1987; Messner and Rosenfeld, 1993; Moynihan, 1965; Grier and Cobbs, 1968; Hope and Shaw, 1988; Redden, 1993).

A Monthly Trend Analysis of Crime in Four Neighborhoods

From the eight neighborhoods previously analyzed, four were selected for monthly trend analyses of crime for the same crime categories and time period. The neighborhoods selected were Hyde Park, two contiguous neighborhoods to Hyde Park (Old North St. Louis and St. Louis Place), and a nearby neighborhood (Covenant Blu-Grand Center). It was felt that demographically similar neighborhoods contiguous to and near Hyde Park were important to look at because of the generally higher crime rates in the city's north side neighborhoods. Also, there was the possibility of crime displacement from Hyde Park to contiguous neighborhoods that may have been caused by the effective crime prevention programs performed in Hyde Park. Frequencies of reported crime in the categories of robbery (Figure 5.2), aggravated assault (Figure 5.3), and burglary (Figure 5.4) were charted monthly for the years 1988 through 1993 (six years or seventy-two months).

The purpose was to analyze monthly fluctuations in reported crime in these categories across the four neighborhoods and any observance of possible Hyde Park crime prevention program effects. The core of the crime prevention program addressing background causes of criminal behavior (the Friedens Haus coalition) was initiated in the fall of 1990 while the Mobile Patrol (addressing foreground causes of criminal behavior [opportunity]) operated from March 1991 through October 1991 and then from March 1992 through October 1992.

For the purpose of visual clarity, Figures 5.2 through 5.4 depict average crime frequencies among the neighborhoods of Old North St. Louis, St. Louis Place, and Covenant Blu-Grand Center (nonprogram neighborhoods). It must be noted that the 1990 population for Hyde Park was 4,917 as compared to the average population of the three nonprogram neighborhoods of 3,398 (1,519 less). It would be expected, therefore, that the number of graphed frequencies would be generally greater for the Hyde Park neighborhood.

Graphed frequencies of monthly crime strongly suggest that there has been a significant effect of Hyde Park community crime prevention efforts on robbery

Figure 5.2
Monthly Robbery Frequencies for Hyde Park and for Three Nonprogram Neighborhoods, 1988–93

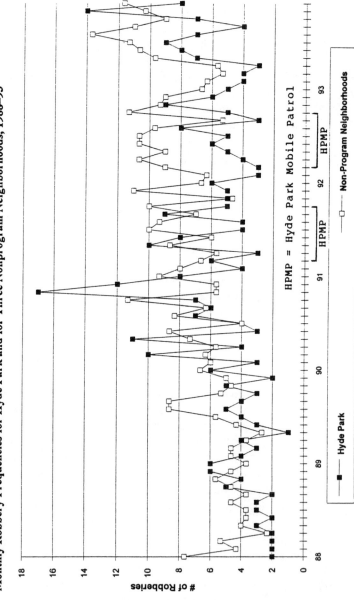

Data for nonprogram neighborhoods (Covenant Blu-Grand Center, Old North St. Louis, and St. Louis Place) are average frequencies.

Source: St. Louis Metropolitan Police Department: Information Service, 1993

Figure 5.3
Monthly Aggravated Assault Frequencies for Hyde Park and for Three Nonprogram Neighborhoods, 1988–93

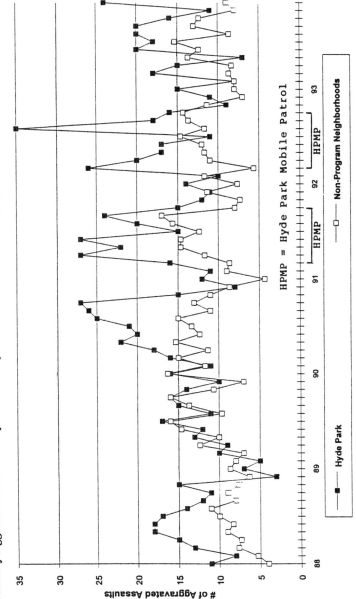

HPMP = Hyde Park Mobile Patrol

■ Hyde Park
□ Non-Program Neighborhoods

Data for nonprogram neighborhoods (Covenant Blu-Grand Center, Old North St. Louis, and St. Louis Place) are average frequencies.

Source: St. Louis Metropolitan Police Department: Information Service, 1993

Figure 5.4
Monthly Burglary Frequencies for Hyde Park and for Three Nonprogram Neighborhoods, 1988–93

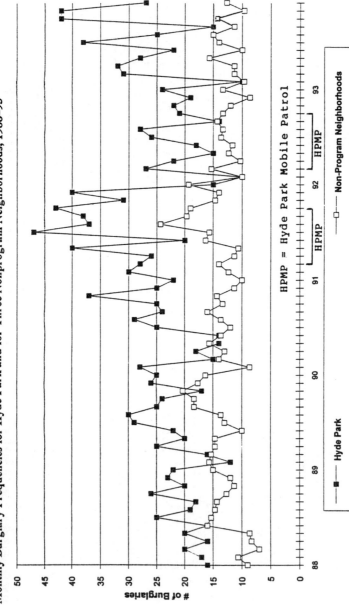

Data for nonprogram neighborhoods (Covenant Blu-Grand Center, Old North St. Louis, and St. Louis Place) are average frequencies.

Source: St. Louis Metropolitan Police Department: Information Service, 1993

during operational years of the Hyde Park Mobile Patrol. Frequencies of robbery steadily rise in Hyde Park before 1991, peaking in November 1990. Frequencies are then lower and more stable after August 1991 (mobile patrol operation) and then rise somewhat in 1993 (post-mobile patrol operation) but remain significantly lower than the average for nonprogram neighborhoods with the exception of one month.

Average frequencies of robbery for nonprogram neighborhoods rise steadily across the six years. Generally, the summer months do not indicate as many frequencies in Hyde Park as they do for the frequency average of the three nonprogram neighborhoods although the average population of the three neighborhoods is approximately 1,500 less. Overall, frequencies of robbery are diminished during the winter months for all neighborhoods.

Number of frequencies for Hyde Park in the category of aggravated assault generally follows the fluctuations of the three nonprogram neighborhoods until 1992 and then again follows in 1993. Generally, frequencies of aggravated assault rise during the spring and/or fall of each of the six years. Average frequencies for nonprogram neighborhoods gradually fluctuate within ten frequencies higher or lower. Hyde Park demonstrates much wider fluctuations, sometimes twenty-five frequencies (more or less), especially in 1991 and 1992. In short, there is no indication of program effect on reported aggravated assaults in Hyde Park.

Number of frequencies for Hyde Park in the category of burglary does not follow the fluctuations of the three nonprogram neighborhoods. Conversely, Hyde Park frequencies in this category fluctuate in the opposite direction until 1991. Average frequencies of burglary fluctuate moderately in nonprogram neighborhoods as compared to Hyde Park, especially in 1991 and 1993. Again, there is no indication of community crime prevention effectiveness for this crime category.

Comparing Crime Rates of Hyde Park and Its Neighbor, Old North St. Louis

As previously stated, after analyzing monthly averages of robbery, aggravated assault, and burglary per 10,000 in eight neighborhoods, it was determined that Old North St. Louis, contiguous to Hyde Park, was the one neighborhood that has higher rates of robbery, aggravated assault, and burglary than its demographic characteristics would indicate. One reason could have been the displacement of crime from Hyde Park because of ongoing community crime prevention efforts in the Hyde Park neighborhood.

The difference between the yearly mean crime rates (Table 5.3) of Old North St. Louis and Hyde Park in the three selected crime categories (robbery, aggravated assault, and burglary) were tested for significance by t-tests for independent samples (1988 through 1993). The directional hypothesis was:

Ha: $X1 - X2 > 0$ (one tailed test)

Old North St. Louis yearly mean crime rate = $X1$

Hyde Park yearly mean crime rate = $X2$

The .01 level of significance was chosen because of the multiple t-tests performed (eighteen). Yearly mean rates and t-scores are listed in Table 5.3 for the two neighborhoods.

For the year 1988, test results indicate there were no significant differences between the yearly mean rates in any of the three crime categories. The same held true for the year 1989 except for the category of burglary where Old North St. Louis had a significantly higher mean rate.

For the year 1990, the first year of the Friedens Haus coalition, initiated in the Fall of 1990, there were again no significant differences between the yearly mean rates in any of the three crime categories. Test results for the following years (1991, 1992, and 1993) show that Old North St. Louis had a significantly higher mean rate for robbery. The yearly mean rate in 1992 for Old North St. Louis in the category of burglary approached significance. (Hyde Park Mobile Patrol was in operation during 1991 and 1992.) Mean rates for the categories of aggravated assault and burglary did not result in significant differences between the two neighborhoods in 1993, although Hyde Park had higher mean rates for burglary.

Overall, test results do not indicate a significant trend of worsening crime rates for Old North St. Louis and improving crime rates for Hyde Park in the categories of aggravated assault and burglary. There were significantly higher crime rates for Old North St. Louis than Hyde Park in the category of robbery for the years of 1991, 1992, and 1993. Both the graphed frequencies and t-tests strongly suggest that the mobile patrol component of Hyde Park's comprehensive approach to crime prevention was making a difference in this crime category. (Robbery may be considered a more overt and outside crime than burglary, the latter occurring inside establishments. Most aggravated assaults are between family members, friends, and acquaintances, again, oftentimes occurring inside various establishments.) The significant difference of mean crime rates for robbery in 1993 when the mobile patrol was not operating can possibly be explained by a legacy effect and/or a gradually increasing influence of the Friedens Haus coalition's efforts. Hyde Park community members purposely did not advertise the mobile patrol's inactivity in 1993 (due to administrative problems) with hopes that criminal activity would remain curtailed by an erroneous perception of continuous mobile patrol operation. Hyde Park reported incidents of robbery did increase somewhat during 1993 as indicated by crime rate comparisons among eight neighborhoods and frequency trend analyses across four neighborhoods, but continued to remain lower than the compared north side neighborhoods.

Table 5.3
Yearly Mean Rates and *T*-Scores for Hyde Park and Old North St. Louis

Mean Rates	Old North St. Louis	T-Score	Hyde Park
1988			
Robbery	9.92	1.65	6.00
Aggravated assault	26.58	0.10	26.17
Burglary	47.08	1.01	40.33
1989			
Robbery	10.66	1.18	8.17
Aggravated assault	33.25	1.92	23.50
Burglary	66.67	4.02	41.00
1990			
Robbery	14.17	−0.27	15.08
Aggravated assault	34.33	−0.77	38.25
Burglary	58.50	1.56	46.50
1991			
Robbery	22.42	3.51	13.83
Aggravated assault	37.33	0.40	34.99
Burglary	64.83	−0.32	67.17
1992			
Robbery	18.25	2.61	10.50
Aggravated assault	34.75	0.02	34.58
Burglary	55.75	2.39	40.17
1993			
Robbery	24.58	2.66	14.17
Aggravated assault	34.50	0.32	32.58
Burglary	47.83	−1.22	56.92

SUMMARY

St. Louis is one of ten most crime-ridden major cities in the United States. Indicating a compounding of this city problem, crime rates in the categories of robbery, aggravated assault, and burglary for Hyde Park and six demographically similar neighborhoods exceeded those of the city during the years 1989 through 1993. The Shaw neighborhood, which had the most favorable demographic characteristics of the eight, fared worse than the city in only one of these categories—burglary. This neighborhood's housing stock was found to be the most favorable. Neighborhoods with the least favorable demographic characteristics were Hyde Park, St. Louis Place, and Covenant Blu-Grand Center, and the neighborhoods with the highest crime rates in the chosen categories were Hyde Park, Old North St. Louis, and Covenant Blu-Grand Center—all north side neighborhoods. The one neighborhood that had comparatively high rates of crime in the above categories but was not among those having least favorable demographic characteristics was Old North St. Louis, a neighbor of Hyde Park. This may have been due to crime displacement from Hyde Park because of the mobile patrol component of a comprehensive crime prevention program and perhaps the gradually increasing influence of the Friedens Haus comprehensive services component that addressed background causes of criminal behavior.

Trend analyses of crime frequencies in the same categories for three nonprogram neighborhoods and Hyde Park support this finding and indicate Hyde Park Mobile Patrol effectiveness on incidents of robbery (a more overt crime than burglary and aggravated assault). Crime in the categories of aggravated assault and burglary were not affected by the Hyde Park comprehensive crime prevention program.

Further supporting the effectiveness of the Hyde Park comprehensive effort, t-test results indicate significant differences in rates of robbery in Old North St. Louis and Hyde Park (higher in Old North St. Louis and lower in Hyde Park). The mean rate difference in this crime category was significant at the .01 level for the years 1991, 1992, and 1993. Rates of aggravated assault were also down in Hyde Park during patrol operating years, but not significantly so in comparison to Old North St. Louis rates. Finally, all three analyses—reported crime incidents per 10,000 monthly averages, monthly trend analyses, and t-tests of mean rates for two independent samples (Hyde Park and Old North St. Louis)—corroborate the finding that reported incidents of robbery were affected by the Hyde Park Mobile Patrol.

Indications are that more *immediate* results of crime prevention efforts at the neighborhood level were effected by the mobile patrol component of Hyde Park's comprehensive crime prevention program because it addressed the foreground causes of criminal behavior such as opportunity. The success of mobile patrol efforts may have been due to a combination of increased resident vigilance, community solidarity (as previously described by Weiss, 1987), and the consequent increase of police involvement and accountability. However, conclusive claims cannot be made that the Friedens Haus program had a positive effect on criminal behavior since its initiation in 1990. If this were so, one would expect that incidents of crime in the categories of aggravated assault and burglary (more or less inside crimes) would also be significantly lower when compared to preprogram incidents in Hyde Park as well as incidents in demographically similar neighborhoods.

Nevertheless, the findings of several previously cited criminologists and social scientists suggest that both background and foreground causes of criminal behavior must be addressed in the form of *comprehensive* approaches to crime prevention. The second section of the book describes programs and practices that address background correlates and causes of criminal behavior, including the Friedens Haus comprehensive services program. The philosophy of community education is examined, and the Friedens Haus coalition in Hyde Park is described as an example of an effective multi-systems, multi-sector community education initiative that has the long-term potential of reducing incidents of criminal behavior at the neighborhood level.

Part II

Confronting Background Causes of Criminal Behavior: A Community Education Approach

Chapter 6

What Is Community Education?

INTRODUCTION

Although community education has much in common with the concepts of
school-linked services, the lighted school house, the community school, citizen
control, community development, and public schooling, it is none of these.
These concepts may be considered elements of community education; however,
the philosophy of community education encompasses much more. It is,
therefore, difficult to describe in one or two sentences. Jack Minzey and Clyde
LeTarte, in their book, *Reforming Public Schools Through Community
Education* (1994), provide the following definition:

Community Education is a philosophical concept which serves the entire community by
providing for all of the educational needs of all of its community members. It uses the
local school to serve as the catalyst for bringing community resources to bear on
community problems in an effort to develop a positive sense of community, improve
community living, and develop the community process toward the end of self-
actualization.

Although this is an admirable attempt at a definition that probably and
adequately describes most community education programs, the community
education model described in this book does not fit this definition. The reason
for this will be explained in the following chapter. This chapter will outline the
elements and sub-elements that are commonly mentioned by community
educators when describing community education, as well as provide a brief
history of the community education movement.

A BRIEF HISTORY AND DESCRIPTION

The community education philosophy in the United States (as espoused by
the National Community Education Association) has its roots in an inconsistent

and evolving movement focused on attempting to connect school and society. In the mid-1600s the intent was to ensure that accepted community life was passed on to future generations, while contemporary thought is to implement a process capable of improving social conditions. Movements toward a school/community approach to education were most evident when the social climate in the United States favored a close relationship between school and community, especially during the decades of the 20s, 30s, and 60s. Movements away from such an approach were most evident during the "back to basics" educational agendas of the early 1900s and then after the Sputnik scare of the mid-1950s (Decker, 1980).

Concurrent with these divergent eras, the coupling of education and community gradually increased through extension service and adult education contributions of the Settlement House and Playground Movement in the late 1800s. Social change implications of education (which are a part of the community education philosophical evolution) gained firm ground during the Great Depression when means and resources were sought to alleviate the social malaise the depression years created (Decker, 1980).

Through the 1920s and 1930s it was not uncommon to view education as a leader for social change. John Dewey's disciple, Joseph K. Hart (1924), wrote, "Social Education works toward interrelated ends: the one, to solve our immediate problems and the other, to build a more adequate social intelligence, and here the rising generations, as well as the present citizens, are also involved" (10). The American Association of School Administrators in 1939 published the statement, "As an integral part of the community the school should join with all desirable social agencies in the continuous rebuilding and improving of group life. . . . The evaluation of the work of the school should be in terms of educational and social outcomes in human lives" (Seay and Crawford, 1954: 13). William Yeager (1939) asserted the "need for educational redirection in regard to the larger problems of society. The public school should be concerned in setting up the school-community as a great laboratory" (499).

Joseph Hart decried schools that often alienated many students:

An unrelated school—a school that is unacquainted with, or indifferent to, the world within which it's attempting to operate, the world from which its "pupils" come each morning and to which they must go back evenings—is an impertinence. A school that compels children to become "pupils" for some hours each day is in the long run an immoral institution. The vitalities of life are in communities, not in institutions! (1924: 427)

The Flint Community School Program initiated in 1935 provided a model for community education programs across the nation. The program evolved over a period of years as community citizens attempted to solve extreme problems of unemployment, crime, delinquency, health conditions, and a shortened school term due to inadequate funds. As the citizen leaders advertised the plight of their community and schools, various agencies and organizations began answering the call for help (Decker, 1980).

C. S. Mott, CEO of General Motors, was convinced to provide funding for recreational and play supervision "if the Board of Education would open five schools for this purpose and supply light, heat and janitorial service" (Manley et al., 1961: 28). The foundation was laid. Since that time the program has evolved from a community school concept into a city-wide plan of meeting the needs of the community through interagency cooperation of social, health, and educational service providers. Although criticized for not changing along with the community and employing leaders not attuned to the community education philosophy, the Flint community education plan is now attempting to meet community needs through a recent restructuring of its program. The results have been both praised and criticized. The school system bears the title, "Flint Community Schools."

The part of the school system's identification entitled "community school" may be broadly or narrowly defined. A broad description of the community school is provided by Elsie R. Clapp (1939), school principal, community educator, and author:

First of all, it meets as best it can, and with everyone's help, the urgent needs of the people, for it holds that everything that affects the welfare of the children and their families is its concern. Where does school end and life outside begin? There is no distinction between them. A community school is a used place, a place used freely and informally for all the needs of living and learning. It is, in effect, the place where living and learning converge. (89)

In short, community education, which most often uses the school as the catalyst for service provision, is an evolving philosophy drawing on an eclectic array of educational theories (Decker, 1980). The backbone of the concept is Dewey's educational philosophy of education as life, learning by doing, and problem-solving. Community education possesses the added element of improving social conditions through an educational process comprised of three overriding elements: community empowerment, community problem-solving, and the effort to involve all community members in the pursuit of lifelong learning.

Community Empowerment

Community empowerment (some prefer to think of releasing power that is already there) is operationalized through citizen advisory councils comprised of community residents, service providers to the community, and political representatives of the community. The council should be truly inclusive and representative of the community. Through this forum of community decision-making in assessing needs, planning programs, and evaluating programs and processes, leadership is developed and political awareness and action are encouraged within the community. The decision-making process that emphasizes community empowerment and people helping people is as important as the implemented programs. The people in the community are solving their own community and personal problems.

Vasil Kerensky and Ernest Melby in their book, *Education II - The Social Imperative* (1971: 102), write about problem-solving by community members as an "education centered" community that provides education for all: "It not only helps people but it also helps people to help themselves. In the school of such a community and in its varied community life, much of the teaching and leadership comes from the people themselves."

Community Problem-solving

This form of problem-solving is possible because community residents have a stake in deciding how their problems will be solved. They are accountable, not the distant federal, state, and even local governmental policy makers.

Because the citizen advisory council develops programs that are designed to meet the expressed needs of the community, the priorities and emphases of community education programs across the nation will vary from one plan to another. One plan may emphasize meeting the needs of "at risk" youth through various programs such as mentoring; tutoring; linkage to the juvenile justice system; recreational and enrichment activities after school hours and on the weekends; conflict resolution, job skills and parenting classes; discussion groups; linkage to social and health service providers; linkage to job opportunities; and parenting classes for parents of youth. Another program may have as its priority economic development through linkages to agencies that could aid in providing decent housing, marketing ideas to encourage new homeowners and businesses to move into the community, and developing entrepreneurial opportunities for community residents. The problem-solving process of both program emphases would necessitate community organization and volunteerism in order to plan, implement, and then evaluate the programs effectively.

In addition to community organization, community educators have embraced the principles of interagency cooperation and networking as viable means to solve community problems whether they be social, educational, health, political, or economic. This synergistic approach reduces duplication of services and allows services to reach the people in most need in the most effective and efficient manner. Through a problem-solving process involving community organization, interagency cooperation, networking, and volunteerism, the people of the community educate themselves.

The Effort to Involve All Community Members
in the Pursuit of Lifelong Learning

Such an effort assumes that no one is left out. Community education embraces people of all ages, ethnicities, and mental and physical abilities. Community members are serviced during day as well as evening hours and, ideally, on weekends with a variety of educational, enrichment, and recreational programming that is easily accessible in terms of service hours and facilities.

Finally, the integration of the K-12 educational program with the community is a part of the lifelong learning process. This integration emphasizes maximum use of school facilities, parental involvement with their children's education, using the community as a classroom, drawing on community resources such as forming partnerships with businesses and area colleges/universities, and involving parents and other community members in K-12 curriculum planning and educational policy decision-making.

Vasil Kerensky (1989) describes community education as a process, not a product. He asserts that it is an educational form that mobilizes all community resources in the development of human potential. It posits new assumptions regarding the governance of public education and the role and degree of participation of the public in the local decision-making process.

SUMMARY

The elements and sub-elements of community education as described in this chapter may be outlined as follows:

Community empowerment
    Political awareness and action
    Inclusiveness
    Citizen advisory boards/councils
    Leadership development
Community problem-solving
    Community organization
    Interagency cooperation
    Assessing, planning, and evaluating
    Volunteerism
The effort to involve everyone in the pursuit of lifelong learning
    Use of community resources and the community as a classroom
    Maximum use of school facilities
    Accessibility (facilities, programs, and services)
    Programs for all
    Parent and community involvement in school governance

Grounded in discussions of theory and national trends, the remainder of this book will assess the extent to which these elements and sub-elements of community education are present within the community education programs of the St. Louis Public School System and the Hyde Park neighborhood. Finally, the type of leadership required for an effective community education program will be discussed and analyzed. Again, Hyde Park community members provide the main ingredients to these discussions and analyses.

Chapter 7

Community Education Models:
A Comparison

INTRODUCTION

This and the following chapters include an examination of how the Friedens Haus collaborative community education initiative (at the time of my study) "measures up" to accepted community education principles as espoused by community educators and the National Community Education Association (NCEA). Elements and sub-elements of community education included in the assessment are outlined in the summary of the previous chapter. They are *community empowerment*, which includes political awareness and action, inclusiveness, citizen councils, and leadership development; *community problem-solving*, which includes community organization, interagency cooperation, citizen council processes of assessing, planning, evaluating, and volunteerism; and the *effort to involve everyone in the pursuit of lifelong learning*, which includes programs for all, maximum use of school facilities, accessibility (facilities, programs, and services), use of the community as a classroom, use of community resources, and parent and community involvement in school decision-making.

First, a tool for measuring levels of community education program-effectiveness provided by two community educators is analyzed. Through this analysis and comparison to the St. Louis community education program operating until 1994, it becomes clear that the community education program in the Hyde Park neighborhood operates at the most advanced levels of effectiveness. The subsequent chapters will provide the evidence.

A TOOL FOR MEASUREMENT

Everette Nance and James Dixon II (1980: 13) write about "community education and the urban dilemma," describing various models of community education. They delineate six component levels of community education (based on Jack Minzey's [1974] program-to-process model) and describe how three models (traditional, program-process, and multi-systems) compare to these levels of effectiveness. The higher component levels are encompassed within a "process" dimension while the lower component levels are encompassed within a "program" dimension (Figure 7.1).

The "traditional model" of community education, as Nance and Dixon describe, includes community organization and development. The authors place this component at the highest level of the "process dimension." The "program-process" model of Jack Minzey (1974 and 1978) achieves the next highest level of "process" with the "community involvement" (program development) component.

Nance and Dixon support their decision of this latter placement, acknowledging that, while Minzey and LeTarte (1979) advocate using the "school to serve as a catalyst for bringing community resources to bear on community problems in an effort to develop a positive sense of community, improve community living, and develop a community process toward the end of self-actualization," Minzey places more emphasis on *program* concerns.

Finally, the multi-systems model as described by George Wood (1977) achieves the highest level of "process" (along with the traditional model) with the "community problem solving" (community based decision-making) component. For example, Wood describes the operational concept of community education as:

the teaching-learning which occurs through the actions of a community's systems, that is, institutions, organizations, and other formalized groups, which are the community's instruments for developing and administering the formal classes, apprenticeships, problem-solving efforts, formal advising, and planned human interactions which constitute much of the educational experience of people. . . . People involvement in participatory decision-making is the central feature. (In Nance and Dixon, 1980: 15)

Wood places more emphasis on the inter-relatedness of community *systems* (institutions, agencies, organizations, and individuals) and less emphasis on the school in order to develop a "fully functioning community."

When reflecting upon Nance and Dixon's comparison, one may reach the conclusion that, although the authors provide community educators with a thoughtful analysis and a valuable tool for assessing community education programs, the placement and selection of the three models appearing on the chart—the traditional, Jack Minzey, and George Wood (the latter two classified as emerging models)—could be debated among community educators as well as

Figure 7.1
Comparison of Traditional and Emerging Concepts

DIMENSION	COMPONENT LEVEL	COMPONENTS OF COMMUNITY EDUCATION (Traditional Concerns*)	PROGRAM-PROCESS MODEL (Minzey)	MULTI-SYSTEMS MODEL (Wood)
	VI	Community organization and development		Community problem solving (community-based decisionmaking)
PROCESS DIMENSION	V	Citizen involvement (program development)	Community involvement (program development)	Community problem solving (system decisionmaking)
	IV	Interagency cooperation, coordination, and collaboration	Delivery and coordination of community services	
	III	Adult enrichment programs	Adult activities / Activities for school age youth	Leisure education
PROGRAM DIMENSION	II	Expanded use of school facilities	Use of facilities	K-12 schooling extended (early childhood and adult)
	I	K-12 programs	K-12 programs	K-12 schooling (youth)

Source: Nance, E. and Dixon, J. (1980). Community education and the urban dilemma. *Community Education Journal. VIII*(1), 15.

education and government policymakers. For example, the authors cite the Flint, Michigan, traditional model as an example of many community education programs across the country. They admit that "while the notion of involvement and facility utilization is inclusive (in the traditional model), it appeals to simplistic explanations and provides little direction to actual practice" (15).

One could argue that because of this statement's validity and because the "traditional model" of community education encompasses the writings, thoughts, and experiences of multiple authors and community educators, this model does not merit inclusion in the highest component level of "process" nor should it be compared to the models of two specific educators (Minzey and Wood). In addition to Nance and Dixon's comparison of a synthesis of writings, thoughts, and/or practices with the writings and thoughts of two individuals, there does not seem to be a publicized "traditional" community education program in the United States where this highly developed community organization and development process is taking place! As Minzey and LeTarte (1994) assert, only 10 percent of practicing community education programs operate within the higher levels of the "process dimension"—delivery and coordination of community services, and community involvement in community problem-solving and decision-making.

For example, Nance and Dixon's cited public school system in Flint serves as the central institution for community education; in fact the school system bears the title, "Flint Community Schools." While the Flint community education program has expanded to include social service delivery and community involvement, one wonders if there is a good amount of community-based decision-making, community organization, and community development. Finally, one wonders if these elements are integral parts of the community education process. The evidence is lacking.

Perhaps using the *school* as the catalyst for traditional community education programs, as indicated in Minzey and LeTarte's definition, has truncated the community education process via the institutionalized bureaucracies found in most school systems:

School systems typify the dilemma of the formal institution; that is, they do not facilitate the initiation of change in the broader community. Because public school systems are the primary agencies used to implement community education, many people wonder if community education through the public school system is a viable mechanism for solving urban problems. (Nance and Dixon, 1980: 14)

Many community educators would agree with this statement! As expressed later in the "Political Awareness and Action" chapter, schools serve more as a reflection of society rather than an agent for social change. Community educators and the authors of community education literature may talk about community organization and development, but the actions of community education practitioners reveal the true story about the traditional model. Jack

Minzey's model seems to have more merit of "process as empowerment" (Warden, 1979) than does the "traditional" model.

The former community education program in St. Louis (traditional model), for example, was included as a component of the St. Louis Public School System (SLPSS) since 1968. At the time of this writing, there were fifteen community school sites out of a system of 105 schools. The program continuously suffered from inadequate funding and lack of philosophical support from the school system's administration and board. This could have been due, in part, to a court mandated desegregation plan for the St. Louis public schools prompting (until the last several years) an extremely factionalized school board. The resistance to a racially integrated St. Louis community was and is apparent as discussed in the "A Theory of Crime Causation" chapter.

Nevertheless, the St. Louis community education plan operated predominantly in the "program dimension" rather than in a "process dimension," providing enrichment, recreational, and educational programming for youth and adults. But even this operation in the "program dimension" inadequately addressed programmatic needs of the community.

Results of a 1992-93 assessment of community needs and community education programs at the fifteen community school sites bear this out. The assessment included focus group sessions comprised of community residents and service providers (including those serviced) at six of the fifteen sites, questionnaire surveys of the same at all fifteen sites, interviews with the fifteen community school coordinators, and surveys of school and city administrators. The prevalent findings from the focus group sessions included the need for cohesive communities, support for families in the way of services, and increased participation. In short, the findings suggested that there was a need, not only for the *process* of community involvement, but for meaningful programs that met community needs. However, it must be noted that *meaningful* programs are a result of all-inclusive community involvement in problem-solving and decision-making:

There was a sense that the disenfranchised, the disconnected and the depressed were not being adequately reached. The question of how to involve these people is, perhaps, the most serious technical question facing community education in St. Louis. It is difficult to see how strong neighborhoods can be built in the absence of cooperation and interaction between residents. (Community Schools Review Panel Report, 1993: 21)

Results of the survey questionnaires supported the focus group findings and contributed to an understanding of these findings:

Reasons for low participation included ignorance and inadequate publicity, consumer apathy and lack of time, inappropriate or unwanted course offerings, inconvenient and insufficient hours of operation, and hesitation regarding entering an unfamiliar school. . . . Respondents supported the notion that community education should focus on

neighborhood problems and employment opportunities for community residents. . . .
Results support the concept of broad involvement of citizens in program development,
implementation, and evaluation. (Community Schools Review Panel Report, 1993: ii)

The survey results also indicated a separation between the regular K-12
educational program and the community schools program.   There were
implications that this separation was due to inadequate communication between
personnel of the two programs as well as philosophical differences in defining
the term "education" and how to best "educate."

Results obtained from telephone interviews with the fifteen community
school coordinators reinforced the feeling of separation between the K-12 and
community school programs. Moreover, there were indications that the advisory
boards at most sites were inadequately small, were not representative of the
surrounding community, membership did not change as the community changed,
and the same people served on the board year after year. Finally, results from
the surveys indicated that many times the advisory boards were just "fronts" for
decisions made exclusively by the community school coordinator.

In short, if one were to add the former St. Louis community education
program to Nance and Dixon's chart, all indications are that it would fit strongly
and comfortably at the third level of adult enrichment programs (traditional
concerns), adult activities and activities for school age youth (Minzey model),
and/or leisure education (Wood model). There were few sites within the St.
Louis system that adequately involved citizens in program development (Level V
traditional concern); but as far as community involvement in the sense of true
representation and inclusiveness (Level V Minzey model) and community
problem solving (Level IV and V Wood model), the focus group, survey, and
interview results did not indicate that this was taking place. The same held true
for interagency cooperation, coordination, and collaboration (traditional
concern) and delivery and coordination of community services (Minzey model)
at Level IV on the chart. These problem-solving efforts were not taking place to
the extent they should have and not to the extent exhibited by the Friedens Haus
model of community education in the Hyde Park neighborhood.

Finally, the multi-systems model of community education discussed by
George Wood was demonstrated in the Hyde Park neighborhood. As will be
shown throughout the remainder of the book, most specifically in the
"Interagency Cooperation" chapter, the public school served as only one of many
institutions working collaboratively for community development.   The school
(Clay Elementary) was not an official St. Louis "community center" as of 1994;
however, community problem-solving, community-based decision-making, and
lifelong learning were taking place through the various organizations,
institutions, and committees within Hyde Park.   Most of this was initiated
through community entities such as the Friedens Haus coalition that had little or
no connection with governmental agencies and that took risks to do what was
needed without the approval of outside agencies or the public school system.

The Clay school principal expressed it this way, "One good thing is that the school district has let me do my thing with the community activities and they have stayed out of my way!" (It must be noted that the decision to make Clay School a community education center within the SLPSS was made during the course of completing this book [1995].)

RESTRUCTURING ST. LOUIS COMMUNITY EDUCATION

The previously described needs assessment and evaluation of the St. Louis community education program was commissioned by a thirteen-member panel of community leaders, School Board members, and city alderpersons. The panel was formed in the spring of 1992, and the study was commissioned after three community meetings were held to provide panel members an overview of community education in St. Louis, orientation to the philosophy of community education, and information about various successful community education programs across the nation. Several consultants and community educators were brought in to assist.

After reviewing survey and focus group results, the panel proposed reorganizing the community schools to involve residents in hiring school principals, devising job descriptions, and planning programs. Those filling the fifteen community school administrative positions were asked to resign and reapply in order to assure that site administrative teams understood and were committed to the new model. A council that included residents was appointed for each of the fifteen sites, and it was involved in the hiring process for these positions. Seven of the fifteen principals and three of the fifteen community school coordinators were newly hired as of August 1994. (Four principals and two coordinators chose not to reapply.)

Part of the reorganizing involved the restructuring of community school administrative lines of accountability. The community school coordinators formerly reported to the "coordinator supervisor" who in turn reported to the Director of Community Schools. The Director was then also director of the SLPSS's vocational education and summer school programs. He reported to the assistant superintendent for curriculum and programs in the SLPSS. The structure was indicative of the "step child" syndrome of community education—an added on program to the K-12 "day" program.

The reformed administrative structure was thought to be a way to alleviate this classification as well as encourage the community education program to become a more integral part of and affect the K-12 educational program. The community center coordinators were to report to the school principal of each community center site, and the Executive Director of the Community Education Centers was to report directly to the SLPSS Superintendent.

In addition to the coordinators, the principals were to be assisted by either an administrative assistant, instructional coordinator, or both. The Executive Director was to be assisted by three specialists: programming, community and parent involvement, and finance. It was thought that the Executive Director would spend a good amount of time establishing linkages to needed resources including businesses, service agencies, and additional organizations. The idea was to expand services at the centers to meet social, health, and economic development as well as educational needs of the community.

The Chairpersons Council, comprised of chairs of the fifteen site councils, was to maintain input at the District level concerning community education center policies. The community center councils were to be comprised of twenty-one community members who were representative of the surrounding community. Composition of the site councils was devised by the Chairpersons Council, community residents, and a representative of city administration. Forty percent of the councils were to be comprised of parents, at least one member was to be under the age of seventeen, and one was to be an alderperson.

The restructured community centers were to continue operating year-round, while the daily hours of operation were to expand. Funding for this and other new program components was procured through additional commitments by the SLPSS and city. Considering that the School Board was faced with a reduction of $7 million projected state funding, the firm commitment of additional funding for the community centers was significant. The private sector also conducted a corporate drive to collect $1.7 million, the Danforth Foundation made provision, and a federal grant of $1.7 million provided twenty-three police officers for protection around center sites. The American Youth Foundation was also involved by way of a $1.6 million federal grant (AmeriCorps) to provide leadership and project involvement for youth in order to establish linkages between communities and schools.

Formative and summative evaluations of the restructured community education program were to be an integral part of the plan. An evaluation design was completed in the fall of 1994 by representatives from city administration; community center central office administration; the American Youth Foundation; the SLPSS research, planning, and evaluation department; an outside consultant; and the University of Missouri-St. Louis. All planning and orientation sessions were documented to ensure a historical account and for the purpose of model-dissemination and use by others.

The plan was to use the fifteen community center sites as pilot programs and to eventually expand the community education program so that services were made available to all St. Louis public schools. Several city service agencies expressed a desire to become part of the sites (Neighborhood Stabilization Office, Health Department, etc.). Commitments from the School Board, city mayor and administration, the corporate sector, and various service agencies were indications that the restructured program would succeed even though there would be bumps in the road ahead.

Problems foreseen by the author included possible ramifications resulting from the exclusion of teachers and custodians as voting council-members, a twenty-one member council limitation, and the 40 percent parent-rule for council composition. These qualifications would possibly preclude full community representation (business, service providers, churches, racial/ethnic/economic diversity). Community educators have expressed that *all* stakeholders be represented as voting members on citizen councils, including school custodians and teachers; however, it was felt that custodian and teacher representation would result in conflict-of-interest issues (union concerns).

Also, it was decided that one necessary component to the restructuring process was ongoing training for the councils in terms of team building and team functions that was to be provided by the American Youth Foundation (a national organization with headquarters in St. Louis). Each council was to work cooperatively with the site administrative team (principal, administrative assistant, instructional coordinator, and community school coordinator) in reviewing the "school improvement plan" and making revisions as needed. A problem foreseen here was that the expertise of the American Youth Foundation was not "community education" even though the technical assistant teams were comprised of several former community school coordinators. However, their tenures as community school coordinators were during the SLPSS's implementation of community education in the "program dimension"; moreover, the former operation was disconnected from the K-12 educational program. This concern was borne out by community education center staff survey results: "Training efforts were well appreciated but they tended to focus on team building and conflict resolution rather than on council functions as they relate to community education implementation" (Nance, 1996: 8).

Additional drawbacks were seen to include possible negative results derived from rushed planning and hiring because of the timing of grant receivership and the fact that many new programs and processes were implemented concurrently. Program evaluation results also validated this concern:

The Community Education office was understaffed. Centers were not given the resources they needed to effectively implement the Center concept. The Community Education Office did not have the capacity to provide ongoing in-service training to the Centers. Space was a problem, and, in some instances, the community education initiative was in direct competition with desegregation efforts and other District programs. (Nance, 1996: 9)

There also remained tentativeness on the part of school administrators and staff in welcoming parent and community involvement in terms of school policy and curriculum decision-making. This may evolve to increased input by parents and community as time goes on. Additionally, only some of the community centers were to be site-based managed, a practice that would seem to be a necessity for all sites attempting to implement a community education philosophical approach to citizen empowerment, community problem-solving, and lifelong learning. Finally, additional duties incurred by site principals was foreseen to possibly become overly burdensome. Structures, processes, and personnel may have to be revised as formative evaluation results are analyzed and acted on.

Another issue that will have to be addressed is the lack of pre-service training for teachers concerning the community education philosophy. For the most part, undergraduate and graduate education courses are grounded in the "four walls" concept of schooling with little inter-disciplinary involvement (health, social work, etc.). The previously cited evaluation survey found that few teachers understood shared governance and how community education could be integrated into the curriculum. Also, teacher interaction with parents and other community members remained in the "traditional" sense, and the observed interaction was mostly negative (Nance, 1996). Without the understanding and support of the majority of SLPSS teaching staff, this exciting restructured community education plan could be truncated before desired results are achieved.

Finally, the community education model found in Hyde Park differs from the restructured model in St. Louis in that the core of the program (Friedens Haus) evolved from the needs expressed by community residents, and locus of control remained with Hyde Park community members. For the most part, the St. Louis former community education plan evolved from top-down decisions, and much of the control remained with the SLPSS. However, the restructured initiative has included a genuine attempt to meet expressed community resident needs and desires for community empowerment, problem-solving, and lifelong learning.

SUMMARY

While the former community education program in St. Louis would be placed at the "program dimension" at Level III on Nance and Dixon's chart (adult enrichment programs/activities for school age youth/leisure education), the restructured St. Louis program may eventually merit placement at the highest level of "process dimension" (community organization and development and/or community problem-solving and decision-making) as well as making a positive difference in the classroom if desired results are realized. Some structure, personnel, and process wrinkles may need to be ironed out before this can happen. The Friedens Haus multi-systems model of community education already merits such placement. Community organization and development, community problem-solving, and community-based decision-making were in progress. However, the *lower* level components in the "program dimension," including expanded use of school facilities, adult enrichment programs, and leisure education, are foreseen to be strengthened by Clay Elementary's inclusion into the St. Louis community education program.

The SLPSS has operated within a traditional schooling mode for many years (with the exception of magnet schools [to some degree]), and the paradigm shift to viewing the community as a classroom has not fully taken place. School walls may come down brick by brick—cracks in the mortar are already evident.

Nevertheless, much could be learned by looking at and studying the community education model practiced in Hyde Park.   Conversely, inclusion of Clay Elementary as a community center site may prove to be an enhancement of the Friedens Haus "multi-systems model" by providing additional funding, staffing, and technical assistance needed for adult and increased youth programming.   In the final analysis, both entities (St. Louis Community Centers and the Friedens Haus coalition) will benefit by a trade off of ideas, processes, and practices.

Chapter 8

The Friedens Haus Coalition

INTRODUCTION

At the time of this writing, the Hyde Park community was serviced by the Friedens Haus coalition; Hyde Park Alliance (a neighborhood organization funded in part by Community Development Agency block grant money); the Hyde Park Housing Corporation (also funded by block grant money); Northside All Combined (interagency cooperation in and among neighborhoods); Hyde Park Business Association; Hyde Park Landlord's Task Force; Hyde Park Safety Committee; city agencies such as the Neighborhood Stabilization Office and Operation Impact; and area churches including Holy Trinity Catholic, Bethlehem Lutheran, Friedens United Church of Christ, and several smaller churches. Some of these entities accomplished much while others were just beginning to be effective or re-effective. In aggregate, it was multiple systems (educational, social, health, economic, and political) and multiple sectors (public, private, not-for-profit, and religious organizations) coming together to meet the needs of community members.

THE FRIEDENS HAUS COALITION

This unique school/church/private social service agency/community coalition was initiated in 1990 by the principal of Clay Elementary ("integrated" St. Louis public school), members of Friedens United Church of Christ, and community parents. The school principal was seeking additional resources for the school, and church members were seeking constructive use of their facilities, which were then being vandalized in the amount of approximately $1,000 per month.

After canvassing area residents, it was confirmed that "something for our kids" was needed. An advisory group comprising parents, community members, church members, and school staff was subsequently convened for the purpose of finding solutions for meeting the needs of Hyde Park children. A commitment was made to establish a permanent advisory board that would create a community program with the focus of "service to children." Consequently, the first cooperative event was the 1990 Clay School fifth grade graduation ceremony held on the stage of the Friedens Church fellowship hall facility.

Connection was then made with the *United Church Neighborhood Houses* (a private social service agency) which provided funding for a full-time social worker (MSW) who served as director, training for social work staff, and other program resources. *Friedens United Church of Christ* made its fellowship hall/gymnasium/stage, kitchen, meeting rooms (office space), maintenance, insurance, security, and custodial services regularly available to Clay School students and, frequently, to the wider community. The facilities are located four city blocks from the school and directly across from the Friedens United Church of Christ.

Clay Elementary served as the primary liaison to children and families of the Hyde Park neighborhood. The school also provided a connection to many St. Louis Public School System (SLPSS) resources, volunteers, educational expertise, and other school-linked services. Finally, but most importantly, *Hyde Park community members* provided knowledge of Hyde Park community life; resident, business, and agency resources and support; and served as a liaison to additional resources. The main entities of the Friedens Haus coalition (Friedens Haus) were: Friedens United Church of Christ, Clay Elementary, United Church Neighborhood Houses, and the Hyde Park community (Figure 8.1).

The philosophy behind Friedens Haus is contained in one of the coalition's grant proposals, "There is a growing awareness that time-worn approaches to helping those at risk (food pantries, rummage sales, etc.) must be revised to reduce dependency and to address causes of need in ways that engage and empower people to take responsibility for their own lives." The main objectives of the program were to secure resources; to provide a program that would help meet specific social, emotional, health, and educational needs of children and their families; and to help bring about positive change in Hyde Park. The multi-level intervention program was targeted at prevention with the theme of "New Hope for Hyde Park."

Since its beginning in 1990, Friedens Haus evolved to become a 501(C)3 organization that employed three full-time social workers (MSW, BSW, and former neighborhood resident), one part-time bookkeeper, one part-time community nurse shared with Friedens Church, and many work hours of student practicums and volunteering. During the years 1993 through 1995, the Friedens staff enlisted the help of one full-time volunteer from Belgium, one part-time social worker by way of an area university's student practicum program, two college student volunteers (computer technology and business administration and urban affairs), and approximately 2,000 volunteer hours from parents, residents, political leaders, business owners, and service providers. During the 1994–95 year, three students from the department of education and four students from the

Figure 8.1
Friedens Haus Model

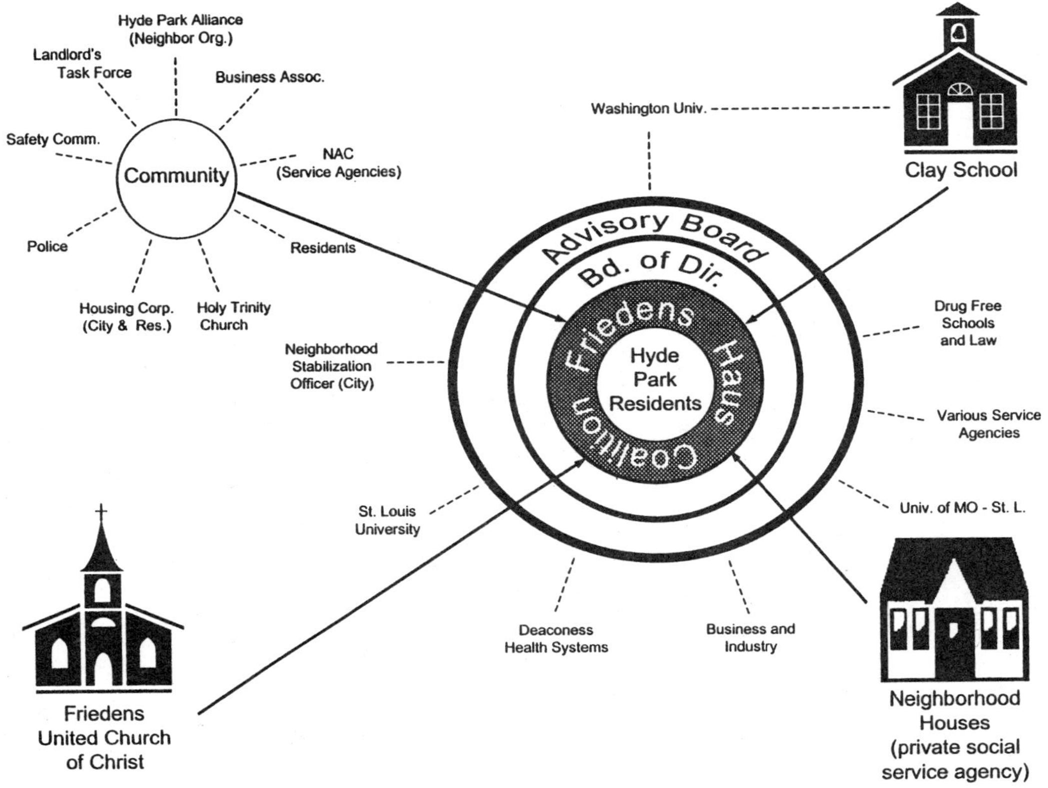

Graphic by Lainie Smith

school of social work at Washington University performed practicums with Clay School and Friedens Haus via a Professional Development School partnership in addition to thirty-eight Washington University education students fulfilling field experience requirements at Clay.

The Friedens Haus program furnished emotional, educational, social, and health needs for the community, especially for students and former students of Clay Elementary and their families. More than 250 children (98% black) were serviced yearly during the school day and through after school and summer activities and services. The program expanded to include discussion groups, leadership training, and activities for teens. A list of activities and services for the years 1993 through 1995 follows:

- Clubs (growth and development groups) for elementary through middle school ages utilized staff trained in group social work techniques to improve social and educational skills and emotional well-being of participants.
- Mentoring and "buddy" programs prepared Clay fourth and fifth graders for middle school through individual attention, motivation, role modeling, and encouragement to improve school attendance and grades; and then provided "follow-up" into middle school (at least three years from start to finish) with support from volunteers, including school certified and support staff, representatives from the business community, city government officials, and other community volunteers.
- A grant administered by the Department of Social Work at the University of Missouri-St. Louis via United Church Neighborhood Houses furnished a drug prevention, cultural awareness, self-esteem enhancement, and decision-making skill curriculum to use with club groups.
- University students and adult volunteers provided tutoring.
- Two St. Louis area dance organizations provided dance lessons.
- SHARP (Students Have the Ability to Reach their Potential) was created to provide tutoring, mentoring, outreach, small group sessions, and other services to fourth and fifth graders (supported via a United Way Priorities Grant).
- EYE (Energized Youth Employment Program) was created to train youth (13-18) in leadership and employment skills and placed them in summer jobs under the sponsorship of Friedens Haus, Hyde Park Alliance, Hyde Park Business Association, and Hyde Park Safety Committee (supported via various grants).
- Boy Scout and Girl Scout troops were formed that met in the Friedens Haus and Clay facilities beginning in 1990.
- A six week all-day summer daycamp provided children (5-12) with crafts, music, games, field trips, recreation, education, and fun activities that included the U.S.D.A. nutritional breakfast and lunch program. The program also provided employment opportunities for Hyde Park residents who were trained as part-time staff.
- A resident volunteer led a weekly art group.
- An International Club provided introductory French and European culture to children in the fourth and fifth grades who were selected to participate based on

their academic achievements. The volunteer from Belgium led this group.
- A Teen Club was initiated in 1991.
- A Reading Club invited teachers, parents, school administrators, city officials, and celebrities to read to children one evening hour, once a week.
- The city's Department of Parks and Recreation furnished sport programs in the Clay facility.
- A parent volunteer coordinated a Coat Room providing clothing to students in need.
- A community nursing program in partnership with Deaconess Health Systems was housed in the Friedens Haus facility.
- Mother, infant, and child health care follow-up was provided in partnership with a health/social service agency (Grace Hill) that furnished a part-time worker housed in the Friedens Haus facility.
- Grace Hill provided health care and transportation for Clay students during school hours for children whose parents could not be reached.
- An SLPSS health grant funded complete physicals for 500 children.
- A Friedens United Church of Christ member provided free eye exams and glasses.
- Conflict resolution training and implementation for teachers and students were available with the assistance of AmeriCorps workers.
- A Bicycle Works program was purchased and a not-for-profit community Bicycle Shop was intended to be located in a refurbished building for the purpose of creating jobs and teaching bicycle repair, bicycle safety skills, and entrepreneurship in partnership with various neighborhood organizations, businesses, and city agencies.
- United Church Neighborhood Houses provided a weekly parent group and child care.
- Social and health outreach and follow-up services for families were available through Friedens Haus via social workers and a community nurse.
- Housing and social/health/educational agency referrals were provided.
- Clay and Friedens Haus facilities were available for community meetings including the Hyde Park Safety Committee, the Landlord's Task Force, police/community meetings, and senior citizens' meetings.
- The Northside All Combined (NAC) organization was initiated in 1991 for area service provider communication and cooperation. The organization was initiated and facilitated by the Friedens Haus director.
- Playground facilities that included a soccer field, playground area, amphitheater, and gardening plots (Gateway to Gardening) were constructed on a vacant lot adjacent to the school. Members of the Assembly of God denomination constructed the playground and a gazebo in 1994.
- The Mallinckrodt Corporation, which is located just outside Hyde Park neighborhood boundaries, provided a science lab housed in Clay School.
- A Danforth grant provided program evaluation.
- Clay became an "official" community education center within the SLPSS (September 1995) that allowed the doors of the school to be opened during evening, weekend, and summer hours for additional basic education, cultural, enrichment, and recreational programs for community residents of all ages (made possible

because of networking, publicizing, and political actions on the part of Friedens Haus advisory board members).

The Friedens Haus forty-member advisory board convened a monthly luncheon meeting in the Friedens Haus facility that was provided by the SLPSS Drug-Free School and Communities, Law, and Citizenship Education Unit. The Board of Directors and most subcommittees met either in this facility or at Clay. The following entities were represented on the advisory board:

- Board of Aldermen, City of St. Louis
- Bremen Bank
- Clay Elementary
- Columbia Community Center (representing an adjacent neighborhood)
- Community residents
- Connector Casting Corporation
- Deaconess Health Systems
- Divoll Branch Library (St. Louis Public Library)
- Friedens United Church of Christ
- Hyde Park Alliance
- Hyde Park Business Association
- Hyde Park Donuts
- Hyde Park Housing Corporation
- Hyde Park Safety Committee
- Metropolitan St. Louis Police Department
- Neighborhood Stabilization Officer (formerly Operation ConServ—city)
- Prevention Partnership
- SLPSS
- St. Louis University
- St. Louis Variety Club
- University of Missouri-St. Louis
- U.S. Marshall's Office
- United Church Neighborhood Houses
- United Way of Greater St. Louis
- Washington University
- Webster Middle School

Fund raising was a constant chore. There were diverse funding sources such as individual donors; private foundations; federal, state, and local grants; and contributions from organizations, corporations, and religious and philanthropic entities.

The Friedens Haus Board of Directors (the core decision-making body) listed eighteen members: thirteen elected members comprising seven community residents, two Friedens church members, two Clay Elementary staff members, and one representative from St. Louis University; two appointed members (Friedens Church Council president and a representative from United Church

Neighborhood Houses), and ex-officio members comprising the Friedens Haus program director, a United Church Neighborhood Houses administrator, and the Friedens United Church of Christ pastor.

The Friedens Haus Board of Directors will be described more fully in the chapter entitled, "Citizen Councils." For now, suffice it to say that the board struggled with changes brought about by Friedens Haus becoming a 501(C)3 organization as well as by Clay becoming a community education center within the SLPSS. The latter required the formation of a proscribed citizen council in terms of community representation and numbers. There remained a continuous concern with control issues, especially concerning insufficient allowances given for meaningful decision-making and leadership on the part of Hyde Park residents.

Nevertheless, Friedens Haus enhanced its effectiveness by the great amount of networking, coordination, cooperation, and collaboration with other neighborhood and outside agencies and organizations. Some of these entities are outlined:

Holy Trinity Catholic Church and School

Located approximately six blocks from the Friedens Haus facility, the school educated over 260 children from pre-school through eighth grade. The church and school offered after-school programs for Holy Trinity children, teen programs, a food pantry, family counseling, and a Headstart program.

Hyde Park Alliance

Hyde Park Alliance (HPA) was a 501(C)3 neighborhood organization initiated in 1987 (then known as Trinity Square Neighborhood and renamed in 1991). The Community Development Agency (city) monitored the organization. The organization's purposes as stated in its bylaws were:

- Developing community, business, and an economic basis
- Preventing crime
- Coordinating services
- Preserving residences
- Dispersing community information to residents
- Providing technical assistance to attain needed resources
- Encouraging historical pride
- Educating families concerning neighborhood living
- Forming a liaison between the city and the Hyde Park community

Hyde Park Alliance served as an umbrella organization for several neighborhood associations and committees for the purposes of sharing information among community organizations, furnishing technical assistance, and providing 501(C)3 benefits. These independent organizations, associations, and committees were:

- Hyde Park Business Association
- Hyde Park Safety Committee
- Hyde Park Landlords Task Force
- Northside All Combined (NAC)

HPA attempted to keep community residents informed through newsletters, brochures, and a monthly calendar of community events. Public relations were also attempted through news releases and networking with political and city entities. Community meetings were held at Clay School or Holy Trinity until the organization relocated to a refurbished building made possible through cooperative neighborhood and city efforts.

Northside All Combined (NAC)

This organization brought social service agencies, religious organizations, schools, neighborhood associations, and businesses together in order to lessen duplication of services and to provide services to the citizens of the Hyde Park, Old North St. Louis, and College Hill neighborhoods in the most effective and efficient manner. The organization was initiated and facilitated by the Friedens Haus director and met in the Holy Trinity rectory.

Accomplishments of NAC included a map that pinpointed area service locations and a resource guide that explained services offered by various organizations. Among several subcommittees was NAC-NET, which was formed to link NAC members into a single computer networking system.

Hyde Park Business Association

This was an effort to bring neighborhood businesses together in order to help the neighborhood, especially children, through mentoring and employment enrichment programs. Members met at the Bissell Mansion (a Hyde Park restaurant and dinner theater owned by a community resident).

Landlord's Task Force

This organization was comprised of landlords who were working toward improving their buildings and learning better ways to deal with landlord/tenant, and community problems. The group met at Friedens Haus or Clay Elementary.

Hyde Park Safety Committee

This organization worked closely with the police and the St. Louis Association of Community Organizations (SLACO) to help maintain a safe and attractive neighborhood. Operating programs included "block watch" and a neighborhood mobile patrol. The group met at Friedens Haus or Holy Trinity, sometimes in conjunction with the SLACO/Trinity safety meetings.

Hyde Park Housing Corporation

This not-for-profit corporation was comprised of neighborhood residents and was assisted by Operation Impact (CDA agency that subsidized funding and provided technical assistance in finance and construction for neighborhood housing corporations), the area's Neighborhood Stabilization Officer, and Hyde Park's three alderpersons. The organization served as a housing resource group and enabled the purchase of property, property rehabilitation, and property resale or rental. The organization met in the Holy Trinity rectory and/or Friedens Haus. The organization owned four buildings and co-owned one building with HPA. At the time of this writing, two buildings were stabilized and one was rehabbed to house the HPA office, a bicycle shop, and residential space on the second floor.

Neighborhood Stabilization Officer

This service provider was furnished by the city through CDA block grant money. The service was initiated under the previous city administration to encourage the formation of neighborhood organizations or to provide support for existing organizations, to assist in strategic planning efforts, and assist in housing development by nonprofit housing corporations. City services such as clearing vacant lots, code enforcement, and additional physical services were delivered.

The Hyde Park Neighborhood Stabilization Officer worked with HPA, the Friedens Haus coalition, the Housing Corporation, and many of the aforementioned committees and nonprofit corporations to improve the community. This is how the officer described his duties:

My job is to work in a proactive as well as a reactive venue for two separate neighborhoods—to implement strategic planning; to be a resource for the different other agencies throughout the community or neighborhood; to serve as a facilitator to get things done; and to facilitate block units, cleanup, and all activities. Basically, it's a wide-open job description. Whatever the area needs and I can supply, I do it. . . .

I serve on different committees—I'm on the Friedens Haus Advisory Board—I serve where I'm needed. One thing I try to do is effectively coordinate city services to the different agencies that need them, serve as liaison to the aldermen in the area, help out with different problems as needed, and try to be available to the community for different resources. I also have helped neighborhoods to write grants to receive money. I just do basically whatever is needed.

SUMMARY

At the time of my study, there were numerous programs, organizations, and agencies servicing the Hyde Park community—many were just beginning to be effective or were in the process of renewal. The five-year-old Friedens Haus coalition was recognized for its increasingly strong presence, inclusiveness, action, program and organizational structures evolving along with community needs and expressed desires, willingness to work with other neighborhood organizations, and the ability to bring in outside resources and to network with city and political entities. All of this was done with funding and evolving operational struggles; however, the program was continuously growing and attracting attention. As one board member stated, "Everyone wants to jump on the bandwagon!"

Weaknesses of the Friedens Haus coalition, at the time of this writing, included inconsistent leadership development of Hyde Park residents and control issues among church members, private social service agency administrators, community residents, funding agencies, and the SLPSS. The most prevalent weakness was the failure to recognize that several community residents were capable of assisting/leading in guiding the coalition through the mine fields of governance, funding, programming, and community relationship issues.

Despite these shortcomings, I found that the Friedens Haus coalition was the core of a multi-systems, multi-sector community education initiative in Hyde Park, emphasizing political awareness and action; inclusiveness; an effective but continuously learning citizen council; community organization and problem-solving; interagency cooperation; assessing, planning, and evaluating; volunteerism; and attempting to involve everyone in the pursuit of lifelong learning. These community education elements are described and discussed in the following chapters.

Chapter 9

Political Awareness and Action

INTRODUCTION

"The obligation of anyone who thinks of himself as responsible is to examine society and try to change it and to fight it—no matter what the risk. This is the only hope society has. This is the only way societies change" (Baldwin, 1971: 285). These words beg the questions: What is wrong with our society? Who wants to change it? What kind of society do they want?

The first question is answered daily in printed and electronic news media and in the day-to-day business of average Americans. Economic, education, human relations, leadership, family, housing, health care, unemployment, injustice, violence, ecological, and disease are a few of the problems we encounter in some way every day. We recognize these problems and often articulate what the ideal should be, so why do we seem to be stuck in the routine of self-satisfaction?

Does everyone really want change? If so, who wants change the most? Those who are the least powerful and the most aware are likely candidates. It is conceivable that the oppressed in our society—including ethnic, cultural, and racial minorities; women; the poor; the homeless; homosexuals; the abused; the unemployed; and the disabled—want their rights and liberties, powers and opportunities, income and wealth, and self-respect.

In our society, social change is attempted via various avenues. The successes and failures of two main avenues for change concerning justice and equality are explored in this chapter. The first avenue is comprised of institutions that many look to as social change-agents. These institutions are the schools, governmental policy-making bodies, and the courts. Secondly the citizenry is examined as a possible avenue for social change. Finally, political awareness and action on the part of Hyde Park residents are revealed through results derived from observing their actions and listening to their thoughts expressed in speeches, comments, and conversations.

INSTITUTIONS AS SOCIAL CHANGE-AGENTS

The Schools

The philosopher Kant (1963) states, "How then is perfection to be sought? Wherein lies our hope? In education, and in nothing else. Education must be adapted to all the ends of nature, between civil and domestic." John Dewey also viewed education and schooling as instruments for changing human conditions. Finally, many Americans claim education (which is usually associated with schooling) to be the promise for a more just and equitable society.

Men and women who fought for school desegregation in the United States also viewed education or schooling as the avenue for positive social change. Today, many see equal educational opportunities for minorities as vehicles for social mobility, full citizenship, empowerment to control individual destinies, and a means to gain part of the economic pie.

On the other hand, many deem the desegregation of our nation's public schools to be a failure. Many of our desegregation plans have not met the needs of our children: racism is all too prevalent; there still exists two societies in our nation, the haves and the have-nots; and many times our desegregation successes, when examined closely, are found to be less than that. What was viewed so optimistically as a solution for the blending of our country's cultures, ethnicities, and races, is now viewed by many as a failure that has resulted in resegregation and even bitterness.

For example, minority children are often faced with the choice of assimilating into the prevalent culture represented in our schools or remaining with their own culture and pulling away from education as a viable, worthwhile pursuit. When interviewed, a black university student expressed it this way, "I realized I was born black when I went to elementary school and they told me about Dick and Jane and Bow Wow and Spot and all that crap and I knew that wasn't me" (Brink and Harris, 1967: 71).

James Baldwin asserts that some of the myths proliferated in our schools are the invincibility of the United States, that any one can become President, and "liberty and justice for all:" "Any Negro who is born in this country and undergoes the American educational system runs the risk of becoming schizophrenic" (1971: 285). According to test results reported by the American Psychological Association in August 1987 (black/white doll test), black children felt as much racial inferiority as their counterparts did twenty years before.

Former Education Secretary, Lauro Cavazos, asserted a few years ago that too many minority students "still attend schools that are both separate and unequal." White flight to the suburbs, white academies in the South, and other private schools have contributed to the resegregation of many inner-city schools. Enrollment in more than-two thirds of the St. Louis public schools, for example, remains 90 percent or more black.

It is not surprising that many question the rationale behind spending huge amounts of money for desegregation plans that include additional administration, busing, compensatory programs, inter-district transfer plans, and magnet schools (all present in the St. Louis desegregation program). Monti (1985) suggests that desegregation money is often used for other than desegregation purposes; is not spent wisely; and, more often than not, benefits the white status quo.

A case can also be made for the "fly paper" quality or backlash phenomena spurred by many desegregation mandates (Rosenberg, 1991). For example, a former member of the St. Louis school board and a member of the Metro South Citizens Council (a group that advocates "white rights") made this rather revealing statement when defending his anti-busing bloc against charges of racism:

All we're doing is engaging in the same kind of activities that are engaged in by blacks—activities that are considered not only acceptable but encouraged. It's a double standard. They've had twenty years to try to implement their ideas and run the school system the way they want to, and it's been a disaster. We've used schools too much as laboratories for social experimentation. (*St. Louis Post-Dispatch*, 1990)

Furthermore, there are some factors in our society that cannot be controlled or changed by the schools such as segregated housing patterns, the dominant culture's hegemony promoted by the media, political influences worsening socio-economic stratification, the lack of importance that several recent federal administrations placed on education, and the plight of many of our nation's families. In short, the schools seem to be more of a reflection of society than an agent for social change.

Governmental Policy-Making Bodies

Many see salvation for civil liberties in the legislative branch of our government. The Constitution *can* be amended, but this is very unlikely considering the cumbersome procedure. Congress passed a Civil Rights Act to make up for Supreme Court decisions making it more difficult to sue employers for discrimination, but the bill leaves many debatable issues and unanswered questions until test cases are brought before the courts. Also, the mood in Congress at the time of this writing to end affirmative action as we know it may bode ill for our nation's minority and female populations. Finally, the compromising and political nature of legislation leaves much to be desired for effective civil liberty laws to be enacted. Congress can do only certain things, and purposeful reform is not one of them.

Besides the compromising and political nature of legislation, Dolbeare (1974) asserts that governmental policy-making bodies in our society are controlled by a ruling class. Congress remains comprised of mostly incumbents who were formerly lawyers representing the "cream of the crop" in their communities. The chairmen of the important power wielding committees are the older members of Congress who serve their own community's special interests.

Dolbeare maintains that the power of governmental institutions is insidious. The ruling class in government is not perceived by the citizenry because of the mythology of the one-man, one-vote principle—all are equal in a democracy. It is assumed that politics are separate from the social and economic systems, that elected representatives represent popular preferences, and that these representatives have the necessary power to influence decisions that would favorably impact the average American. Furthermore, it is perceived that democratic pluralism requires that people are represented by interest groups, and that the government reacts to all groups equally and according to the merits of an issue.

Dolbeare states that these perceptions are myths because there is an integration of the corporate economy with the political system. The few key banks interlock, members of the board of directors of one bank or corporation sit on the board of directors of one or several other corporations or banks, and the federal government and businesses are mutually supportive and globally involved. Additionally, the President must engage in some partnership operation to get nominated and elected. His cabinet and other key office memberships are predominantly found among his political supporters in the business world (Dolbeare, 1974).

Added to what Dolbeare claims, campaign financing in support of federal legislators serves to influence congressional decisions. Former U.S. Representative Dan Hamburg describes the mounting pressure to raise huge amounts of money as his political career progressed. The following quote taken from his article "Inside the Money Chase" (1997: 24–25), provides a revealing account of how our legislative body works:

I had been at the annual picnic of the Operating Engineers, a union that had "maxed out" to me ($5,000 each for primary and general elections). At the picnic, several of the union leaders spoke to me about a problem they were having—getting the go-ahead for a freeway-widening project in the district. I said I'd do what I could. The next day, there I was at the White House, arguing for more money for "infrastructure," including, of course, the project the Operating Engineers were pushing.

This is the kind of thing members of Congress do routinely. After all, this is how the system is supposed to work. The member goes out into the district, talks to his constituents, finds out what they need, and then fights to get it, especially if it's for a group that's good for $10,000 in the next election. I knew lots of reasons that the widening project was a bad idea, at best unnecessary. In fact, as a county official, I had voted against it several times. But it wasn't hard to conjure up reasons to be *for* it either: primarily, jobs and campaign money.

Dolbeare asserts that all of our political institutions, the Constitution, and legislative procedures are really an integrated barrier to significant reform. The myths that surround these political institutions serve as their security.

Nevertheless, even if one does not share this view, it can probably be surmised that, as with the schools, governmental policy-making bodies are reflections of society and act in conjunction with other agencies when and if they perform to effect social change.

The Courts

Because political institutions seem to more readily respond to those with power and money, the courts are imbued with the ability to respond to the disadvantaged. Most judges at the local level and all at the federal level are not elected and do not have the same pressures put upon them from political arenas and bureaucracies. Also, complaints must be taken seriously, because the courts supposedly rule by precedent and have certain procedural rules to follow. The courts are deemed to be an escape from rigid bureaucracies, ossified institutions, and reluctant or biased citizenry.

Moreover, the courts can be used to dramatize and publicize injustices, and some would say that the courts encourage groups to mobilize (Rosenberg, 1991). Some claim this power for the courts, especially concerning the *Brown* decision as a precursor to the Civil Rights movement in the late fifties and early sixties.

Rosenberg (1991) contests this theory and asserts that the *Brown* decision may have delayed rather than encouraged American citizens to support civil rights for blacks. Resistance to the Court's order to desegregate with "all deliberate speed" may have foreshadowed the delays in providing equal opportunities and/or practices in the work place, legislative bodies, and the criminal justice system.

Thurgood Marshall said of the *Brown* decision upon being interviewed shortly after *Brown II* in 1955, that the decision was "very clear." "If the decision were violated anywhere on one morning, we'll have the responsible authorities in court by the next morning, if not the same afternoon." He also stated, "it might be up to five years for the entire country" when speaking about how long it would take for full implementation in desegregating the nation's public schools. He predicted that by the time of the 100th anniversary (1963) of the Emancipation Proclamation, segregation in all its forms would have been eliminated from the nation (NAACP, 1954: 16 as cited in Rosenberg).

We now know that the future justice of the Supreme Court was overly optimistic in his predictions. De jure school segregation lasted another ten years in the South and de facto school segregation is still the norm rather than an aberration. Even though the *Brown* decision was unanimous as most of the subsequent school desegregation decisions and the Supreme Court confirmed *Brown* in these subsequent decisions, action was not taken nationwide until ten years later! Rosenberg (1991: 156) claims, "By stiffening resistance and raising fears before the activist phase of the civil rights movement was in place, *Brown* may actually have delayed the achievement of civil rights."

Civil rights for blacks is not the only issue where the courts may have been a reflection of society rather than a leader for social change. The courts have made little difference in other civil liberty arenas such as women, homosexual, and other less powerful group issues. Rosenberg (1991) asserts this must be true because of the constraints put upon the courts by the limited nature of constitutional rights, lack of judicial independence, and lack of judicial powers of implementation. Additionally, the courts did not have much impact on the desegregation of transportation, voting, housing, accommodations, and public places until Congress and the Executive Branch acted in concert with the courts (Rosenberg, 1991). Needless to say, there remains segregated housing patterns within most American urban communities.

The Citizens

Although political scientists have not studied social movements very much, they have found that citizen dissatisfaction coupled with the necessary resources and the existence of leadership that is able to motivate a group to take action, can influence the public and politicians, and be a major source for change (Walker, 1968). Agreeing, Dolbeare (1974) suggests that instead of our unit of thinking being the individual, it should be the community or, better yet, humanity. He talks of this way of thinking as a new consciousness or what neo-Marxists call, "new critical theory:" "Only when people begin to see systematic causes for their circumstances, and to connect these with their own values and ways of thinking—and, therefore, to make demands that go beyond the existing system—can social protest become a part of the consciousness change process" (119).

The value we place on individualism in our society and our preoccupation with materialism and property may be blocks, but not the *only* blocks to this consciousness change-process to effect social improvement: "A deep sense of inevitability about all things American pervades our thinking linking up with a sense of how fortunate we are to enjoy such a standard of living and relative individual freedom; therefore, we should muddle through, somehow. It is better to seize what pleasures one can find in the immediate present" (Dolbeare, 1974: 86).

However, Dolbeare maintains that the limitations in our governmental system in terms of reform "saps" those who are *willing* to act. The costs of time, money, and internal conflicts obfuscate shared needs and goals. This leads to a sense of hopelessness that may in turn lead some to vent their frustrations upon each other. Dolbeare ponders if our governmental system was designed so that people have to work themselves up to a near hysteria or violence to make a point. Kenneth Clark relates, "Whenever we found any attempt at significant community action as part of the anti poverty programs, almost invariably political considerations intervened to truncate or control or restrict the extent of community action which local political figures would permit" (1970: 22).

Moreover, Dolbeare (1974) points out that although there are more people at the bottom of the "power-structure pyramid" in this country, and that these people should have greater political power than those few at the top, this large group is neither self-conscious of its strength, inclined to use it, nor organized to do so if it were. He asserts that there is a ruling class that gets its way and orchestrates popular acquiescence besides. This ruling class operates collectively but is not necessarily apparent to the public because it shares values, interests, experiences, and goals with the populace. It is not all-pervading or all-controlling, but it is there.

Nevertheless, instances of grass-root citizen action that spurred political, legislative, judicial, and educational change are numerous. During Franklin Roosevelt's administration, it was black leaders who threatened a massive march on Washington D.C. for jobs (Brotherhood of Sleeping Car Porters). Roosevelt then issued an executive order establishing a Fair Employment Practices Committee to prevent discrimination in federal employment and vocational training programs. Rosenberg claims that blacks demonstrated that they maintained power to exert pressure on the government and, consequently, "the pot was boiling" before the 1960s' Civil Rights movement. In fact, "there were more civil rights demonstrations in 1943, 1946, 1947 and 1948 than in any year following until 1960 (1956 and 1958 excepted)" (Rosenberg, 1991: 1668)!

Rosenberg reminds us that the Civil Rights demonstrations, beginning with the Montgomery bus boycott in the early 1950s, galvanized a series of demonstrations and boycotts, including the boycott in Baton Rouge in 1953, the sit-ins, and the Freedom Ride organized by CORE in 1961. Black groups such as SNCC, CORE, SCLC, and the NAACP capitalized on the success of the Montgomery bus boycott. Martin Luther King was elected president of SNCC in 1960 and organized students for the sit-ins. These groups, with the exception of the NAACP, put little faith in the courts and admired several African nation liberations. But, most importantly, daily injustices perpetrated upon blacks brought on resentment.

In Little Rock (1957) political mobilization spawned by resistance to court decisions also brought positive results. King saw the courts as too slow and costing too much:

Rank and file blacks, themselves, could act to advance the race's goals rather than relying exclusively on lawyers and litigation to win incremental legal gains. . . . Only when the people themselves begin to act are rights on paper given life blood. [Blacks] must not get involved in legalism [and] needless fights in lower courts because that is exactly what the white man wants the Negro to do. Then he can draw out the fight. (quoted in Garrow, 1986: 91)

Because of the Civil Rights demonstrations, financial support of black organizations increased. White contributions went up, it seems, because of threats of violence (Rosenberg, 1991). The demonstrations had a nationwide impact because the violence of the status quo white power was seen through the electronic news media. The entire nation was becoming aware of the injustices perpetrated upon the black race. Ira Glasser provides further credence to grass-roots power. He reminds us,

When the Court struck down a federal law prohibiting slavery in the territories in 1857, litigation did not overturn that infamous decision; the Civil War did. When women were finally enfranchised in 1920, it was not due to any action by the Court, but because women organized for years until they had created enough pressure to force a constitutional amendment that guaranteed them the right to vote. Working people who wanted to form labor unions in the 1930s won recognition of their First Amendment rights to free speech and peaceful assembly the same way: through political struggle and organizing. Their efforts forced passage of the National Labor Relations Act and, thus, altered the climate in which the Supreme Court viewed freedom of expression. (1992: 2)

(This view of freedom of expression was also exhibited by the anti Vietnam War demonstrators who pressured politicians to end the U.S. role in another nation's war.) Glasser goes on to say, "today, gay men and lesbians understand very well that rights are won as often in the streets as in the courts. . . . History shows that rights come to those who fight for them, with or without the Supreme Court's help."

CITIZENS FIGHTING FOR RIGHTS IN HYDE PARK

Following is an example of political awareness and action on the part of the citizenry in Hyde Park. Hyde Park residents played the leading role in organizing their community and surrounding neighborhoods to block construction of a halfway house/honor center near the Hyde Park neighborhood.

In the summer of 1991, the Lafayette Square neighborhood (just south of downtown St. Louis) held a rally to protest the reopening of the Malcolm Bliss Hospital to house an honor center for convicted criminals. Subsequently, the decision was made to have the center built near the Hyde Park neighborhood between the River and Interstate 70. It wasn't until February 1992, when a Hyde Park resident read a small notice in the *St. Louis Post-Dispatch* reporting the changed site-plans, that the community was notified (the resident claimed it appeared in the *sports* section). The battle was on!

Community meetings were organized; fliers were distributed; block captains and others made numerous phone calls; many letters were written to federal, state, and local politicians and agency administrators (some also written by children); fourteen community members traveled to the State capital to support their representative; and investigations and research were tediously and thoroughly carried out. Hyde Park residents led all these efforts and involved residents, service providers, and business owners from several surrounding neighborhoods; industry owners on the river front; and political representatives.

The honor center facility was proposed to house 400 to 450 convicted criminals who would be released to seek employment and work in the St. Louis area. The State was given the property by the City of St. Louis, which bought the property with federal HUD block grant monies ($500,000 worth).

Complaints expressed by community members included:

- citizens were not notified in a timely and adequate fashion;
- information was withheld and/or hidden;
- city administration representatives lied to community residents;
- most of the elected politicians were not representing and working for community members;
- north St. Louis was being "dumped" on again;
- block grant money was improperly spent and should be spent to help and uplift neighborhoods;
- the honor center would have an adverse impact on neighborhoods, industries, businesses, service agencies, and residents; and
- the city administration agreed to have an honor center built at the river front location mainly for political reasons.

Apparently, the alderpersons representing the affected neighborhoods had voted in favor of the proposed site. They stated that community members did not object before the vote was taken. As one Hyde Park resident expressed it, "We didn't know about it! What kind of representation is that? None!"

The alderpersons then worked out a compromise with the residents indicating that they would help block the construction of the center on the river front site if the residents would support keeping the honor center at its present location. This would prevent moving the center to Malcolm Bliss in the Lafayette Square neighborhood in south St. Louis.

The day after this agreement, one of the alderpersons called a Hyde Park community leader and stated that the deal was off. This action prompted the following speech made at the third community meeting by a Hyde Park resident and business owner (schooled through the 12th grade and life-educated through the 43d year):

Once again we are being shafted. The bottom line is—these people (politicians) work for us. They are our employees from the Board of Aldermen to the President of the United States. They have been hired by us to work for us.

We interview potential candidates to fill the position and we evaluate who will be the best by what they tell us they will do for us. We then hire them by using the voting process and we are responsible to pay these employees through the tax process. But something happens after we hire these people. The majority forget who their employers are and forget their purpose and their responsibility to their positions. That is known as "I've got them where I want them—so screw you process!"

In any other business, I don't know of any employer who would allow the employee to maintain a position where the employee does not do the job he was hired to do, who works against the business that the employee was hired to serve, who approves a program that is detrimental to the business without even researching the program, and who refuses to appear before the employer when requested to do so. I know of no employer who would allow these things to happen except for us.

We also allow these employees to give themselves numerous perks, give themselves raises without being evaluated, and, last but not least, we have allowed these people to confuse, bully, and intimidate us into thinking that they are in control, that they have power over our lives, and there's not a damn thing we can do about it. But we can, and that, my friends, is "the hit the road Jack—you're fired process!"

The Community Meetings

Three community meetings were convened so that people could air their concerns to political representatives and city administrators and for the purpose of organizing and carrying out strategies to block the proposed honor center. The meetings were held in the Friedens Haus facility.

The first meeting (February 23, 1992) was televised by the three major St. Louis TV stations and shown on that night's 10:00 news programs. One station entitled the spot "Not in our Back Yard." The meeting was very well organized and included speakers from business, industry, schools, and the Hyde Park residential community. Information was distributed, charts were displayed, and empty chairs were placed on the stage with boldly printed placards positioned in front of each chair. Names of missing political representatives were well in view.

One Hyde Park school teacher displayed a chart explaining the distance in walking time from the proposed honor center to various businesses, homes, schools, and churches (four to twenty minutes). This presentation and others showed that the potential impact on the community would be great. Complaints from the audience included, "We get what others reject!" "Why does it have to be on the north side?" "I'm a product of Hyde Park and north St. Louis. When someone puts Hyde Park or north St. Louis down, I consider it an insult! I'm working to help children in the area have the kind of life I had as a child in the neighborhood, and I don't want to see it go down the drain!"

One industry owner stated, "When you work some place for eight hours a day, it's like living there. We have to protect our employees!" The area had just been designated as an enterprise zone, and it was felt that businesses needed to be attracted and not detracted from the area: "We don't want to make north St. Louis the dumping ground for someone else's problems!"

When the director for Public Safety spoke for the St. Louis administration, he stated that he felt a little like "a cockroach in the punch bowl!" That was the only statement he offered with which the audience agreed. When the director asserted that the state was holding the cards and the city didn't want the center, the disbelief was apparent and the shouting began. The speaker "gave up" within five minutes. The voices of the people were heard! "We're tired of being prisoners in our own neighborhood! We already have one of the highest crime rates in St. Louis!"

Several of the political representatives who arrived late acknowledged the concerns of community members. Promises were made to look into this and that and to be present at the following week's community meeting. One alderperson told of a plan made years ago to maintain a "do nothing" policy for north St. Louis and let it fall.

The second community meeting featured slides of the proposed site (eighteen acres) and showed the various community locations that would suffer the greatest impact. Community members made presentations that were well thought out, short, and to the point. Children held up a banner that expressed "thanks" to one state representative for his assistance. The same representative explained to the audience what he had done during the week, whom he had contacted, what he told them, and what their responses had been. He then told whom he planned to meet with during the next week concerning the issue: "We will get a restraining order if necessary!"

By the third meeting it was discovered through research and investigation that the state should have reviewed an impact study before building an honor center facility on a site purchased with CDA money. HUD officials maintained that the city was responsible for implementing the study. It was decided that the community members would present their own impact study, collect signatures, and then deliver the study to HUD officials the following day.

Community members then talked about specific impacts to industries, businesses, schools, churches, real estate, and so on. All of this was included in the impact study delivered to HUD. Charts were displayed comparing insurance costs, and costs were mentioned concerning added security, loss of customers, loss of business due to existing city policies, and bad experiences with hiring previous work-release inmates on the part of local industry and business establishments. One resident expressed it this way, "I'm all for giving people a second chance in life, but, hey, give us a chance first!"

The importance of registering to vote was mentioned. People were asked to sign a petition and volunteer to go to the HUD offices the next day. One resident asserted, "This is the first time in a long time that we feel we have a chance to make a difference!"

The "community investigator" from the Hyde Park neighborhood (schooled through the 12th grade and life-educated through the 45th year) spent over 100 hours in the library researching the honor center issue. He began his investigation by trying to find out who previously owned the proposed site, when it was transferred, and who presently owned it. He sifted through the listings of HUD and found out how HUD went about acquiring property, how block grant money was to be used, and then perused city ordinances. As he stated it, "We tried to hit every angle! You can never get anywhere because there's too many people hiding things! The government's supposed to be working for you—well, that's a big laugh—they're working for themselves!"

The community investigator made several trips to the state capital and spent one week conversing with various representatives and senators. Strategy meetings were held at a neighbor's house, and several community residents developed and implemented their plans in the Holy Trinity school kitchen where one of the community leaders worked. It was decided that the investigator should visit the proposed site and try to find something that would block construction of the honor center facility. He found black "stuff" oozing out of the ground and took pictures. He then wrote a report describing "noxious materials coming out of the earth." This forced the Environmental Protection Agency to initiate an environmental study. The investigator boasted, "We were like little ants, and we were just causing these people a great deal of pain!"

No one knows what happened to the honor center proposal. As the lead investigator said, "It just died." He was sure of one thing, the community's actions *made* it die.

Continuing Political Awareness and Action in Hyde Park

When asked about issues that could bring the community together again, the lead investigator had this to say:

Well I was hoping that all these kids getting shot would get somebody to moving—but, so far, nothing. The only thing that's going to get everybody together again is going to be a crisis situation like perhaps the possibility of an honor center-type facility going in on Salisbury. That could turn into a crisis situation. People around here do not like to hear anything about being "dumped" on. They do not like to hear anything about criminals coming into the neighborhood.

Although considered to be a community rather than a political matter by some, ears of community residents and leaders really perked up about this issue. It was learned that a small business on Salisbury was bought by a church entity in order to house several single men as well as a few families. The possibility existed that there would be ex-offenders living there—one resident was reportedly wearing an ankle bracelet indicating that he was under house arrest. Community members talked about actions in the form of protesting or looking into keeping the City Building Division aware of building violations and other ways to perhaps force the establishment out of the neighborhood. Many hours were spent strategizing about this issue.

Other political action focused on keeping additional negative factors out of the community. For instance, petitions were signed and resident and agency representatives attended a meeting at City Hall to block a local store from obtaining a liquor license. Community members felt that neighborhood children frequented the store, and the owners were not responsible in following existing laws.

There was an awareness on the part of some community leaders of a "turning point election period" (Iannaccone, 1983). One leader asserted that with new administration at all governmental levels, the Hyde Park community needed to take advantage. During one Housing Corporation meeting it was stated, "We need to move forward on buildings and do as much as possible so we can cash in on this new mood towards affordable housing" (1993).

Political action was also taken by the Friedens Haus coalition in approaching the St. Louis School Board and the Board of Aldermen concerning consideration that Clay Elementary become a "community center." Letters and program descriptions were sent to school board members; one board member was invited to visit Clay School and the Friedens Haus facility; the neighborhood organization sent a letter of support; the 3d Ward alderman, the mayor, and the president of the school board were spoken to; and letters were sent to the SLPSS superintendent. Finally, the Clay school principal, the president of the Friedens Haus advisory board, the director of the Friedens Haus program, and the interim director of Hyde Park Alliance spoke before the Board of Education.

The effect was noticeable. During the meeting, four of the twelve board members spoke in favor of making Clay a community center sometime in the near future. There was mention of the Friedens Haus coalition serving as a model for community education. School district and city representatives (four months later) subsequently announced that the restructured community education program would include one additional elementary school during the 1995–96 year—Clay Elementary.

SUMMARY

If one adopts the definition of politics as, "the authoritative allocation of values and resources in society" (Wirt and Kirst, 1989: 82), then the issues of community empowerment, community problem-solving, and the effort to involve everyone in the pursuit of lifelong learning are very much political processes. All of these issues are dependent upon resources and/or values—they concern power and control.

Hyde Park neighborhood problems are multiple, varied and great, and many of its residents represent the oppressed of our society. However, the schools, the courts, and governmental policy-making institutions serve, more or less, as reflections of our society rather than agents for social change. Political awareness and action on the part of the citizenry is essential, and Hyde Park community residents are capable.

Nevertheless, the community's political structure in terms of outside agencies entering the neighborhood to "serve" may be "elitist," modifying inputs from residents so as to subordinate them (Wirt and Kirst, 1989). "In place of a sense of Gemeinschaft—genuine community of values—there intrudes pseudo-Gemeinschaft—the feigning of personal concern with the other fellow in order to manipulate him the better" (Josephson and Josephson, 1962: 43). Consequently garnering facts about salient issues such as the decision-making processes concerning the honor center and the SLPSS community center locations was essential.   As one community resident asserted, "Empowerment starts with holding people accountable!"

Finally, there is not a single solution to multiple societal problems. It will take a combination of education, leadership, and informed citizen involvement to bring about social change in the face of the resistant status quo. Monumental tasks such as social change are evolutionary (with the exception of revolution or a catastrophic event), require persistence and risk, and the use of our courts, other political institutions, the schools, and the organization of critical masses of people. The most important ingredient for social change, however, is a citizenry who is aware of its social condition and is willing to act. Thus, we come full circle and return to the words of James Baldwin, "The obligation of any one who thinks of himself as responsible is to examine society and try to change it and to fight it—no matter what the risk. This is the only hope society has. This is the only way societies change" (1971).

Chapter 10

Community Empowerment

INTRODUCTION

As maintained in the previous chapter, because the basis for positive social change is a citizenry that is aware and willing to act, community education is foremost concerned with community empowerment or, as some would prefer, maintaining the power already present within a community. Without this, community problem-solving and the effort to involve everyone in the pursuit of lifelong learning will be nonexistent, truncated, or at least greatly diminished no matter the possible Herculean efforts of outside agencies and service providers to better the community. This and following chapters address the issues of outside agency involvement for community betterment vs. community empowerment, the role community advisory boards play in the community empowerment endeavor, and the necessity of inclusiveness and leadership development within the community for this empowerment to be effective.

COMMUNITY EMPOWERMENT VS. COMMUNITY BETTERMENT

It must be noted that interagency cooperation may *exclude* community members as well as inclusive decision-making processes that improve community life. The previously mentioned multi-systems model of George Wood *includes* community problem-solving and decision-making and has much in common with the writings of Arthur Himmelman (1992). Himmelman adds to the discussion by noting the difference between interagency linkages for community *empowerment* and interagency linkages for community *betterment*. He advocates that the community betterment model (when an outside organization comes in to improve the community and uses community members as participants and advisors) evolve into a community empowerment model (when community members make the important decisions for improving community life and outside organizations are used as participants and advisors).

In support of this philosophy and when attempting to define the function of a recently formed Friedens Haus committee comprised of service providers and residents, one Hyde Park resident stated, "Think of this . . . as a 'tool' for the community." She admitted that the connection to outside resources was "vital" to the neighborhood, but that citizens needed to be empowered to take control. A service provider then expressed that people and institutions on the outside needed a sense of *giving*: "People at both ends of the giving benefit by what is being done." Another resident was mindful that with this giving there was sometimes "implied control." Finally, an outside community participant asserted that "do-goodniks" should not impose their "do-good" philosophy on someone else.

Outside agencies coming in to better the Hyde Park neighborhood instead of empowering community members to improve their own environment was a constant source of frustration. As one service provider observed:

There are so many wonderful things about Hyde Park, but it seems as though all of those entities are entities from without—not within. Because I don't live here, how can I say I want something good for Hyde Park? I work here--it's a job for me. . . . So if I'm not even conducive to even the community and what they think,—people who live here, who may have a business here, who have invested their lives here, they should have some say.

I have a Masters degree, but who's to say a Masters degree or a Ph.D. is going to solve community problems? You may not even be able to get an entree in. It's the community people who have the base and heart of the community.

A Hyde Park resident expressed his feelings concerning outside agencies blocking resident control of the neighborhood in the following interview.

What were the greatest efforts to stabilize the community during the last 10 years? Have they been effective?

Not really. Private institutions like Friedens Haus and North Side Team Ministry have done more than the city has. The Housing Corporation has been virtually ineffective. That was set up, I think, to give the local people the notion that they had some control over development, but it was bullshit.

The Housing Corporation, initiated in 1989, hasn't developed a damn thing yet out of their $225,000 even though they're working on a couple projects. The ties to the federal money that the city has necessitates a grass-roots type effort. It really is a sham, because the Housing Corporation can't do anything the city doesn't want to do. We tried to initiate some things that we thought would work for Hyde Park that *were* a little different, because we had been through this before—we knew what didn't work.

The Bike Shop, for instance, is taking two years and $140,000 to develop a 2,000 square foot building (not to mention the hidden staff costs). I think the Bike Shop will eventually do something for economic development here—tying in with the River Front

Bike Trail, but not very efficiently, and it is not cost effective. If there was some way to take a little building like that and give some guy twenty to fifty thousand dollars and say, "Here, put a bike shop in--we don't care how you do it as long as you get the permits—do it out of sweat equity—do a lot of it yourself—we'll get out of your way—we won't bullshit you to death with inspections, heritage commissions, and architectural plans that give the bureaucrat a sense of control, I guess. That's pretty threatening to those guys—you don't need them then.

What could the community members/organizations do to make you want to stay [in Hyde Park]?

It ain't going to happen. You've got to figure out a way to get this out of the hands of the professional bureaucrats downtown. You need to develop a public-private partnership where you can take CDA (Community Development Agency) money and give appropriate oversight to the city and do with it as you see fit. Friedens Haus can do things development-wise that the Housing Corporation can*not* because it's exempt from a lot of the rules and regulations.

I'm enough of a dreamer to believe that something still can be done here. You can get the police, the building division, city agencies, churches, neighborhood organizations—all these people working together—and let them work out what they want to do [in cooperation] with the residents. It's just never happened, even with nuisance-type issues. The police don't deal with it--the system doesn't work.

I'm about to give up. I've been here fifteen years and I don't see any prospect of things changing. I don't think you can change things until you get the grass roots, local control, and I think that's impossible. That threatens the politicians, and it all comes back to politics—it really does.

The former director of the neighborhood organization, Hyde Park Alliance, expressed her frustration this way:

What do you see as the biggest disappointments?

The relationship with CDA and their two-sided and two-faced activity of competing with us for grants and not giving us any technical assistance and simply monitoring us for mistakes but never praising us for success—never caring that we exist. I don't like that at all.

Anyway, that's a little of my thinking of the usefulness of downtown people and the lack of usefulness to us these people become. CDA is a good case in point. I mean they have monitors, they have *monitors*, I mean even the word is an unalliance kind of word; "Oh well, we're going to monitor and we're going to slap their wrist when they go astray, but we're not going to be there to help them expand."

I think a big problem with the Housing Corporation is that it's a political beast that's not a free-standing agent of this office. Its motivation is entirely to be a puppet to this downtown money. Everybody on the board is appointed by a politician and approved by the mayor and they have meetings that have certain ground rules and bylaws that are big enough to choke a horse, and yet they have the appearance of being neighborhood-based because the people are neighborhood people. But those neighborhood people are not educated in terms of how to make that organization function for their purposes.

Downtown wants to have all the control over neighborhood development. The more they can make it look like Hyde Park can't get their act together, the more they have the power. Keep the pot boiling—have to go back to CDA and ask, have to go back to Impact and ask. We can never just move on something. Our hands are constantly tied by bureaucratic bullshit. It's the same in any bureaucratic institution, they are not about to allow for visionaries to come through the rank and file. They're into control and power. They're not afraid that neighborhood people would mess it up, they're afraid of having their own jobs at stake. What if we know how to do it better than they know how to do? What about their salaries? When you really look at it, they can't afford to have us look good.

(The other side of the story is contained in the chapter entitled, "Citizen Councils.")

An interview with the Friedens Haus director reveals what she views as the negative factors of higher education's involvement and what would be an ideal college/university partnership with Hyde Park. Her views add to the discussion of outside agencies' linkages from the perspectives of community betterment and community empowerment:

Universities are used to teaching rather than interacting. That's when there has to be enough people around to say, "OK, we want your expertise, but you have to work with us and not run everything." Other agencies can do the same thing—the ones who have the expertise. Universities probably tend to do this more. That's their kind of format.

What is an ideal involvement of higher education with a community in your opinion?

If they could do research and evaluations for us and keep that expertise level, but not telling us how to do things. They could give us the data and then we can decide how to change things to make things better. That's what bothers me about one university's study, because they are telling us that we're suppose to do this and that in a group and this kind of thing—not based on *after* we've been doing it, but based on to fit their study to give them the data to give to the government. We just want knowledge and expertise and encouragement for their students to get involved—all different levels of involvement.

AN EXAMPLE OF COMMUNITY BETTERMENT

The Housing Corporation, which was described as a "political beast" by the Hyde Park Alliance director, convened a meeting on December 1, 1993 (annual meeting to elect officers and to announce membership appointments by alderpersons with mayoral approval). The meeting serves an example of a "community betterment" as opposed to a "community empowerment" process. There were seven members present.

At the previous month's meeting, the city agency representative had problems with one board member. The member suggested that time be set aside during the December meeting for making future plans. The representative asserted that the bylaws would have to be changed in order to do this, because the purpose of the annual meeting was to introduce new members and officers. The member asserted, "We can change the bylaws for this corporation if we want to—this is America!" The representative retorted, "You can do what you want to, but the bylaws will *have* to be changed!" The member then exclaimed, "There's no thought police out there!"

Consequently, prior to the December meeting the same member was informed that he would not be reappointed. He submitted a letter of resignation at the December meeting. One member asked, "If we can't *appoint* members, how can we accept a resignation?" The city representative then asked for a motion to accept the member's resignation. (It must be noted that the city agency representative was presiding instead of the board's president.)

One member then asserted that the city representative was to *assist* the board in conducting business. Another member cited the bylaws, "the *board* makes election of its members." The city representative then maintained that, in order for the organization to keep its 501(C)3 status and continue receiving city support, the "procedures" had to be followed.

The point was then made that the city had an amount of money to spend but needed a 501(C)3 organization to do it—the Housing Corporation board was developed for that purpose. One board member stated, "We're just a facility to use money for housing." Another member expressed, "The only changes are the hoops we have to jump through from CDA. We have had to play with politicians in the past, and it has been back and forth, back and forth."

Another board member just then learned that he, too, had not been reappointed (identified from here on as Member I). A lengthy discussion then ensued about what the bylaws really said about length of terms and so forth, the fact that the organization operated outside of the bylaws in the past, and that some members did not know when their terms expired.

The alderperson who made the new appointments then entered the room and was asked why some members were not reappointed. (Three alderpersons represented three portions of Hyde Park.)

Alderperson. To start out fresh and because the Hyde Park area may be declared a Conservation District in the near future. We need people that are not of the old order, who cause friction.

Member I. So if you cause friction, you're out!

Alderperson. I realize you're busy and you never approached me to indicate interest, and these others have approached me and have shown interest.

Member I. Last meeting, I just wanted a meeting with you!

Alderperson. Political organizations aren't allowed to handle federal money so a corporation had to be created to mirror the aldermen—to take us some place—and if you don't take us someplace, then you need to be replaced. There is something wrong with how this organization functions. Hyde Park can turn out to be the best historic district—other historic districts have left Hyde Park far behind. I need people who are willing to take chances; you've got to be able to work together. Being obstinate or just opposing things just because they are different is counter-productive.

Member II. (the first ousted member) At first, you never even made appointments; we had to depend upon the ConServ (city) officers who were very slow to act. You never made any recommendations then!

Alderperson. (after acknowledging this laxity) Now I'm here!

Member II. In the beginning, it was like twisting arms to get members, you weren't here for us!

Alderperson. Yes, you're right, I didn't know you were here.

(Member II then stated facts indicating that this was not so.)

When the city representative tried to change the subject, Member I asked, "Who is running this meeting? The representative should be keeping us *apprised*!"

Representative. There is a danger of losing money from HUD because of our lack of movement on anything. We need to spend the money that we're allocated. The auditors will be coming in. If we don't get going, we will be endangering the whole program. The inconsistencies in the bylaws were not addressed until personal issues of not being reappointed to the board came up.

Member I. (trying to remain calm) We have been moving as quickly as we can considering all the factors!

Member III. We could be losing support of _____ Church which has been a bulwark in this community and making it a tolerable place to live. The board, here, is largely because of previous leaders of this church getting the neighborhood association started, and then the [former] mayor decided that he could throw a Housing Corporation in here (in an election year, of course). I can see another rift coming in this neighborhood if this obtains [referring to the church leader not being reappointed].

Board business then resumed, and a board member residing *outside* Hyde Park was elected president after the alderperson spoke in his favor after two "tie" votes. When Member II was asked to write something about himself for a proclamation ceremony, he claimed that he wasn't "in the mood." Member I seemed disgruntled and stated that he would no longer be available to let members in the church for future meetings.

AN EXAMPLE OF COMMUNITY EMPOWERMENT

The struggle to maintain community power was also witnessed during three housing meetings initiated by Hyde Park Alliance and held in connection with the strategic planning efforts guided by a city agency. The meetings were held July 17, August 10, and September 14, 1993 at Clay Elementary and were well attended by Friedens Haus/Clay program leaders and staff, Hyde Park Alliance members and staff, community residents, and several area service providers.

Because the Hyde Park city agency representative had recently moved away from the St. Louis area, there was no city representation at the July meeting. A free flow of ideas abounded during this first meeting and excitement was the prevailing emotion. One Hyde Park resident put it this way, "The synergy in this room literally scares me! . . . Dream big!" The discussion centered around local control, de-emphasizing outside owners of Hyde Park property, the community's purchase of buildings, and the community serving as the money lender for property acquisitions.

The tone of the following meeting was in complete contrast. The director of the city agency attended the meeting in place of a yet to be replaced representative. The director "directed" the meeting. When community members attempted to offer ideas, the director debated their feasibility or offered his own suggestions. The excitement exhibited during the previous meeting was gone, and there was a general mood of resignation among meeting participants.

The *third* meeting was attended by both the city agency director and the newly hired representative. There were substantially more community members in attendance. A Hyde Park Alliance staffer announced at the start that this meeting was to be conducted following the *consensus* model, a procedure that was new to strategic planning committee members. An agenda was distributed, time limits were set for reports, and minutes were read. One community member's responsibility was to observe the process and report how participants fared in emulating the model. There was little room for one person to direct or control the meeting. Consequently, via a structured meeting process, the *community* regained control. It must be noted that the city agency director left after approximately thirty minutes, having offered only limited input.

SUMMARY

Similar to residents of many communities, especially inner-city neighborhoods, Hyde Park community members continuously struggled to maintain control of their own affairs either within and among neighborhood organizations or between these organizations and outside service providers. Hyde Park residents were capable of solving their own problems with the *assistance* of outside agencies and resources. It is doubtful that effective community problem-solving can happen without community members taking ownership of, not only their problems, but the solutions.

Ownership, locus-of-control, or empowerment was at various levels within and between the multiple Hyde Park community organizations and outside agencies. However, *maintenance* of community power was especially witnessed within the Friedens Haus coalition, because it was a grass-roots effort that involved community members organizing themselves to focus on a purpose and then integrating outside organizations in *support* of that purpose (Himmelman, 1992). This is borne out in the following chapters.

Chapter 11

Inclusiveness

INTRODUCTION

Although Hyde Park's population is approximately 68 percent black and 32 percent white, the community organizations were made up of white home owners until the last five years. When talking with some white community residents, racial remarks were expressed, although not very often. We have to put up with "the elements" in this neighborhood, "those people," and other generalized statements were made. Some said they felt tension between the races and that Hyde Park seemed like a segregated neighborhood within an integrated neighborhood.

When asked why his church was not represented at any of the community meetings, the pastor of Bethlehem Lutheran offered this view as part of his explanation:

The other thing is—there's never been any desire to come up our way [southwest Hyde Park] to start anything. Everything has been around Holy Trinity [southeast Hyde Park]. It's interesting—everything is in the white pocket. That's the white pocket of the neighborhood. The people of the community who come here are almost 100 percent African-American. Also, the economic lines are very different. We're working with people here who are below poverty level income. That's not the case totally over there.

As recently as four years ago, when campaigning for a black state representative in a predominantly black part of the neighborhood, one white community resident was told, "You know, you're living dangerous." When he asked why he was answered, "Son, you're white! Be careful!"

This resident asserted that many people did not participate in community activities because of racism; however, this was not perceived to be so, because people who had these feelings were not visible—they were not involved.

COMMUNITY POWER STRUCTURES

Inclusiveness has much to do with the structure of power within organizations, communities, and other entities. It is, therefore, relevant to talk about a community's power structure when looking at the level of inclusiveness within that community. Before looking at the evolving power structure in the diversified and rapidly changing Hyde Park neighborhood, it is useful to examine community power structures as defined in the literature. Donald McCarty and Charles Ramsey's study (1971) of fifty-one cities of varying size categorized community power structures within four classifications:

- The power structure is elite if the community is dominated by one small group that shares the same values.
- The power structure is bifactional if the community is dominated by two divergent groups, each of which share the same values within the group.
- The power structure is pluralistic if the community has a number of groups, each important in shaping policy in one domain, or has shifting coalitions that form temporary majorities on each issue area.
- The power structure is lacking or is unpatterned.

Johns and Kimbrough (1968) found that citizens tended to drastically misperceive the power arrangement in their communities, seeing more competition than actually existed. Merle Sumption and Yvonne Engstrom (1966) assert that, typically, those holding power want the community to grow and prosper economically, and they exert influence for their own selfish ends while the welfare of the community is incidental. The authors maintain that it is only natural that groups formed within a community would have a primary interest in one or two issue areas with only a secondary interest in others.

Sumption and Engstrom trace an evolutionary process of community power structure:

- The newly established community or one with great population mobility has only a rudimentary power structure consisting of several or many groups, each operating independently in one to four issue areas.
- As time passes, the issue areas for each group are likely to be reduced to a single issue—the one in which the group demonstrates superior power. Weaker groups will consolidate with the stronger ones until a pluralistic structure develops.
- The more stabilized communities exhibit power groups which tend to be fused into a single unit.
- An aroused citizenry revolting against a corrupt situation would bring about the breakdown and subsequent fragmentation of the community's power structure.
- The cycle begins again in the reformation of independent groups: "Characteristically, indignation tends to die down, and a more or less lethargic

attitude is assumed by the community, allowing the cautious but insistent reformation of the power structure." (22)

The authors assert that members of the power structure are often found in the upper regions of the socioeconomic scale, and many are quite wealthy and intelligent. Additionally, some of the power holders work behind the scenes and are not known to the general public.

THE POWER STRUCTURE IN THE HYDE PARK COMMUNITY

The power structure of Hyde Park recently evolved from an elite-type in the 1960s, 1970s, and 1980s to a more pluralistic structure that showed indications of becoming bifactional or even authoritarian via one powerful alderperson. Like Sumption and Engstrom's findings, neighborhood residents experienced indignation and lethargy due to feelings of powerlessness, disillusionment, and/or being excluded by the elite-type power structures of the past. Unlike John's and Kimbrough's findings, however, Hyde Park community members gave a rather fair assessment of the neighborhood's power structure during the time of my study as being pluralistic. The community was at a point where the power structure may evolve to a bifactional and then on to an elite model if steps are not taken to preserve pluralistic power.

Community residents who grew up in the neighborhood remembered the organization entitled Historic Hyde Park, Inc. in the 1960s—a predominately white home owners' group. The residents asserted that the purpose of this organization was to "keep the undesirables out"—blacks and those of lower socio-economic status (hoosiers). Long-time community residents described Historic Hyde Park, Inc. as the power-holder in the community and as a group that exerted its power to garner resources for organizational members while other community residents were more or less "left out."

Some of the same community members belonging to this neighborhood organization were also subsequently members of the Hyde Park Renovation Effort (HYPRE). Both organizations existed during several concurrent years. The focus of HYPRE was to rehab and sell homes in the neighborhood. Although less exclusionary, this organization was geared to home ownership and, subsequently, maintained the real power in Hyde Park.

Several years after HYPRE died out, the Trinity Square Association was formed (1987), which was also somewhat exclusionary. One community resident and former member of both the Historic and HYPRE organizations described this evolving power structure:

When things were really clicking in Hyde Park in the mid 70s to mid 80s, we became convinced that we could control our own destiny, so to speak (HYPRE). There was a lot of cronyism, some were involved with kickbacks to aldermen in cash, and a lot of very crooked things. There is a lot of that background. I guess the leader of that project had to do that to keep things going. [There is an outstanding HYPRE debt of $84,000 owed to the Missouri Department of Revenue. All properties owned by HYPRE that were not sold at the time the organization was considered defunct were reclaimed by the city.] Then Trinity Square was formed. There was some connection between the priest at Trinity to City Hall. It targeted the area right around Trinity church and was very exclusionary. Hyde Park Alliance has widened neighborhood participation, but there is a leadership vacuum.

Because the Trinity Square Association excluded a good part of the community at first, smaller groups were formed to address specific issues (alienation and frustration leading to an unpatterned power structure). The newly formed committees, associations, and organizations were the Safety Committee, the Landlord's Task Force, the Business Association, Northside All Combined (NAC), and the Friedens Haus coalition (the latter two organized in 1990).

After the Trinity Square Association acquired a new director, the name was changed to Hyde Park Alliance (HPA) and the smaller committees and associations began working under this organization's umbrella in order to acquire technical assistance, make use of HPA's 501(C)3 status, and have a format for sharing information while retaining their independent identities. The Friedens Haus coalition (six blocks from Holy Trinity) had by then become a major neighborhood organization servicing mainly the children, parents, and former students of Clay Elementary. The Housing Corporation was formed at about the same time by city political leaders. The main community entities working together at the time of my study were the Friedens Haus coalition, Hyde Park Alliance, the Housing Corporation, and New Holy Trinity Church (pluralistic power structure).

The inclusion of wider community participation within Hyde Park Alliance was an important step to a pluralistic power structure. The former HPA director gave this explanation of the changeover from the Trinity Square Association to the Hyde Park Alliance neighborhood organization:

What are the greatest accomplishments of HPA during your tenure?

Changing the name, changing the board structure, officers, who they are, changing the bylaws and mission, changing the concept that this is a totally open-to-everyone community organization with no political ties. We changed from being just a little tiny mission of being a code violation expert.

The organization originally started for home owners in these three blocks, so it had a very narrow focus, just around Trinity Church. The Trinity Square organization was very white, elitist, and narrow. It was pretty defunct when the name was changed to Hyde Park Alliance. There were people who didn't want to change the name—at first I wasn't too interested—that was a big thing.

Over the two years I've been here we've concentrated on bringing people together that didn't know each other, that didn't have a clue about one end of the community knowing the other end, and knowing that that's part of their community. What happens on block 1689 affects block 1421. You can't just live in your own little world and expect things to get better.

I gradually see the people coming together. We have a racially integrated board, for heavens sake, that wasn't there when I came on. And coming together, neighborhood-wise, different parts of the neighborhood—that's just critical.

Hyde Park's power structure was accurately described by community leaders and residents. One community leader had this to say: "The power structure is definitely pluralistic. I see really three very dominant groups and one that I think, if there is a particular issue, that they can pull it through if necessary."

One community resident gave this realistic account explaining that many community residents still viewed the residents around Holy Trinity as having the power or at least getting most of the attention and resources focused on them:

Describe the power structure of this community—elite, bifactional, pluralistic, or lacking and/or unpatterned—who has the power?

I look at it as pluralistic but that's because I'm not one of the "old guard" Hyde Park residents. The old guard tends to look at it as if Trinity [church] is the one. Ignorance is bliss. That's not part of my mind set. I look at it as we have a lot of different agencies that do a lot of different things, and, yes, at any one given time we can build one up higher than the others, but I don't see where one is a bit better than the other. . . . You have Friedens Haus, you have Hyde Park Alliance, the people at Trinity Church, the Safety Committee, the Landlord's Task Force, and all the other committees.

I think the old guard within Hyde Park still sees the Trinity Church area getting the attention focused there. There are pockets of Hyde Park where people feel totally neglected.

Holy Trinity's priest described the gradual inclusion of the wider community:

When I came, I began hearing that Trinity Square was too exclusive—they would only allow home owners to join. So I brought it up to the board regarding community-minded people living in north Hyde Park. "If they're willing to help out, why not let them join? The more people we have, the stronger we'll be!". . . This upset a few people—that renters were going to be allowed to join and people north of Salisbury. . . .

I would say Trinity Square [HPA] wouldn't be doing as well as it is if we hadn't gotten more connected to Friedens [north of Salisbury] and all that. There is strength in numbers.

It must be noted that at the time of my study, the most recent director of Hyde Park Alliance *seemed* to be focusing on inclusion and community involvement. The community meetings prior to her employment were attended by approximately ten community members while the first meeting after her employment was attended by approximately thirty (Spring, 1994).

There remained the question if these additional resident-participants would be allowed to vote for Board of Director members and officers. The organization's bylaws stated that yearly dues ($10) were required in order to obtain voting privileges. Since dues-paying members were few in number, there was little chance that the voice of the community would be heard concerning the election. It was decided at the June 1994 community meeting (attended by forty community members) that a subcommittee would meet to rewrite the bylaws.

The subsequent meeting of the bylaw subcommittee resulted in three options for the upcoming board election: (1) no dues requirement to vote, (2) dues of $10 required to vote, and (3) dues of $10 or community service (if unable to pay) required to vote. Also, it was determined that the two office-holders nominated at the last meeting would remain nominated. One resident expressed that it had been decided the nominations were to be entirely redone. (My notes substantiated this.) There ensued a hot exchange of words, and the director indicated to this resident that she would be furnished with a taped recording of the community meeting as evidence that this was not so. (The tape was never furnished.)

The following Board of Directors meeting (open to the public) was determined to be a "closed" meeting after two nonboard members (one was the previously mentioned community resident) were sitting in the meeting room for approximately ten minutes. The minutes were written by the HPA director instead of the secretary, they were not read, and they contained several substantial errors concerning meeting proceedings and decisions made. The idea of keeping the previous year's officers was discussed as well as postponing further community meetings until the Fall. It was eventually decided to postpone the June 1994 community meeting to either July and possibly August (the meeting was postponed to May 1995—one year later!). It was also decided the bylaws were to be completely rewritten and the elections were to be possibly held in September (postponed until May 1995 and still awaiting rewritten bylaws as of August 1995). Meanwhile, the current officers were to remain in their positions.

Circumstances were not looking very optimistic for inclusiveness in HPA, a neighborhood organization that was required to be inclusive in order to maintain funding from the Community Development Agency. It was obvious that several individuals desired to maintain control. Some residents became so frustrated at not being included that they were seriously thinking of supporting one of the smaller committees to become the official neighborhood organization (an aroused citizenry revolting against a corrupt situation as described by Sumption and Engstrom). This did not happen, in my opinion, because the Friedens Haus coalition served as an avenue for diminishing resident frustration by providing alternate opportunities for community service and decision-making.

Consequently, there was evidence of increasing friction between HPA and the Friedens Haus coalition, which could eventually lead to a bifactional community and/or even to an authoritative structure controlled by one powerful city alderperson. (The three aldermanic wards within the Hyde Park neighborhood boundaries had recently been redrawn, allocating the largest section to one powerful alderperson.)

SUMMARY

Although the Hyde Park community power structure was described as pluralistic at the time of my interviews with community members, there remained certain sections within the neighborhood that did not seem to be a part of community-wide efforts for improvement. The words of the pastor at the beginning of this chapter expressed the reality. While there may have been a greater amount of inclusion in one section of Hyde Park, the other section of the community remained separate and unequal. The fault may have lied somewhere between the two constituencies, but most fault usually lies at the feet of those who have the most power. In this case, the "haves" (relatively speaking) resided in the eastern part of the neighborhood where Holy Trinity, Hyde Park Alliance, The Housing Corporation, and the Friedens Haus coalition were located and/or met. It must be noted that the size of the Hyde Park neighborhood may, in itself, have been a deterrent for full inclusion in decision-making processes.

Added to this separatism, which was permeated with racial and economically prejudicial undertones, the more recent and persistent exclusionary actions of the neighborhood organization, Hyde Park Alliance, was a significant block to community involvement, empowerment, and community efforts to solve problems. If the status quo maintains on the HPA Board of Directors, most community members will remain without a voice concerning business proceedings of this organization. Although there was evidence of a multi-systems model of community education operating in the Hyde Park neighborhood, the recent lack of inclusiveness on the part of HPA truncated effects of such a community education initiative and encouraged frustration and alienation on the part of residents. Finally, with the recent change of Holy Trinity's priest, inclusion of several additional neighborhoods within the Holy Trinity parish, and withdrawal of one powerful alderperson's support and city money from the Housing Corporation, Hyde Park was at risk of becoming a bifactional community comprised of HPA and Friedens Haus factions. The possibility also remained that the aforementioned alderperson would exert authoritative power, leading to an elite neighborhood power structure. At the time of my study, multiple pieces of evidence indicated that this possibility was not unlikely.

Chapter 12

Citizen Councils

INTRODUCTION

One identifying factor of a viable community education program as advocated by the National Community Education Association is the citizen advisory board/council. The essential duties of the council are to assess community needs, assist in devising programs to meet these needs, ensure that the programs are implemented as designed, and then evaluate to determine if community needs are being met through the implemented programs. The problem, as Jack Minzey and Clyde LeTarte (1979) assert, is that the process is usually blocked at the after-school-programs level before attaining a true community and school partnership. This partnership would include community involvement concerning school policies and curriculum decision-making and attempting to solve community problems such as social, health, and economic needs through collaborative efforts.

A TYPOLOGY OF CITIZEN ADVISORY BOARDS/COUNCILS

Sumption and Engstrom (1966) suggest that advisory boards/councils may be classified as either independent or school sponsored and then further categorized as temporary or continuing boards and "overall" or "phase" boards. The overall board is concerned with the total school system and its program while the phase board is concerned with one particular phase of the school system or program. Most community education advisory boards would be classified as school sponsored, continuing, and overall, although "overall" does not necessarily mean a meaningful connection to the K-12 school program.

For example, this connection may have existed at one time or another in Flint, Michigan, where all schools in the system are community schools (Flint

Community Schools) but did not exist in the St. Louis Public School System's (SLPSS) former community education program where the community school operations were, for the most part, independent of the "day" (K-12) school operations. This was true even though the community schools are physically connected or within the same facility as the "day" school. Advisory board members were not included in making policy and curriculum decisions concerning the K-12 school program, and school staff were not usually included in the decision-making process concerning after school and/or community programs.

Conclusions reached from a recent survey of SLPSS school administration and staff, community school staff, and community residents indicated this type of community decision-making connection to the schools was not generally desired in the St. Louis Public School System. This was especially true of the SLPSS K-12 administration and staff (Community Schools Review Panel Report, 1993).

Nevertheless, most community educators express a different point of view about this issue. Vasil Kerensky (1989), among many others writing about community education, advocates that the citizenry be involved in school policy and decision-making. He writes that community education posits new assumptions concerning the governance of public education and the role and degree of public participation in the local decision-making process.

Sumption and Engstrom (1966) also maintain that citizens should play a role in decision-making processes within public schools. They assert, first of all, that public schools belong to the people. Second, it behooves the schools to take advantage of sound advice that can be offered by a wealth of resource people who are available within communities. Third, program evaluations coming from the community can effectively supplement the judgment of professional people. Finally, advisory boards can serve as the conduit for accurate communication between school and community.

The authors view the role of citizen advisory boards concerning public schooling as:

- aiding in the development of educational policy;
- aiding in the development of long-range plans;
- helping to solve school-community problems;
- assisting in the evaluation of the work of the school; and
- helping to maintain two-way communication between community and school.

Sumption and Engstrom also warn of the following dangers:

- boards that do not represent the entire community;
- members expressing opinions and making pronouncements without adequate information;
- boards that stray from their proper duties (e.g., making textbook, instructional, or School Board type policy decisions); and

• boards that assume a complaint bureau role.

Another danger could be added: meetings that are conducted without modes of operation. Lack of structured ways of conducting business may encourage confusion, mistrust, disrespectful conduct, frustration, and antagonism.

Some of these dangers were evident within the SLPSS community school advisory boards (before restructuring). Interviews with the fifteen community school site coordinators (Community Schools Review Panel Report, 1993) revealed that most site advisory boards were not representative of the community, were comprised of few members or many of the members were inactive, were ossified in their memberships, and did not actively recruit new members. Survey results also revealed that several boards did not function as they should have and sometimes were just "used" by the site coordinator.

THE FRIEDENS HAUS BOARD

The *Friedens Haus Advisory Board* (independent, continuing, and overall) listed approximately forty members with usually thirty in attendance at the monthly luncheon meetings. Board members included numerous resource agency people, political representatives, service providers, and community residents (listed in the chapter entitled, "The Friedens Haus Coalition").

There were various subcommittees that were to meet on a monthly or as needed basis. These included: Long-range/Strategic Planning, Fund Raising, Evaluation, and Policy-Making. In reality, the subcommittees rarely met during the time of my study, and a complete list of policies and procedures were not developed until 1995. It was eventually decided that completion of this task was necessary for effective organizational and Board of Director meeting procedures, identifying the structure of the Friedens Haus coalition and its function, facility use, personnel issues, and additional administrative functions. The added structure proved to be beneficial, especially for a complex organization comprised of four main entities: church, school, private social service agency, and community.

The *Friedens Haus Board of Directors* met monthly and, at the time of my study, listed eighteen members—thirteen elected members comprised of seven community residents, two Friedens church members, two Clay Elementary staff members (principal and teacher), a representative from St. Louis University, and one outside volunteer; two appointed members (Friedens Church Council President and a representative from United Church Neighborhood Houses); and ex-officio members comprised of the Friedens Haus program director, a United Church Neighborhood Houses administrator, and the Friedens United Church of Christ Pastor. The newly elected president (Hyde Park resident) demonstrated herself to be a very competent meeting facilitator, fact finder, and organizer.

Conversely, prior to April 1994 the Board of Directors was comprised of twelve members that included only one community resident. The only office was that of president, which was held by the same person (Friedens Church member) since the fall of 1990. United Church Neighborhood Houses was then represented as well as Friedens Church, St. Louis University, Clay Elementary, and the Friedens Haus director and staff. Program decisions were usually made by the director and staff, and some administrative decisions were made by the director and staff in conjunction with the Board of Directors. The larger Advisory Board served as a sharing and resource gathering body. Although a summary of the previous meeting's proceedings, an agenda, and necessary handouts were provided, there was no additional structure to either the Board of Directors or Advisory Board meetings.

The restructuring of the Board of Directors may have been prompted by the results of focus group sessions comprised of Advisory Board and community members. The director of the Friedens Haus program had been thinking and talking about the necessity of restructuring for some time, but the black and white account of board member perceptions may have served as the galvanizing factor. Members of the Board of Directors seemed willing to acknowledge what was said by Advisory Board and community members and to take action based on their criticisms and suggestions.

Service provider and community resident focus group participants expressed an apparent shifting of the board's focus from community empowerment to attracting outside agencies for the purpose of helping with resources and meeting needs. Some felt that this was one reason for the lack of high levels of citizen involvement. One resident expressed that board members needed to "empower" Hyde Park residents instead of "serving" them. (A complete summary of the Friedens Haus Advisory Board focus group session is included in the chapter entitled "Assessing Needs, Planning, and Evaluating.")

It must be noted that the Friedens Haus Board of Directors continuously struggled with control and turf issues, especially concerning the transfer of a fair amount of control to Hyde Park residents. Sometimes, control seemed to be emanating from funding agencies and at other times from Friedens church members and/or the private social service agency, Neighborhood Houses. The desire and need for outside resources as well as program ownership seemed to take precedence over the need for leadership development among community residents. This is said with the realization that community residents may also exhibit "controlling" behaviors toward their neighbors and others, negating benefits and expertise that could be derived from individuals, outside agencies, and service providers.

Nevertheless, when comparing the functions of the Friedens Haus Advisory Board to those previously listed by Sumption and Engstrom, the board rated well in helping to solve school-community problems and maintaining two-way communication between the community and school. It also functioned well in assessing needs, making program suggestions, evaluating programs (there was an evaluation subcommittee), and attempting to address community-wide needs such as housing and economic development. It did not aid in the development of educational policy and long-range plans or assist in evaluations concerning the school. Indications were that the Friedens Advisory Board was waiting for Clay to become an "official" St. Louis community center before serving in an advisory capacity in terms of school policies and curriculum.

This is what the Clay School principal had to say about an advisory board that would have input concerning school issues:

How would you go about having community resident and parental input regarding school policies and curriculum?

I think that's important and that's another reason we're pushing for that community school. I think that parents and people in the community—business, industry, and everything else—all these people need to be involved in telling us what it is our kids need to be successful in life.

We've got educators now making decisions for our kids that haven't been in classrooms, haven't been out into the community, and don't know what's going on out there. They're doing this stuff because book companies say this is what they need. So many times we're listening to book companies rather than the reality of life regarding what these kids need to know to be successful in life out there in the community. John Dewey was right on target. Experience is the key. . . .

We would need real representation from the different groups on this advisory committee.   Some committees, when they're formed, they get people who the administration wants on that team—they want "yes" people and people who see it their way. I think you need a real representation of, not only the people who view everything the way you view it, but people with diversified views.

What about input regarding how things are taught?

Well, if anybody said that they've got the absolute way that anything should be taught, they're mistaken. There are different ways to teach everything—there's so many different methods.

I had a parent once who was a teacher, and she came in and was concerned about reading. She thought that the teacher should read more to the kids which I kind of agreed with, too. She took it a step further and came in and developed a schedule where she came in and read to the kids on a regular basis for kindergarten, first, and second grades. That was some input that a parent had directly with the curriculum and instruction. The kids loved it and the teachers thought that was really good.

I've had parents who have told me that teachers may be too strict—maybe they need to loosen up a little bit. I've had parents tell me that teachers aren't strict enough and that there's confusion they think should not be in those classrooms. I honor that, and I use that input.

I've had a couple classrooms where I've had people in there who had no business being teachers—they needed to be in another field. I can observe, I can write and make documentation, but there's nothing as powerful as when parents start coming up and saying, "Hey, this is happening in that classroom and we don't like it!" Then I say, "You put it in writing," and I use that along with mine to help solve some of the problems I have with incompetent teachers.

Parents have come to me and demanded that something be done! I think they should! I always look at it as, "Would I put my child in that classroom?" I have brought my child to our preschool which I think is one of the best in the city. I have a few teachers that I wouldn't have my child in their classroom. So I have to take my time and a lot of effort to work to see that they get some place where they are more "suited."

What if the council came up with something you personally found objectionable?

We've had some issues where parents wanted to do some things against Board policy. First of all, parents need to be educated, too. A lot of times they come up with some great ideas, and they're ideas that wouldn't work with the school policies. It's more informing and teaching the parents what can be done through Board policy.

Now if it's something that would be permitted by Board policy that they thought would work and even if I felt 100 percent against it, if it was a majority and it didn't violate any Board policy or ethical considerations, I guess, moral issues, I would bend and let them try it. But you've always got to remember that to come up with these good ideas and then implement them, you have to be knowledgeable about what the ramifications are going to be. They have to think it through and they have to take into consideration how these people are going to react.

I think the more educated they are and the more they find out about it, the more they will adjust rather than you saying "no," you can't do it this way—do it that way. You try to get them to become educated so that they make the right decision.

THE HYDE PARK ALLIANCE BOARD

The Hyde Park Alliance (HPA) Board of Directors differed from the Friedens Haus Board in that it was more concerned with housing, economic, marketing, historical pride, and safety issues. Although efforts were made to support and to collaborate with the educational, health, and social endeavors of Friedens Haus (under the direction of the former Executive Director), the focus of the board was not with these concerns. The HPA community meetings were attended by Hyde Park community members with little representation from outside agencies.

The HPA Board of Directors was hampered with a problem that the Friedens Haus board decided to address—the same people directing or serving as officers for several consecutive years. This was especially a problem for HPA in that the organization may not have been guided very wisely. During the 1993–94 year, several residents believed there was evidence of poor judgment concerning financial management and some say dishonesty on the part of the former Executive Director.

After the former director left, the position was filled by an interim director.

He strongly defended the integrity of the former director and felt that she truly gave herself to the neighborhood. Following are his views concerning HPA board problems and the need for structure to enhance organizational and meeting functions:

Getting back to trust as the greatest barrier to working together, that's where the structure comes in. I feel that there are tools that could really help build this atmosphere of trust. The former director was used to an organization where she had the full trust of her board. She pretty much had a free hand. But I think that same kind of trust needs to permeate an organization. The whole purpose of structure is to create a safe environment that's as predictable as possible and to create that environment where trust can grow.

All this stuff about governance that Himmelman talks about where I feel Hyde Park is lacking is in its structure, and individuals are vulnerable because of this lack of governance structure. We threw out the Roberts Rules of Order two years ago, but they were never replaced with the consensus model. Now there is a kind of arbitrary governance—consensus when it's only convenient. That is a very volatile situation.

Both with Friedens Haus and Hyde Park Alliance, the attitude seems to be, "Let's get together and have a community meeting and have input"; but because there is no formal structure, it kind of comes down to whoever is the most tenacious about getting their way, runs everything! It really becomes just a very few people that are making the decisions.

I think that's why there's so much apathy is that people don't feel like they really have any kind of sustained impact on the direction of the organizations, and it's not even clear how you become a part of the organizations. Clarity needs to be created. People need a place where they can go and really be heard.

One of the HPA Board of Directors meetings and subsequent community meeting (June 1994) are salient examples of undesirable and almost volatile situations caused, in part, by lack of structure. In addition to a poorly written and structured set of bylaws, meeting minutes omitted important decisions and information, and were sometimes not even written. This, along with a newly hired director who did not share necessary information with board members, allowed for confusion, manipulation, and control by a few board members and the director. Additionally, the bylaws were not adhered to, even as written.

First of all, the nominating committee to nominate Board of Director officers was not chosen properly (according to the bylaws), and the slate were not presented to the community in a timely manner. Two nominating committee members nominated themselves to hold the same offices as they currently held. The other nominees were also sitting officers.

During the Board of Directors meeting, the vice president remarked that if the slate were accepted as presented, there would be no need for nominations from the floor. One board member insisted that election procedures be followed at the upcoming community meeting in order that nominations *could* be taken from the floor and votes could be counted in a proper fashion (this had not been done the previous year).

The community meeting to elect Board of Director officers and members was held the week following the Board of Directors meeting. By that time, news had leaked concerning the slate to be offered. Because the meeting room's configuration in Holy Trinity included pews facing toward the center of the room, it looked as if there were two sides of the community ready to "face off." Relatives and friends of the HPA board president and treasurer were on one side of the room, while friends of the "revisionists" were on the other side (more or less).

The vice president chaired the meeting, explaining that the president should not preside since she was being "elected." (She was nominated for her held position as was the vice president for his held position.) The slate was then presented and the vice president had to be reminded that election procedures were to be followed as discussed during the Board of Directors meeting. After two nominations were taken from the floor (sitting treasurer and president), the presiding officer (sitting vice president) made a motion that the nominations be closed. This motion was quickly seconded. The vice president then said he would be calling the role of all dues-paying members (those few allowed to vote).

One board member then reminded the vice president that it was previously decided to rescind the dues-paying rule in favor of a community-meeting-attendance rule for voting privileges. None of the board officers could remember this incident. The newly hired director stated that she had read the previous year's minutes and could find nothing about a vote taken concerning this issue. (There *was* a vote taken to change the voting qualification rule as I was present at the Board of Directors meeting in question and took extensive notes.) The complaining board member then left in anger.

Several community residents expressed their frustration and surprise to learn that they would not be allowed to vote. Information had not been disseminated to residents who had recently become active in community affairs during the past year. One resident remarked, "I've paid my ten dollars over and over as donations to the Safety Committee, and I can't vote? People should be informed of dues requirements!" One member related that when she tried to pay her dues the previous year, HPA refused to take her payment. She suggested that the election be postponed, because the slate were not presented a month prior as written in the bylaws: "This kind of thing causes resentment!"

The discussion became heated, and several residents expressed that all who were Hyde Park residents should be allowed to vote. One resident exclaimed, "We're not children fighting over this neighborhood—this is our neighborhood! We need to be fighting drugs and crime!"

It was then suggested that the bylaws be rewritten and the election of officers be postponed until this was completed. One resident expressed that this would give people a chance to dialogue and have input. As previously mentioned, the bylaws were *not* rewritten. A community meeting was finally scheduled and new

officers were elected in May 1995—a year later! A ten dollar fee was required
to vote. Indications were that HPA would remain an exclusive neighborhood
organization.

RECOMMENDATIONS

Conclusions may be drawn from the previously described Friedens Haus and
Hyde Park Alliance citizen councils in terms of what an ideal council should
look like. Indicators of an effective citizen council are:

- Inclusiveness (gender, ethnicity, socio-economic status, pertinent entities) with the
  right people at the table. For example, if the council is assisting with the
  governance of a community education center/community school program, members
  should include: the principal, the community education coordinator, and
  representatives from the following groups: teachers; parents; community school
  staff; students (depending on grade levels included in the school) and neighborhood
  youth; support and custodial staff; service providers such as health, social service,
  and police; businesses in the community; area colleges/universities; residents; and
  other community members such as church leaders
- Regularly scheduled meetings
- Designated roles such as president, vice president, secretary, and treasurer
- A common mission or purpose that is in written form and often revisited in order to
  maintain the council's focus and curtail the possibility of sidetracking on individual
  or individual organizational issues
- Commonly developed policies and guidelines if not already in place via the school
  district or other responsible entity
- Commonly agreed upon meeting procedures
- Information (including agenda) sent to members well in advance of scheduled
  meetings so that facts and pertinent information are well thought through, allowing
  for meaningful discussion before informed decisions are made
- Problem-solving procedure similar to: conduct a needs assessment, identify the
  problems or issues; prioritize; assign roles (perhaps subcommittees for each priority
  problem); formulate hypotheses (causes) for each problem; select the most probable
  hypothesis; discuss possible solutions; identify resources; select the best solution;
  plan the solution's implementation process; assign roles and timelines; implement
  evaluations, both formative (during the process in order to make corrections) and
  summative (to determine if the problem has been solved)
- Record keeping and sharing of conducted business and information with all
  members
- Lack of assumptions made about individual members—everyone listens and makes
  judgments based on others' *actions*
- The other person is given the benefit of the doubt
- Multiple intelligences and various learning styles of adults are respected and valued
  just as they should be when interacting with children and youth

- Expertise of community members is valued and used before soliciting outside expertise
- Willingness to bring in consultants and/or arbitrators when expertise and/or conflict resolution is needed
- Planned socialization, recreation, and team building among council members
- Tenacity on the part of council members, weathering storms and disappointments on the way to realizing goals while remaining focused on the mission

SUMMARY

With changes in terms of Board of Director membership, Executive Director, and bylaws, some of the lacking and scewed structure within Hyde Park Alliance could have been remedied. This added and reformed structure would have provided a way to lessen control and manipulation by a few people. It did not look as though this was imminent. Hyde Park Alliance also maintained a history of sanctioning community friction that festered, in part, because the organization lacked proper monitoring by the city's Community Development Agency. The net result was abuse of the Hyde Park community, especially residents, by its own neighborhood organization whose charge was to *uplift* the neighborhood. The organization's practices became antithetical to even its name—Hyde Park *Alliance*.

Because the Friedens Haus Board of Directors underwent reconstitution and reorganization, community residents regained some control. Also, written policies and procedures, including meeting procedures, provided needed structure that had been lacking. However, relinquishing control by community members who lived outside Hyde Park and leadership development within the neighborhood and among Hyde Park residents remained pertinent issues that needed focused attention.

Nevertheless, the Friedens Haus Advisory Board functioned as many community school advisory councils even though it was not school-connected. Unlike many councils, however, it excelled with networking and drawing in outside resources to meet community needs. Assessing needs, devising programs to meet these needs, and program evaluations were also superior and became stronger during the 1994–95 year with the implementation of an outside evaluation commissioned through a grant. These strengths were especially evident when compared to what the St. Louis community school citizen councils practiced in these areas. (Needs assessment and evaluating procedures of the Friedens Haus program will be explained in the chapter entitled "Assessing Needs, Planning, and Evaluating.")

Finally, parent and community input concerning school policies and curriculum remained a forthcoming issue for the Friedens Haus board to address. Optimistically, this issue will also be fully addressed by the newly restructured St. Louis community center citizen councils. As Sumption and Engstrom (1966) remind us, citizens should have a say concerning what goes on inside *their* schools.

The authors summarize a good and convincing case for the citizen advisory council as it pertains to schools: (1) The school needs the community's advice on policies, plans, and problems; (2) both the school and community benefit from direct, clear, and accurate communication between school and community; (3) the school benefits from appraisals and judgments coming from the community about its programs; and most importantly, (4) parents, community members, teachers, and school administrators should collectively act on the realization that the public schools are theirs.

Chapter 13

Leadership Development

Leadership within communities is often developed via community residents serving on citizen councils/committees and/or by attempting in other ways to solve community problems. Citizen leadership development within the Hyde Park neighborhood proved to be uneven across community organizations. Factors that entered into the equation were: (1) individual readiness to assume leadership roles and (2) processes used by service providers to encourage or thwart residents in leading their neighbors to solve community problems.

WHO ARE THE CANDIDATES?

Individual readiness for leadership roles have to do with stages of personal concerns and moral reasoning. These may be identified in relation to needs that motivate humans to act as outlined by Maslow's (1954) hierarchy of needs. These needs from most crucial (lower level) to least crucial (higher level) are: physiological, safety, belonging and love, esteem, and self-actualization. Stages may also vary and/or regress depending on a given situation. Many Hyde Park residents were hindered in terms of their concerns for the community and their desires to assume leadership roles, because they found themselves lacking those factors listed by Maslow as lower level needs—experiencing physiological, safety, belonging, and esteem needs.

Maslow lists Level I needs (physiological) as: hunger, thirst, sex, taste, smell, touch, and sleep. Level II needs concern safety and security issues: protection against danger and threat; freedom from fear, anxiety, and chaos; and need for structure, order, law, limits, and stability. Level III needs include belonging and love concerns: satisfactory associations with others, belonging to groups, and giving and receiving friendship and affection. Level IV needs have to do with esteem: self-respect in terms of achievement, competence, and confidence; and deserved respect from others in terms of status, recognition, dignity, and appreciation. As one former community leader expressed it:

We have an expressed interest in community residents wanting to become leaders. Whether they follow up on it, I see a far smaller number. That's related to where they are in their life, how much free time they have, how much energy they have, how many crises, how many kids.
 Certainly a blockage would be . . . the situations that occur in people's lives that are crises taking away from the concentration of decision-making that one has to attend to on a regular basis if you're going to solve problems adequately or continuously. I think that this is a crisis-driven community—I mean every night there's another problem that faces someone in the leadership. On the street there's so much drug activity, breaking-in, and car theft—and all those things in this community are at an outrageous level.

Given adequate time for involvement and lack of family and neighborhood crises, community residents who described themselves as self-actualized or self-fulfilled (the highest level of Maslow's needs) were most likely those who desired leadership roles within the community. They were seeking realization of their potential, and desired maximum development of their creativity and problem-solving abilities. Within the Hyde Park neighborhood, however, residents who were ready to assume leadership roles were often blocked; and those whose leadership qualities should have been encouraged and developed were hindered by processes and leadership styles implemented and exhibited by service providers.

WHAT ARE THE PROCESSES?

By observing and talking with many community residents, it was concluded that one of the significant problems with leadership development in the Hyde Park neighborhood was the limited room and allowance given to those who were seeking self-actualization through developing their creativity and self-expression in problem-solving efforts. Several resident-leaders decided to take a "back seat" because of limited and blocked opportunities. As one resident expressed it:

I can see where you will stifle the creativity of maybe a less powerful group. You will not have people stick around long if you stifle their creativity. I think to improve any neighborhood you have to empower it and really get down with the people and into the gutter with folks. That's a lot of work. There is a lot of untapped potential in our neighborhood—people-wise—whether they are renters or owners. Maybe what we need to do is human resource development within the neighborhood.

A study completed by Frederick Herzberg and colleagues (1959) speaks to the empowerment issue by differentiating between "dissatisfiers" (which could be associated with Maslow's lower-level needs as Carl Glickman [1985] suggests) and "satisfiers." (Figure 13.1) The authors assert that dissatisfiers (hygiene factors such as poor salary and less than adequate working environments) may lead to job dissatisfaction, but elimination of these dissatisfiers does not lead to motivation. Motivating factors include achievement, responsibility, recognition, advancement, and the possibility of growth. Although the study was for business management purposes, the findings are relevant to "community leadership development."

Figure 13.1
Comparing Herzberg and Maslow

	Herzberg	**Maslow**
Motivating Factors	Achievement Responsibility Recognition Advancement Possibility of Growth	Self-Actualization Esteem
Hygiene Factors	Status Interpersonal Relations Personal Life Job Security Working Conditions Salary	Belongingness and Love Safety Needs Physiological Needs

Sources: F. Herzberg, B. Mausner, and B. Snyderman. (1959). *The Motivation to Work.* New York: Wiley; and A. Maslow. (1954). *Motivation and Personality.* New York: Harper & Row.

Pajak and Seyfarth (1983) agree with Herzberg and colleagues when asserting that there are two types of environments—controlling and informational. Informational environments allow for individual choice, promote autonomy, and encourage commitment to improvement. Elaborating on this idea, Herzberg (1968: 54) describes the controlling environment as KITA—Kick him In The Pants (the "A" word is never used) and as having three drawbacks: (1) It is inelegant; (2) it contradicts the precious image of benevolence; and (3) since it is a physical attack, it directly stimulates the autonomic nervous system, and this often results in negative feedback—the recipient may just kick you in return.

Herzberg also distinguishes between negative and positive KITA:

Why is it that [leaders] are quick to see that negative KITA is not motivation, while they are almost unanimous in their judgment that positive KITA is motivation? It is because negative KITA is rape, and positive KITA is seduction. This is why positive KITA is so popular; it is a tradition, it is in the American way. The [leader] does not have to kick you, you kick yourself.

Why is KITA not motivation? If I kick my dog (from the front or the back), he will move. And when I want him to move again, what must I do? I must kick him again. Similarly, I can charge a man's battery, and then recharge it, and recharge it again. But it is only when he has his own generator that we can talk about motivation. (54-55)

Many of Herzberg's principles for job enrichment are relevant concerning community leadership development. Motivation for leadership development is directly linked to the removal of controls while retaining accountability, providing complete units of work (projects), granting additional authority, and introducing new and more difficult tasks. The Clay school principal found this to be true. He explained his philosophy of leadership development:

One of the keys is letting these parents run with it—giving them jobs and tasks and letting them come up with some ideas and let them follow through with them until completion so that they can come back and say, "We did this, this is what we've done, and this is how we did it!" That's the key! We have had teachers that have said, "When these parents come, we need to have specific things for them to do," and I was totally against that. I thought that if the teachers needed parents, they needed to let the parents know what they needed and then let the parents decide who would do what, how they would help rather than just trying to delegate them into something that they may not enjoy or even want to be involved in.

The mother who was [the former] PTO president who was selected because people looked on her as a leader and wanted her to be president, didn't necessarily want to be the president. She didn't feel that she was assertive enough. She knows how she is—she knows what she's all about. She came to me several times and said that she just didn't want to be president of the PTO. I tried to talk her into it and that she could change, it would be good for her and that she would meet a lot of people and do a lot of things. But she wasn't happy with that—that's not the kind of person she is.

She still does a lot of things around here. As a matter of fact, she organized the Mother and Daughter Banquet for the fifth graders and the Father and Son Banquet, and they turned out to be super programs. She had a lot of fathers, sons, uncles, and even mentors who came, and she thoroughly enjoyed that! She just doesn't feel comfortable in that top leadership role, but she's good at what she does. She had to get caterers, she had to organize and send invitations, she had to call people and make sure they were coming, she had to get the room ready, she had to get the guest speakers—she had some top notch people come in as guest speakers for these programs! She didn't ask me for a lot of help—she just went about her business and pulled it off, and both of them were outstanding programs!

The principal related that one very reticent parent's leadership development evolved through participating in the parent-teacher organization, becoming the PTO president, directing several projects, earning her GED, taking part in a presentation at the Missouri Department of Elementary and Secondary Education Association's yearly conference, and subsequently securing employment. The principal told of several similar success stories.

Norman Sprinthall and Lois Thies-Sprinthall (1983: 27) add to the principal's expressed concept of motivation and to Herzberg's model. They list six factors toward an "instructional model" that may be useful concerning leadership development. They are:

1. significant role-taking experiences
2. experiences that are neither beyond the reach nor below the grasp of an individual
3. careful and continuous guided reflection
4. balance between experience and reflection
5. continuous leadership development
6. personal support and challenge

Giving credence to several of these suggestions, one former neighborhood service provider explained her idea of leadership development:

One good way is to just know people and when you know someone is a leader, pull them aside and recommend, highlight, or give them a task or something that will use that part of them, and see if you can push people into places that they may not think of being. To me, that's my job as the leader, to be observant of other peoples' capacity to lead instead of being threatened or being concerned.

Leaders lead best when they sit back and let others do the talking. That is sometimes hard for leaders to learn and that is, you provide another person with the opportunity to give the report, and it's surprising how that will draw somebody into being thought of as a leader. People look to that person for some answers instead of always to you. I think training for leadership is often being a good listener.

Role models were also mentioned by several Hyde Park residents as contributing to the process of leadership development. Piaget (1962) offers a psychological theory in support of modeling in the context of education and describes imitation as a generative and creative act, making the action one's own. He asserts that the ability to differentiate among various features of a modeled activity involves the learner in a highly analytical act, and the process of matching those features with his or her own action requires a highly creative act. Davidson (1989) adds that the role model offers support and encouragement. One community resident described her role model this way:

I admire this particular leader because she's smart, and I admire smart people. When I first started getting involved, she just always knew the right people to contact.

Knowing the right people is important for information resources. Information is just like a commodity—it's salable, it's marketable- and if you know where to go to get it, it's great.

This leader is a person I can look up to, admire, and respect. She has been a friend to me and has been very encouraging. I lack a lot of confidence in myself. I don't consider myself a real smart person—I consider myself an average person. She always told me that I could do it and I could make a difference, and she just helped put some of those leadership qualities in me. She made me realize that it's not going to happen just by sitting back.

The same resident described how a "project" (Herzberg, 1968) or concern was instrumental in her leadership development and then "reflected" (Sprinthall and Thies-Sprinthall, 1983) upon her mistakes and achievements:

After my break-ins, I noticed that the neighbors were not paying attention to what went on in my block. I tried to form this neighborhood watch where the neighbors got together and we just met each other and began to watch out for each other. My theme was, "Good neighbors are made—not born." I wanted everybody to know that to be a good neighbor we had to pull together and watch out for each other. I did that in front of my apartment. I sent out flyers and I called around and got information from different people who lived in the community. The Fire Department was really helpful—they gave me a lot of names. I borrowed chairs from my church, I served refreshments—I did all this on my own. I had like thirty people turn out that first night and the police captain of the 5th District, a captain from the Fire Department, and an alderperson spoke.

Then I started being invited to different things in Hyde Park. Before, all the time I had lived in Hyde Park, I can't ever remember being invited! I learned then that different organizations were set up in Hyde Park, and then I was encouraged to get involved. The director of Hyde Park Alliance was the first to invite me to something Holy Trinity was having, and she allowed me to speak about the meeting I was having. I started talking to another leader about some of the things I would like to see happen in Hyde Park.

After that, I got involved with the Safety Committee, and the chairperson asked me to be cochairperson. Then I became chairperson and she became secretary. She thought I had the time, and I was excited about safety and doing safety things. She saw I had some good ideas about the Hyde Park area, so she thought it would be a great opportunity. So we went on to do the clothing drive and have the safety meetings, and the meetings turned out to be great!

When I first started up with the Safety Committee, we only had two or three people attending the meetings. Our very last meeting we had was about home burglary and we had at least twenty-five people to turn out. You have to work.

What leadership qualities have you developed?

I have a problem with public speaking. I feel a little more confident that I can get the message through in my approach in speaking. When you have confidence in what you're doing and saying, you're able to develop and you're able to reach the people better.

My organizing abilities have developed more. Being consistent is really important in organizing. I try to be more consistent and do everything on a timely basis and make sure everything is done in a proper way. My church activities have helped with organizing, following through, and returning calls.

I don't really consider myself a leader. I consider myself as a resident of the neighborhood who is trying to make a difference. When people keep saying that I'm a leader, it hits me.

What would you do differently as a leader in the neighborhood?

I would target more areas. I limited myself to certain streets, and I find myself being a little selfish because I was really concerned about the area where I lived. The Hyde Park neighborhood really stretches much further. I didn't go to certain blocks. I would have made more phone calls and put out more literature about what the Safety Committee and other organizations are trying to do to better the community. I would try to reach more—I would go door to door. I still have that plan to go door to door. We should meet the residents in the neighborhood. The Mobile Patrol kick off and the Mobile Patrol itself wouldn't have happened without the help of neighborhood residents.

What do you enjoy about being a neighborhood leader?

Meeting new people. I enjoy the success both personal and reaching the goals that we're trying to reach and have achieved. I think we've gotten a lot more people involved. I don't feel like the crime has gone down since I've been a part of it—I think we have to give a lot of credit to the Police Department, because I think they're patrolling more. Most of all, I'm glad to witness all the activities of the Safety Committee, Holy Trinity, and the 5th District Police.

SUMMARY

Besides the needy circumstances in which many Hyde Park residents found themselves, the lack of optimal *opportunities* for leadership development was a hindrance. For that reason, this chapter about leadership development is concomitant to the chapter describing desired characteristics of community education leaders ("Leadership for Community Education").

As an observer and participant in the community, I found that many actions of service providers contradicted what they expressed in words. I found only one service provider who seemed to have the "track" on leadership development (at least with parents), not only with words and philosophy, but with actions: "One of the keys is letting these parents run with it—giving them jobs and tasks and letting them come up with some ideas and let them follow through with them until completion." This one sentence and the observed actions of this leader when dealing with parents, speak to autonomy, responsibility, creativity, challenge, accountability, risk taking, encouragement, strengthening self-esteem, allowing for mistakes, and reflection. In short, these words are about lifelong learning and community education in that they address a "learning by doing" and problem-solving educational approach as advocated by the educator and philosopher, John Dewey.

As explained further in the "Leadership for Community Education" chapter, service providers often entered the Hyde Park community and attempted to assume leadership, not considering viable community projects led by community residents. Many service providers' actions were geared toward proving themselves omniscient, delegating and speaking from positions of authority, and establishing themselves as unique change-agents for the community's benefit. Other service providers gave the appearance of *facilitating* but instead were *manipulating* (positive KITA or seduction) and surrounded themselves with reticent and/or supportive program participants and/or included "token" residents who were content to be led.

Those community residents who expressed creative ideas and/or questioned decisions of those in leadership positions were sometimes maneuvered off decision-making bodies, ignored, and/or not acknowledged. Community residents are quoted throughout this book, expressing frustration and giving reasons for dropping out of leadership positions due to pervasive controlling environments. Observations found this to be true even to a more extreme extent than some interviewees were willing to express.

Effective leaders and/or service providers in any community should view their roles and the processes they use to fulfill their roles as requiring artistic and flexible skills rather than managerial or administrative techniques. In inner-city neighborhoods where there may be an abundance of individuals lacking physiological, safety, belonging, and esteem needs, an instructional/facilitative leadership style, matching individual readiness and learning styles with specific levels of responsibility and types of duties (that Sprinthall and Thies-Sprinthall [1983] write about) is essential. I observed several instances within the Hyde Park neighborhood where residents were given leadership and/or employment roles that were beyond their capabilities or levels of self-assumed responsibility and accountability for a particular stage in their lives and/or individual learning style. The results were disappointing and discouraging for all involved. Conversely, many residents who were ready to assume productive leadership roles were denied opportunities for such roles by authoritative and manipulative service providers. A facilitative-type leader would have been best suited for situations where such resident-leaders were involved.

It must be noted that citizen advisory councils featured in community education programs provide forums for community residents to develop leadership capabilities. Service providers included on these councils, however, often prove to be intimidating. (In Hyde Park, several service providers fulfilling board membership roles were labeled "suits" and only a few were considered to be role models.) If optimal program results and problem-solving efforts are realized, locus of control must remain within the community, especially with community residents. With this basic premise accepted and serving as background, service providers would more readily adopt leadership processes and perspectives that would encourage and facilitate this locus of control.

Nevertheless, expanded opportunities for adult education, leadership development, and lifelong learning existed in the Hyde Park neighborhood. Clay Elementary recently became an "official" community education center within the St. Louis Public School System. This allowed the opening of school doors beyond regular school hours for community use in terms of educational, cultural, enrichment, vocational, and recreational programming. A nominal fee is paid (if able) to cover instructional costs, and classes and activities are offered during evenings and weekends as well as yearlong. Residents who serve on the advisory council assist in planning the programs based on expressed community needs, and then have a part in evaluating programs to determine if community needs are being met.

In addition to extended formal educational opportunities for adult learners, the problem-solving and decision-making efforts that engaged Hyde Park residents provided opportunities for leadership development and lifelong learning. Residents became members and officers of advisory boards, boards of directors, and committees (Safety Committee, Landlord's Task Force; Hyde Park Business Association; and policy-making, strategic planning, and personnel committees, among others). These problem-solving and decision-making activities offered Hyde Park residents a "learning by doing" avenue to leadership development and lifelong learning.

Finally, a facilitative style of leadership on the part of service providers that offers recognition as well as opportunities for growth is then an added ingredient for leadership development and lifelong learning possibilities within inner-cities. This will be explored more fully in the chapter entitled "Leadership for Community Education."

Chapter 14

Community Organization and Problem-Solving: The Economic Problem

As explained in a previous chapter and at the time of this writing, the power structure within the Hyde Park neighborhood was determined to be pluralistic. This pluralistic power structure offers an explanation of the community's organization and thus its ability to address multiple community problems. There were four predominant community entities (the Friedens Haus coalition, New Holy Trinity, Hyde Park Alliance [HPA], and the Housing Corporation [the city]) and then several committees operating under the HPA umbrella (NAC [area service agency representation], Hyde Park Safety Committee, Hyde Park Business Association, and the Landlord's Task Force). Each focused on specific issues and at the same time worked collectively with the other Hyde Park organizations to solve neighborhood problems. Bethlehem Lutheran on the other side of the neighborhood was more or less on its own, attempting to meet parishioner needs.

Hyde Park community members talked about the themes of this chapter—community organization and problem-solving. For example, a service provider who also serviced another St. Louis neighborhood explained Hyde Park *community organization:*

Hyde Park is a lot more organized. They have a lot of things and people in place, so I serve more as a facilitator. O'Fallon doesn't have the committees—we just started a youth program. We don't have a Friedens Haus, so we're trying to get those kinds of programs started and let the neighborhood start coordinating things together to get some things done. One area is very far advanced in the organizational stage, and the other area is not very organized, but the people are interested.

One former community leader defined community *problem solving:* "Well to me, it's a sense of getting the community aware of itself and aware of its good points, aware of its weaknesses, aware of how to address both the strengths—

which means having fairs, having markets, or having events so that you can show off as well as the weaknesses, having committees, having problem-solving sessions."

As previously described, the problems confronting the neighborhood were multiple and varied. This and following chapters discuss two of the problems on which Hyde Park community members focused (in addition to crime)—the economic problem and the housing problem; how the community attempted to solve these problems; the levels of interagency cooperation exhibited in attempting to do so; and the various methods used to assess needs, plan, and evaluate. First, some background information is provided in order to more fully understand Hyde Park's economic problem.

THE ECONOMIC PROBLEM

Author, James Michener states, "But I still believe that society prospers most when there are laws that bring . . . wealth back into circulation, when there are taxes to provide social services that otherwise might not be available, when there is governmental surveillance to ensure proper business practices and to prevent manipulation of financial markets, and when profits are plowed into research and the education of new generations" (1992: 7).

Elliiott Currie (1985: 169) notes that industrial societies that have done most to blunt inequities produced by the market system have low rates of crime, particularly when compared to the United States, which has done the *least* to address inequities: "Around the world, at every level of economic development, increasing equality goes hand in hand with lower risks of homicide." The alienated of our society must be given a reason to start at the bottom and believe that they can rise to the top or get ahead.

Nevertheless, we may be developing into a society where the "haves" care less and less about the "have-nots" and don't want to assume any responsibility for the latters' well-being—no matter that their "have-not" status may have resulted from a market system with inadequate cushions for the "left outs." Currie states, "We have the level of criminal violence we do because we have arranged our social and economic life in certain ways rather than others. . . . We have decided that the benefits of changing those conditions aren't worth the costs" (1985: 19). Supporting Currie's link between equality and homicide risks, Richard Fowles from the University of Utah found that the average percentage increase in the national homicide rate for every 1 percent increase in the unemployment rate is 5.6 percent (*Harper's Magazine*, 1996). The following information adds to the "economic problem" background.

Attending the Economic Summit of the Eight in Denver (June 1997), a Dutch labor ministry official emphasized that the United States spends more on prisons than on welfare, and if prisoners were counted as lost workers, the U.S. unemployment rate would be nearly double its officially reported level. A German social benefit expert mocked Americans' pride in low tax rates, emphasizing that privately financed health insurance also takes money from wages; and the cost of the American health care system is nearly double that of Europe. In short, we pay less and get less in terms of our low minimum wage, social programs, and health care (Sawyer, 1997). The International Institute for Management Development reported in 1996 that the United Sates came out on top in the areas of economic strength, new technology, and financial services; placed second in international trade; but placed fifteenth in people skills—education and training.

In a discussion with former Labor Secretary, Robert Reich, and former CEO of Scott Paper, Albert Dunlap, as well as others, Ronald Blackwell maintains that since 1973, family incomes have stagnated and, for 60 percent, incomes have declined in spite of the fact that workers are working longer hours, are more productive, and the country is richer than it has ever been: "This is the first recovery in the postwar period in which wages are still falling in the fifth year of the recovery. And that wage data is important, because what's going on here is a redistribution of income from employees to employers, from people who work for a living to people who own" (*Harper's Magazine*, 1996: 36). The ratio of pay for a typical worker to that of a typical CEO in Japan is 1:16; Germany, 1:21; the United Kingdom, 1:33; and the United States, 1:120 (*Harper's Magazine*, 1996). (See Figure 14.1.)

Secretary Reich asserts that American corporations have abrogated their social contract (when companies do better, the workers do better). He maintains that most corporate layoffs are now strategic maneuvers instead of responses to economic difficulties:

[Corporations] reflect laws, social judgment about how we're going to organize ourselves. Those judgments reflect some choices, made implicitly or explicitly, about the kind of society we want. And we can't avoid those choices. . . . Profitable companies may contribute to a good society, but ultimately the end is not profits. The end is several other things. For example: We want to have a society in which most people have a chance at a high standard of living. We want a society that has a moral character, in which there is a degree of trust among people and a deepening sense of what it means to be a human being. (*Harpers Magazine*, 1996: 37)

Nevertheless, at the time of this writing, the economy was booming: unemployment hit a twenty-three year low, the deficit was shrinking, and Congress and the President had recently agreed on balanced budget legislation. However, a survey conducted in 1997 by the Pew Research Center for the People & the Press reported that 30 percent of respondents said they worried a lot about suffering a pay cut or losing their job. This was down from 47 percent in March 1996, but up from 18 percent in 1988.

Moreover, when the United States' economy is not booming and may even be in a recession, many believe this results in a *depression* for black Americans. *The Wall Street Journal* cited blacks as the only racial group to suffer a net loss of jobs during the 1990–91 recession. During that same period, whites, Hispanics, and Asians gained thousands of jobs. The *Journal's* report was based

Figure 14.1

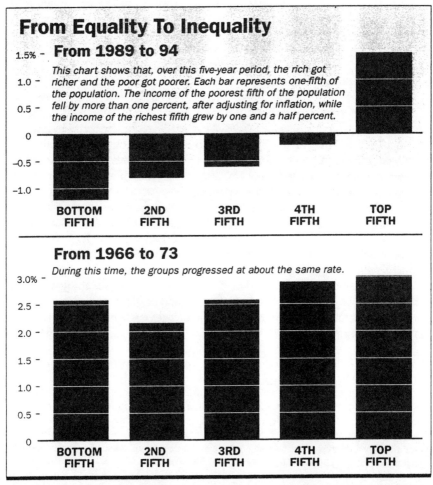

Source: Committee on Economic Development   Tom Borgman/*Post-Dispatch*

on employment statistics filed with the Equal Employment Opportunity Commission in 1993.

In his book, *The Black Power Imperative: Racial Inequality and the Politics of Nonviolence* (1987), Theodore Cross writes about the tremendous gap between black and white median incomes. He maintains that capital and wealth inequities are equal handicaps to income inequities as well as the prevalence of poverty among black Americans. It is interesting to note that the percentage of all employed black American men with a college degree who earned poverty-level wages in 1979 was 9.5 percent and the percentage as of December 1991 was 14.8 percent (*Harper's Magazine*, 1992).

Additionally, many economists agree that the recent NAFTA agreement, while producing improved long-term economic results for the United States (economic dynamism), will produce more job loss for many black Americans who depend on low-wage, low-skill jobs. Clarence Page (1993: 15B) warned,

Economic dynamism, it must be remembered, created slavery and kept it alive. Economic dynamism prompted the government at the end of the Civil War to break its promise to give land to blacks as compensation. Instead, it was given to the railroads, to mostly white settlers in the West and to land-grant colleges, most of which did not admit blacks, while freed slaves were left tied to land they didn't own in the near-chattel condition of share-cropping. Economic dynamism was the excuse given by trickle-down economists for subsidizing business, the natural constituency of Republicans, with big tax incentives in the 1980s.

Theodore Cross (1987) adds to the debate as he dismisses the liberal attempts of missionary-type projects in the 1960s and 1970s to help blacks economically. He maintains that blacks were still not "let in" to the corporate world and that these attempts grew out of a charitable view toward black America. Cross asserts that "do gooders" in the political arena give, but don't seek to empower the disenfranchised.

A PERPETUATING CYCLE

Lewis Lapham (1992: 6) adds to the discussion when he writes about the plight of American cities: "Americans take pride in the building of roads and weapons systems as well as in their gifts for violence. We know how to mount expeditions—to the Persian Gulf or the California frontier or the moon—but we lack a talent for making cities."

Everette Nance and Mathew Foggy, Jr. recognize the urban plight in the United States, the role racism plays in negative urban socioeconomic cycles, and the importance of empowering the disenfranchised (1992: 23). They maintain that, "the *effects* of no business development are used as the *reasons* for no business development. This cycle perpetuates and reinforces itself" (emphasis added). (See Figure 14.2.)

The authors zero in on specific economic redevelopment strategies for cities. They advocate that block grant monies be used more to benefit lower income persons, banks be required to comply with the terms of the Community Reinvestment Act, the practice of redlining be ended, capital be made available for financing small and large retail businesses, public dollars be spent on rebuilding the infrastructure, and finally, local community members be involved in the planning and use of targeted appropriations and in attracting new retail business. They assert, "Enterprise zones and other such strategies will not be effective unless the community becomes involved in the process" (28).

Theodore Cross (1987) agrees with Nance and Foggy in that he recommends a strategy similar to the Community Development Corporation (CDC) introduced in the 1960s that served as an instrument for building economic and

Figure 14.2
Negative Socioeconomic Cycle

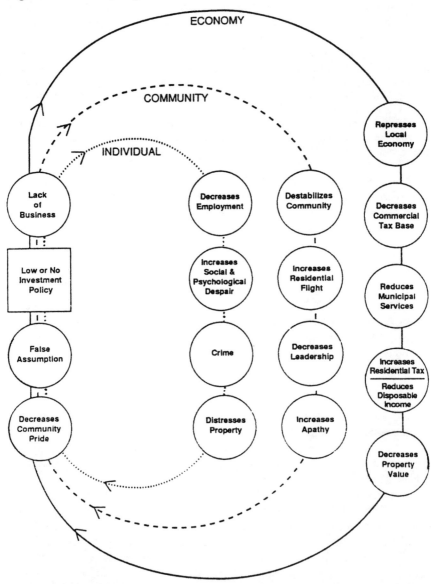

Source: Mathew Foggy, Jr.

political power. The CDC was a federal program that provided funding for housing and local business self-help efforts and financed efforts by blacks to form locally owned and controlled enterprises. He maintains that this type of program would be effective in lessening the economic gap between blacks and whites and would be superior to outside help such as enterprise zones. For example, there are many neighborhoods in the northern part of enterprise-zone St. Louis where residents, a large percentage who are black, have to travel miles outside their communities in order to shop for basic necessities. Most retailers have moved out. St. Louis ranked twentieth of twenty-five cities in black-owned businesses per 1,000 black residents in 1987, and only one city out of twenty-nine had a higher unemployment rate for blacks in 1990. St. Louis, with 17 percent, ranked twenty-eighth (Schlinkmann, 1991).

Moreover, St. Louis is considered an "inelastic" city as compared to "elastic" cities such as Kansas City, Nashville, Little Rock, Phoenix, and others. The United States Census Bureau released a report on November 18, 1997 that revealed the City of St. Louis was losing population faster than any other city in the United States. David Rusk (1993), a former New Mexico legislator and mayor of Albuquerque, cites fifteen "elastic" cities that have expanded their city limits more than 700 percent. Some of these cities can be described as "cities without suburbs." He asserts that elastic cities have more racially integrated neighborhoods, equal average city and suburban income levels, and maintain municipal credit ratings four grades better than inelastic cities. He writes, "In short, multiple, independent suburbs are machines to keep poor blacks and Latinos trapped in inner cities away from middle-class America" (1993: 3B). Rusk recommends either expanding inelastic cities to include their suburbs, or making suburbs accept their fair share of responsibility through various metro-wide programs.

Metro-wide programs and regional cooperation are solutions that cities are presently implementing to alleviate "inelasticity." This type of cooperation was advocated by mayors from around the country in San Francisco, June 21-22, 1997 at a mayors' conference. Detroit served as one example of "a saga of a glorious past, a fall from grace and now a glorious rebirth," as Mayor Dennis Archer explains. Disagreeing with previously cited authors, Mayor Archer believes that Detroit's enterprise zone, which was sought by the city and Wayne county, played an important role in the city's "rebirth." Detroit city officials maintain that their new optimism had everything to do with city-county collaboration (Associated Press, 1997[b]).

Zoning is another solution that Richard Moe, president of the National Trust for Historic Preservation, advocates: "Our communities should be shaped by choice, not by chance. . . . We can let the highway engineers and the big-box retailers determine our communities' futures for us, or we can take a more active role ourselves" (1996). His recommendations are: (1) downtown housing; (2) mixed-use zoning that reduces the distances people must travel between home and work; (3) land-use planning that exhibits a strong bias in favor of existing communities; and (4) looking to cities such as Portland, Oregon as models of maintaining urban vitality.

For example, Oregon passed legislation that requires every community to calculate the amount of land it needs to accommodate growth during the next twenty years. A circle is then drawn (an urban growth boundary) and

166   Community Education and Crime Prevention

development is concentrated inside the circle. Moe reports that "a 1991 study showed that Portland's urban growth boundary had expanded by only two percent in the preceding seventeen years while containing 95 percent of the area's residential growth." Moe explains that, also, *The Wall Street Journal* noted that, "the number of downtown jobs has doubled since 1975 without the city [Portland] adding a single parking space, widening roads or building new ones." Nevertheless, several urban designers and academe of urban policy assert that the Portland plan may not be the answer for most metropolitan areas that exhibit "urban sprawl." They maintain that because each metropolitan area has its own history, physical environment, and set of problems, each must develop its own solutions.

ECONOMIC DEVELOPMENT WITHIN THE COMMUNITY

In addition to the previous suggestions for urban revitalization, the following emphases by the former mayor of St. Louis provides "food for thought." The former mayor urged that the city shift emphasis from downtown to *neighborhood* economic development. A special committee appointed by the mayor to study economic development made the following recommendations: (1) rezone blocks of vacant residential lots to be marketed for attracting or expanding business; (2) improve incubator programs that help small businesses; and (3) increase efforts to attract small businesses and not focus all recruiting efforts on large, well-known businesses.

The mayor believed that several neighborhoods in the city could be stabilized by retail stores and industrial operations. He predicted that north St. Louis would boast two new shopping centers within his four years of administration (housing meeting, 1993). Good intentions were then followed by a concrete plan to establish a shopping area in north St. Louis with a major discount store chain and a major local grocery chain making commitments. Additional smaller retailers would complete the center, furnishing over 500 jobs with a commitment of over 20 percent of those jobs going to residents in the immediate neighborhood (Holleman, 1994). The mayor asserted, "If we can show people they can do well in their own neighborhoods, then they will *stay* in their own neighborhoods" (housing meeting, 1993).

Nevertheless, without *comprehensively* addressing urban economic problems, business and industry will not be attracted to and stay in distressed communities. For example, businesses will most likely be lured to an area where there is less fear of crime, where the schools are good, where there is adequate housing, and where there is a "sense of community" free from racism and prejudices. In other words, an approach that addresses economic concerns must be accomplished in tandem with addressing housing, education, safety, social, recreation, health, and community beautification concerns.

Gregory Squires, a professor of sociology and a member of the Urban Studies Program faculty at the University of Wisconsin, agrees. He asserts:

Given the severity of problems in the most distressed areas . . . proposed incentives are insufficient to encourage business to move in. . . . Bigger and better incentives . . . would [result] in a massive unintended subsidy of the private sector by the public sector in a collective race to the bottom as every community tries to outdo each other by offering increasing unaffordable subsidies. . . . Enterprise zones don't work. Numerous studies have documented that tax incentives are relatively insignificant factors in business decisions to start up, expand or where to locate. (1992: 3B)

Squires goes on to say that a community must be made livable and be a decent place to work in order to attract business. He also advocates that specific commitments be agreed to in advance such as the number of jobs to be created for residents, construction of low- or moderate-income housing, creation of day-care facilities, and so on.

The former mayor of St. Louis expressed this same view concerning the necessity of a comprehensive approach to community development in numerous talks at various community gatherings and in television and newspaper interviews: "The community is the foundation to improving the quality of life in this city, and all issues are tied together [housing, education, safety, economics]. This is what the Friedens Haus concept is" (Friedens Haus 1993 Anniversary Celebration).

ECONOMIC DEVELOPMENT IN HYDE PARK

As described in the chapter entitled "The Hyde Park Community," most of the industry and many businesses moved out of the neighborhood. Salisbury Street was the center of business activity years ago where Hyde Park residents could take care of most of their daily needs. Many shops operated on the first floor while the second floor served as residential space. At the time of my study, there were approximately seventy small businesses throughout the neighborhood and approximately forty industries along Broadway, east of Interstate 70 (considered outside Hyde Park boundaries).

One of the remaining businesses was a small food store on Salisbury owned and operated by a long-time Hyde Park resident. Fresh donuts were sold daily along with convenient items such as milk and bread. Prices were kept unusually low in comparison to other shops carrying the same items—the shop catered to neighborhood residents. Candy sold for a penny a piece (the customer got to choose) and a cup of coffee sold for thirty-five cents.

The owner explained that profit came from volume rather than individual sales—half of the gross income was derived from food stamps. Brochures, flyers, and sheets of information could be found on the front counter notifying residents of Friedens Haus, Hyde Park Alliance, and Holy Trinity news and activities as well as other community happenings. The shop was a place to catch up on the latest. Children stopped in on their way to and from school—they had to attend school regularly in order to be a store customer. The owner kept an eye on them, and they knew it.

The owner's philosophy of business and economic development is contained in a letter of support included with a grant proposal written approximately six years ago:

As an officer of the Hyde Park Business Association, I initially assisted in the formation of our organization in order that we as business owners utilize one another as a means of encouraging business success and growth. What we as an organization began to realize was that our business success and growth, for the most part, depended upon and was determined by the neighborhood's success and growth. Consciously, we have always known that economic growth and prosperity are better obtained through team effort, but we forget . . . that for business progress our communities need to be included as team players. . . . Goods and services cannot be sold unless there are buyers, buyers need jobs in order to have the money to purchase the goods and services, and just as important, a buyer needs to feel secure in entering a community to purchase.

    As business owners, we can and should provide skills, employment opportunities and challenges necessary to educate, encourage, and create the self-esteem that is vital to youth development. Too often our young people are given "band-aid" programs that accomplish nothing more than "just keeping them off the streets."

    Through a [collaborative effort], we intend to provide our youth the opportunity to assist in the development and use of a bicycle trail that will be routed along the outskirts of this neighborhood. . . . [The Hyde Park Business Association] is involved in a collaborative effort with Hyde Park Alliance, Friedens Haus, Bicycle Works and the Hyde Park Safety Committee in creating a bicycle shop entrepreneurship. . . . This bicycle shop will include bike rental. The development of the Bike Trail will enhance the Bicycle Shop and vice versa. Our organization believes and is committed to this type of programming.

    Many hopes of Hyde Park residents and service providers were "pinned" to the Bike Shop endeavor. One resident foresaw that the Bike Shop could serve as a "benchmark" showing the Hyde Park neighborhood as bankable—she believed that it would serve as a model for getting businesses initiated in distressed St. Louis neighborhoods.

    This possibility was in line with the prevailing economic philosophy of involved Hyde Park residents, community leaders, and several service providers—to keep the money in the community. As one leader expressed, "There is a need for people to be able to do their full range of shopping here so the money is staying in the community."

    Discussions among residents, business owners, and interested parties included ideas about shares of businesses and/or properties being bought and sold within the community to keep control and money in the neighborhood. Figure 14.3 demonstrates this philosophy working, to some degree, when the Bike Shop would be completed and in operation. The diagram was drawn by the previously mentioned Hyde Park resident and business owner. Although the flow of money and joint efforts among the various community organizations may not be fully understood by the reader, one gets the idea of money and benefits continuously flowing within the community (an antithesis of the negative socioeconomic cycle presented by Nance and Foggy) and the necessary collaborations among organizations to get the job done. Community members eventually entitled the diagram, "The Loop System."

Figure 14.3
Loop System (as depicted by Hyde Park resident)

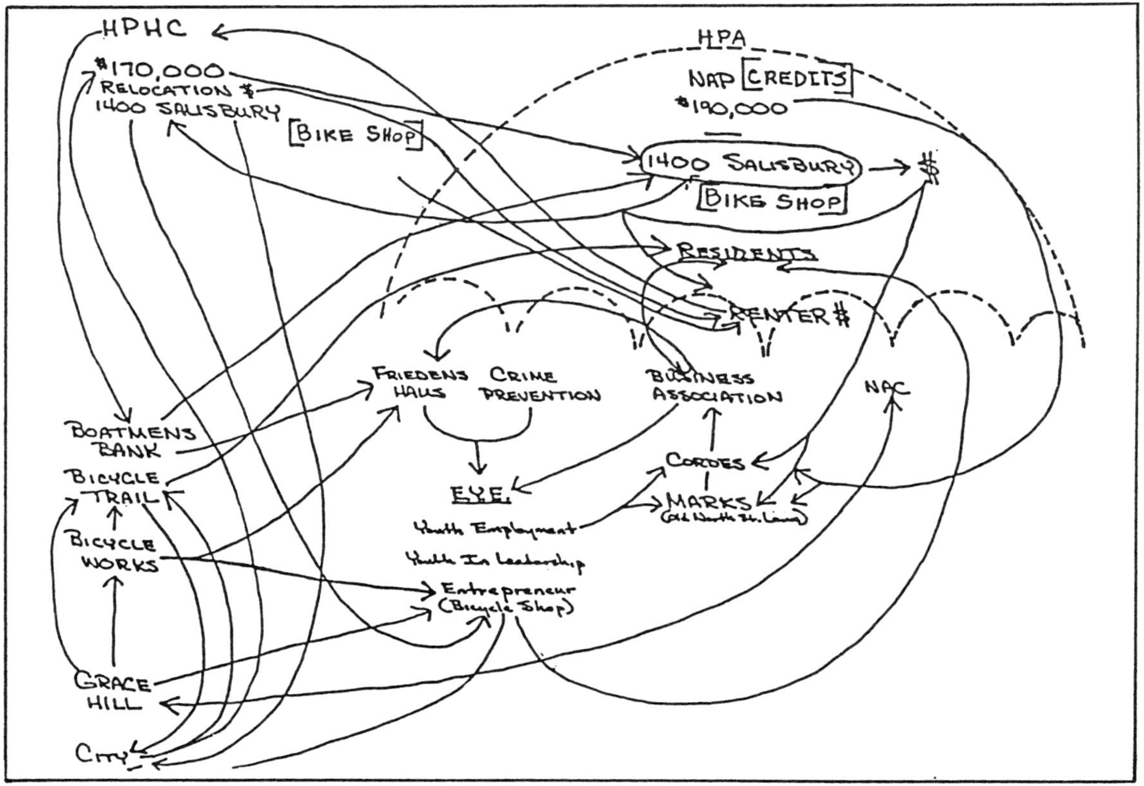

INDUSTRY INVOLVEMENT

Most industries along the river front had not been involved with the Hyde Park residential community since the 1950 construction of Interstate 70 that served as a psychological as well as physical barrier. An exception was the period of political activity surrounding the potential construction of the "honor center" along the river front. Mallinckrodt had been somewhat involved because of the necessity of maintaining a good relationship with environmentally aware constituents. A former Hyde Park resident and community leader had this to say:

Mallinckrodt is a superfund site [one of the most environmentally hazardous locations in the United States for health concerns and a priority for cleanup], so potentially they kind of need to watch themselves. If you have a really activist neighborhood group, they might demand that Mallinckrodt abate the problem that they created.

In a sense, Mallinckrodt is partially responsible for the low property values in Hyde Park. There are certain environmentally conscious middle class individuals that would not live in Hyde Park—not because of the crime—not because of anything else—but because of the proximity to the superfund site at Mallinckrodt.

A neighborhood resident gave the following reasons for lack of neighborhood involvement by river front industries:

I don't think what happens in Hyde Park really affects these industries that much. It's too easy for them to just close their doors and go on. "We have no financial obligation to you at all." Mallinckrodt does work with us. They fund various things. We have talked to them about the contamination of the soil around here from Mallinckrodt.

The industries on the river front see Hyde Park as a ghetto. This is north St. Louis and only bad things happen in north St. Louis. They think most of the people are on welfare or on AFDC—you have all these women with ten kids. If we could give them a better impression of what goes on here . . .

Another resident and business owner added, "One of the problems is that when some of the industries *do* fund certain things for the community, the projects are not that successful and the industry doesn't get much PR benefit. If the projects were more successful, more money could possibly be gotten from the contributing industry."

SUMMARY

Federal, state, and local policies have contributed to and exasperated inequities undermining our society and that are magnified in our cities. The Hyde Park neighborhood exemplifies this. The cycle of socio-economic and psychological despair will continue unless it is broken by individual communities as well as innovative governmental policies that have as their aim the narrowing of the economic, social, health, and educational gaps between those who have and those who have not. Moreover, institutionalized racism dictates that blacks are disproportionately represented in the group of "have-nots."

As President Clinton expressed in his State of the Union Address (1994) and referring to the "new American community," "We have seen a simultaneous breakdown of community, family, and work. We must give youth something to say yes to." In line with this statement, the plans for economic development in Hyde Park included planned opportunities for neighborhood youth to participate in the Bike Shop project and the Energizing Youth for Employment program.

In short, Hyde Park community members did not lack creativity. Moreover, the Bike Shop and its possible tie-in with the River Front Bike Trail were more than just dreams. At one time, the Bike Shop was well on its way to becoming a reality, and construction of the Bike Trail was inching its way toward the Arch (one section located along the river front near the Hyde Park neighborhood).

However, more often than not progress is realized from a two-steps-forward-and-one-step-backward approach. It must be noted that, at the time of this writing, HPA had moved into the section of the refurbished building intended for the Bike Shop. It is a continuing saga of control by a few people, "feigning . . . personal concern with the other fellow in order to manipulate him the better" as Josephson and Josephson assert (1962). However, the story has not ended, and the Bike Shop or a similar community enterprise may still become a reality. There were continuous and frequent brainstorming sessions about keeping Hyde Park money in Hyde Park, and ideas for comprehensive approaches prevailed.

Staff of the various Hyde Park neighborhood organizations were also making renewed efforts to effectively communicate with local business owners. Safety was a major concern for businesses, and this worry was being addressed by a comprehensive effort to improve the community, including keeping the police accountable to neighborhood residents, continuous efforts by the Safety Committee that included a mobile patrol component, and the provision of comprehensive and multi-systems efforts to improve quality of life for neighborhood children and their families.

The lack of industry involvement (on the border of Hyde Park) was a different matter. Community members and federal, state, and local leaders had yet to fully and energetically address this problem. It is definitely a foreshadowing issue that could make a tremendous impact on the economic redevelopment of the Hyde Park neighborhood.

Chapter 15

The Housing Problem

INTRODUCTION

The *St. Louis Post-Dispatch* series, "Slum Landlord," (1991) revealed some troubling facts. Of the twenty-eight city wards, the twelve most northern had one of every five housing units vacant—more than 100 housing units a month were destroyed or left vacant in the preceding decade. These same wards had 77 percent of the city's abandoned buildings and 64 percent of the city's vacant lots. In contrast, the city's central corridor claimed 69 percent of the city's *abated* property and was responsible for 28 percent of the real estate taxes (1991). In short, the neighborhoods in north St. Louis, heavily populated by blacks, suffered neglect when compared to the central corridor where tax abatements were attracting the more affluent populations and businesses.

Boarded-up buildings and vacant lots were a significant sign of economic decline in Hyde Park, one of the north St. Louis neighborhoods. For example, when looking out from the Friedens Haus director's office, one was able to view vacant lots, two boarded-up buildings, and one dilapidated four-family flat. Absentee landlords (one owned approximately five rentals in the area), the problem of determining who these landlords were, people continuously moving out when they could, and the lack of decent, affordable housing for low-income residents were major neighborhood problems. Added to this, property in the Hyde Park community appraised for less than one-half of rehabbing costs.

These were not exclusively Hyde Park problems, but problems for the City of St. Louis and large urban areas across the nation. Andrew Cuomo, Housing Secretary, asserts that there is a large and growing gap between home ownership in cities and suburbs.

This chapter explains that, similar to the city, the housing problem in Hyde Park evolved over a period of years. Surprisingly, recognition as a Historic Neighborhood proved to be somewhat of a hindrance to solving the problem as was the potential designation of Hyde Park as a Conservation District. Community members engaged in numerous problem-solving and planning efforts in order to find solutions, but the implementation of these solutions proved to be difficult and slow.

HOUSING PROBLEMS—CITY AND NATION-WIDE

One issue debated among St. Louis as well as Hyde Park residents was Section 8 housing. The intent of the program, set up some twenty-five years ago, was to give low- and moderate-income tenants the chance to obtain housing in stable neighborhoods. The program gives private landlords subsidies so they can charge lower rents. Some of the buildings involved are apartment complexes erected by private developers with government help. Also, many tenants receive vouchers or certificates for the purpose of finding a place to live. In 1994 more than 4,300 St. Louis families were housed under the Section 8 program and another 13,000 were on the program's waiting list (*St. Louis Post-Dispatch*, 1994a).

Several Hyde Park community members expressed that a high concentration of Section 8 housing presented a major problem for the neighborhood. A good number of residents maintained that many property owners, while pocketing Section 8 money, were negligent in bringing their properties up to Section 8 standards and were poor property managers.

One St. Louis alderman agreed that many St. Louis neighborhoods were adversely affected by high concentrations of Section 8 housing. He cited sharp crime increases in some areas where Section 8 housing had been concentrated and recommended dispersing this type housing throughout the city, restricting the number of units on one block, tightening application procedures to include police checks, and giving the St. Louis Housing Authority more clout to enforce Section 8 rules (Todd, 1994a). (See Figure 15.1.)

A housing task force appointed by the former mayor agreed when making the recommendation that St. Louis increase the use of Section 8 certificates that could be used anywhere. Several aldermen also urged frequent inspections of Section 8 housing and that landlords and tenants be held more accountable (Todd and Holleman, 1993).

The housing task force's final report also included evidence of needed affordable housing nation-wide as well as in St. Louis. The task force cited the Washington-based Center on Budget and Policy Priorities' finding that housing expenses consumed at least half the income of 64 percent of St. Louis area's poor white households and 60 percent of poor black households. In some instances, the Center found that poor families were paying 73 percent of their income to housing expenses. The task force found decreases in the supply of affordable housing attributable to an increase in the number of poor families, a decline in the average income of poor families, and a reduction in the number of low cost rental units.

Figure 15.1

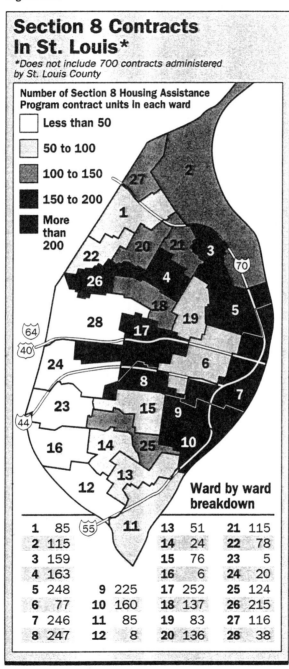

Section 8 Contracts In St. Louis*

Does not include 700 contracts administered by St. Louis County

Number of Section 8 Housing Assistance Program contract units in each ward

- Less than 50
- 50 to 100
- 100 to 150
- 150 to 200
- More than 200

Ward by ward breakdown

1	85		**13**	51	
2	115		**14**	24	
3	159		**15**	76	
4	163		**16**	6	
5	248	**9** 225	**17**	252	
6	77	**10** 160	**18**	137	
7	246	**11** 85	**19**	83	
8	247	**12** 8	**20**	136	

21	115
22	78
23	5
24	20
25	124
26	215
27	116
28	38

Most of Hyde Park is in Ward 3.

Source: St. Louis Post-Dispatch. (1994). February 3, 6B.

Possible remedies discussed among St. Louis as well as Hyde Park residents included affordable housing incentives launched federally and locally. It was reported that the Federal National Mortgage Association (Fannie Mae) increased the amount of money invested in low- and moderate-income housing to $1 trillion and spent millions more to address bias in mortgage lending (*St. Louis Post-Dispatch*, 1994b). Several St. Louis community members felt that St. Louis could get the most out of this program if the mortgage money were used to complement already initiated redevelopment plans or help to revive whole neighborhoods.

Federal initiatives more recently introduced include (Associated Press, 1997b):

- Federal Housing Administration cuts in mortgage insurance premiums that will enable 50,000 low-income families to buy homes. To qualify, first-time homeowners must successfully complete a sixteen-hour education program that includes information on selecting a home and mortgage, household budgeting, credit management, and home maintenance and repair.
- On top of $4 billion made available earlier, a Government National Mortgage Association (Ginnie Mae) $1 billion initiative to assist 15,000 families in inner cities in buying their own homes.
- Department of Housing and Urban Development provision of $10 million to create new Homeownership Zones in blighted urban neighborhoods and attract local investment.

One St. Louis public/private housing initiative is the Murphy Park development of 160 (to be expanded to 400) garden-style apartments and town houses in the inner city of St. Louis, offering housing for people of mixed incomes. Approximately 55 percent of the units are set aside for residents who qualify for public housing, while the remaining units are for those who can afford to pay market rate. Residents have to face tough screening procedures. The project's private developer manages the property, and the St. Louis Housing Authority owns the land (Parish, 1997). The project is funded by HUD, the state, and private entities. HUD Secretary Andrew Cuomo maintains that this development is an important step in HUD's nationwide transformation of public housing in inner cities.

One resident and property owner expressed his views concerning the future for housing in Hyde Park in terms of one of the aforementioned programs:

The Fannie May policy is a good thing; however, you have to fund that to the extent you can make a difference. You get into the issue of race where research has shown whites get uncomfortable when you have more than 25 percent to 30 percent black population. In the mid 80s I was part of a project which did twelve home-ownership buildings, but they were *scattered* sites in the Hyde Park historic district and most of those original people aren't here any more.

The Fannie May program will be good if it can stabilize the neighborhood. Hyde Park presently does not have much of a core of strength left. You have a few pockets . . . where you have stable owner-occupieds. I think you have to build on those areas of strength—you can't do one or two buildings on the worst streets in Hyde Park. The owners would be driven out in no time. It's a very tough thing to do because you get into steering and legalities.

Putting people together who own their homes works, but it doesn't work for the Section 8 program where you have a large concentration of people who don't own their homes and don't have a stake necessarily. I'm not saying that all tenants in Section 8 housing don't care—that certainly is not true. I've observed a lot of problems with Section 8 large-family units. It also has a lot to do with management and tenant selection.

AN EVOLVING PROBLEM IN HYDE PARK

One community resident, property owner, and landlord attempted to explain the historical evolvement of Hyde Park's housing problem.

Why did the housing stock deteriorate more so in north St. Louis than in south St. Louis?

Steering was a large part of it. Maybe this was conscious or done passively? I don't think there was a grand conspiracy—but there were programs in the 60s and 70s where the city did repairs to houses in south St. Louis in order to keep people in their homes. This was done in south rather than north St. Louis because of racism. The politicians who were in control were basically south side politicians—so some of this may have been by design and some by benign neglect.

Team IV did a study for the city back in the 70s and proposed that the city let the north part of the city fall down and then rebuild from there. It was not very well received in this part of town.

There were numerous community and outside efforts to solve the housing problem in Hyde Park. One such effort was attempted by Historic Hyde Park, Inc. that was initiated by rehabbers who were joined by other residents interested in the history of the neighborhood (late 1960s to early 1980s). As explained in the chapter entitled "Inclusiveness," this organization was geared toward home ownership and was rather exclusionary.

In the late 1970s and early 1980s, Hyde Park Restoration Effort (HYPRE) was active. This organization was also geared towards home ownership. The organization conducted house tours, street markets, made long-term plans, involved people and outside entities, and resisted government involvement. Members of the organization felt that restoration of the Hyde Park neighborhood could be done on the market. The organization maintained an office and staff, and published a neighborhood newsletter. However, there were kickbacks, other illegalities, and speculation resulting in great losses and broken dreams for some, a huge outstanding debt to the State of Missouri, and many buildings taken over by the city for nonpayment of taxes. The charismatic leader of this endeavor took up residence in another country.

Concurrently, in the early 1980s a project initiated from the mayor's office entitled "Hyde Park Partnership" was involved with rehabbing and investment in the neighborhood. Entities included in this endeavor were Mercantile Trust, Neighborhood Housing Services, and the Community Development Agency (CDA), which provided for several independent consultants for research purposes and funding. Hyde Park was assisted with public relations, graphics, finance, enhancement of positive public opinion, and housing (Jones and Horn, 1985).

The "Partnership" referred to the joint effort of the bank and four associations active in the Hyde Park area. These associations were Historic Hyde Park, Inc., HYPRE, North Side Team Ministry (NSTM), and the Water Tower Group (all now defunct). The purpose of the endeavor was to encourage and facilitate long-term involvement and investment in the neighborhood. The project was begun in 1980 and lasted until the end of 1983. Jones and Horn (program participants in 1985) write that the partnership was the catalyst for the rehabbing of 250 apartment units and over sixty buildings. The authors explain that seventeen units financed by the Bank and CDA were designed for low- and moderate-income families.

Participants felt that the residuals of the project would exist for an indefinite period of time; however, one of the authors relate that the project had an impact on rentals but not home-ownership (Jones and Horn, 1985). Also, an outside criticism was that more time should have been spent on rehabbing efforts rather than public relations and marketing.

The Partnership's prediction that the project's residuals would last for an indefinite period of time was not identifiable at the time of my study, except for the annual Mallinckrodt-sponsored Antique Fair held in the park (initiated as part of the project). It is interesting to note that the criticism of too much money, time, and effort being devoted to marketing instead of rehabbing was again a criticism of HUD (Housing and Urban Development) in 1991 when it was discovered that block grant monies were being used for "City Living" ad campaigns rather than for housing. Hyde Park's brochure was featured on the front page of the *St. Louis Post-Dispatch* (Linsalata and Novak, 1991) as an example of thousands of dollars spent to promote living in a St. Louis neighborhood. The article maintained that the brochure gave a false impression of Hyde Park—not depicting the typicality of the neighborhood. A picture of a boy walking by two boarded up buildings with graffiti scrawled across one brick wall was juxtaposed with the picture on front of the brochure showing a family enjoying a peaceful afternoon in the park.

HISTORICAL HYDE PARK: A HINDRANCE TO IMPROVEMENT?

Paradoxically, the fact that Hyde Park is a nationally registered Historic District became one constraint to improved and affordable housing in the neighborhood. This held true in terms of several "historical" structures that needed to be demolished in the citizens' view, and for several others that needed rehabbing. For example, because of Hyde Park's Historical District designation, only certain types of fencing could be used (wrought iron) to enhance and protect several properties.

Conversely, Stephen Acree, Executive Director of the St. Louis Community Development Agency (1997), writing in support of the Historic Homeownership Assistant Act, asserts that the stabilization of neighborhoods depends on home ownership. If a tax credit encourages the purchase of historic homes, it needs the support of everyone. He maintains that the initial cost is minimal and more than offset by a subsequent growth of the tax base.

Giving credence to this view, there were several Hyde Park residents who moved into the community because Hyde Park was an architecturally historic neighborhood. During one community housing meeting, one resident inquired, "Why aren't historical preservation rules being enforced?" She had previously reported three buildings to the ConServ office that were not in compliance with historic codes: "I'm not paying money to live here when things aren't historically correct!" The ConServ officer related that he would get someone out to inspect building exteriors and would eventually bring property owners into court for not abiding by the rules. The resident suggested educating Hyde Park residents about what is "historically correct."

For residents who were barely able to pay their bills (a large segment of the Hyde Park population), maintaining a building to be "historically correct" proved to be a huge burden. As one resident and business owner observed,

A lot of times the community has wound up short changing itself because of certain ways of thinking. An example would be blocking building improvements because it's a historical building, and years ago it was used for this and so on. All of these buildings, even though they are old, weren't built during the same time period. They just didn't spring up overnight!

. . . I think some people get stuck on this historical authenticity and the charm. That's fine, but we have to look to the future, too! We have to do things and maybe build things that serve the needs of the community if you want it to grow. If you want it to stagnate, you won't build anything new and you're going to work with nothing but old. There has to be sort of a merging between old buildings, new buildings, old ideas, and new ideas. You want to utilize what works!

CONSERVATION DISTRICT: HELP OR HINDRANCE?

It was one Hyde Park alderperson's view that the neighborhood should become a Conservation District. At least one property owner expressed that she would have a better chance to secure no-interest or low-interest loans for the purpose of rehabbing homes to rent for $100 to $200 a month. Becoming a Conservation District would have meant housing code enforcement and would have forced many owners to board up their buildings—"We should not give property owners reason to rent out dilapidated buildings!" On the other hand, many residents were fearful of what this would mean in terms of forcing people out of their homes. One community leader addressed this concern:

Further on down the road I think one of the things they're going to have to address here is housing code violations like this becoming a Conservation District. Do you really want to see improvement in housing stock, or do you want everything to be just OK?

How is this going to put someone out of their house? If you have an absentee landlord, or even if the landlord lives in the property, you want that property to be maintained. If you are a renter, you want that property to be maintained. You pay your rent—you want decent, adequate housing. To me that's a very common thing that you want first. Then you move on to the other thing in that you are protecting the market value if you're purchasing. If you have all the houses sitting around you with gutters falling off, needing painting, needing chimney repairs, all kinds of things going on—these are things you have to think about. These are *important* things!

No one has to be put out. It is implemented over a very long period of time. Usually if you have some sort of neighborhood organization in your area, they can pretty much work with the system to identify pockets that they want to deal with first. A lot of times you have to have some sense of accord to how your housing is going to be in your area. It's not "ok" for people to rent some place for $350 a month and you don't have a decent heating facility, you don't have adequate water pressure, you're subject to endangerment by the electrical system, it rains in your apartment—this is not fair housing—it is not!

I know what has happened is that because some landlords didn't want to do it, they sold their property. That was "ok," too, because the people who bought it came in and repaired it. Now the tenants may or may not have wanted to stay—we don't know that. The people may or may not have raised the rent, but not likely. Most times they didn't because the people usually paid adequate rent anyway, but they just weren't getting anything for their money. I think people don't understand all of the different facets of housing code restrictions. You have to look at the whole picture—don't look at part of it!

RESIDENT EFFORTS

Providing decent, affordable housing was a major problem-solving effort in the Hyde Park neighborhood. Rehabbing, upgrading, and providing decent housing for community residents and promoting low-income housing ownership were the goals of Hyde Park Alliance, were the major concerns of the Housing Corporation, and were becoming increasing efforts of the Friedens Haus program.

Ideas discussed at the July strategic planning meeting concerning housing (facilitated by Operation ConServ) provide some indication of the concerns and creativeness of community members. There were approximately fifteen present including the Clay school principal, Friedens Haus and Hyde Park Alliance staff, local business owners, community residents, property owners, and a real estate agent who had been successful in selling Hyde Park properties. Ideas discussed included:

- applying for federal grants for low-income home ownership
- converting four family flats into two town houses
- lease/purchase arrangements
- concentrating efforts in one area
- local control, de-emphasizing outside ownership
- marketing the community
- subcommittee planning
- concentrating on places where there were already numerous homeowners in order to keep them in the community
- the possibility of making a recently closed elementary school into a community, day care, senior housing, or job training center
- addressing the problem of buyer credit worthiness

The following meeting in August added to the list of ideas:

- tie in with ACORN and Catholic Charities to secure loans for low-income buyers
- keep track of who is selling and buying
- develop a listing—offer better buildings to those who want to sell
- develop different strategies for different buildings—those ready for move-in, those needing moderate rehabbing, and those needing major rehabbing (map in these buildings)
- provide an address map
- also provide low-income rental property
- use rent for renovation or down payment for other buildings (if Hyde Park owned the property)
- provide home-ownership education
- encourage local residents to be trained as real estate agents to sell properties in the community
- churches could keep track of property in their immediate areas

(It must be noted that eleven buildings around Holy Trinity were subsequently renovated via seed money coming from two St. Louis county parishes, based on the idea of building around a stable core.)

Another idea that was discussed at several community meetings, Housing Corporation meetings, and in various homes in the community was the possibility of establishing CoHousing in the neighborhood. A description of CoHousing is offered by The CoHousing Company in Berkeley, California:

Pioneered primarily in Denmark and now being adapted in other countries, the CoHousing concept reestablishes many of the advantages of traditional villages within the context of late twentieth-century life. Each household has a private residence but also shares extensive common facilities with the larger group such as a dining hall, children's playrooms, workshops, guest rooms and laundry facilities. Although individual dwellings are designed to be self-sufficient and each has its own kitchen, the common facilities, and particularly common dinners, are an important aspect of community life both for social and practical reasons.

I would add that, for inner-city communities, an attraction of CoHousing was that it provided increased security and safety.

Although the CoHousing concept was well researched and presented by a HPA staff member for adaptation in an urban setting and using city blocks as a natural CoHousing design, there seemed to be little interest and a reluctance to "give up" a sense of autonomy on the part of Hyde Park residents. The HPA staffer then explained that residents could keep their own yards and gardens, and the plan could evolve into developing trust for sharing such areas.

It was also pointed out that the "undesirables" on the block would self-select to move out if the majority on the block imposed self-rules and lease-rules. The possibility of exclusion was there. In a community where the neighborhood organization had only recently become racially integrated, this was an important consideration. Finally, Hyde Park residents suggested that a CoHousing plan should evolve from the people living in Hyde Park and not be a plan already developed for them. In short, residents remained suspicious of this "out of the box" solution to neighborhood problems.

IMPLEMENTATION PROBLEMS

One constraint was the actual "doing" of community housing plans. At a meeting held September 28, 1993, sponsored by Adequate Housing for Missourians, the former mayor of St. Louis expressed it this way,

Community Development block grants should produce brick and mortar. Up to now, we have been spending a lot of money on administration, and so on—where is the beef? Where is the house? . . . If a building is given to a neighborhood organization, how much time do you give them to turn it around? Goals, objectives, and accountability must be important to these groups. This is a touchy issue, because some of these groups are linked to the constituency which is linked to alderpersons.

The mayor went on to say that economic development is linked to housing:

The goal should be a plan that is best for the city as a whole, while at the same time encouraging neighborhood incentive by recognizing neighborhood-initiated plans as the primary guiding documents for policy purposes as they apply to a particular neighborhood.   Together these plans should outline a blueprint for completely refurbishing the physical environment, rebuilding the social infrastructure, and restoring health and prosperity to the entire population of St. Louis.

Of the many ideas offered at various Hyde Park community and strategic planning meetings, only a few had been implemented at the time of my study. Hyde Park Alliance wrote several grant proposals for major amounts of money in support of improved housing.   Many community members felt that these were "pie-in-the-sky" efforts, and that proposals for smaller amounts of money should have been written to aid ongoing projects.   Friedens Haus was effective in finding housing for families—rentals and property purchases. Finally, the Hyde Park Housing Corporation owned four properties and co-owned one property with HPA.   Two buildings were stabilized, and the rehabbing of one was completed in 1994.   This property housed the relocated HPA on the bottom floor, a residential renter on the second floor, and was, at one time, intended to house the Bike Shop in the remaining bottom floor space.

SUMMARY

The housing problems in Hyde Park remained and continuously worsened in spite of outside agency and business efforts, a few favorable governmental policies, and a few property owners who established residency in order to rehab and realize a profit.   Others intensified the problem by buying property for speculation.   Moreover, there were minimal *inclusive* efforts to solve the problem from within the neighborhood. The Hyde Park Housing Corporation maintained the facade of a "grass-roots" effort to improve housing in the community, but this organization remained a city solution using federal money. Progress was being made, but five years and only one finished project was not much to showcase. There remained the problem of establishing the Bike Shop within the completed refurbished building.

The more recent governmental policies and regional efforts to subsidize low- and moderate-income home ownership may aid the Hyde Park community, but connections have to be made. As mentioned previously, during a turning point election period, results of long-time efforts may be realized. The debate remains whether designation of Hyde Park as a Conservation District will add to or detract from the housing problem and neighborhood stabilization. Nevertheless, the concept of mixed-income housing as well as multi-sector involvement could be added solutions to a continuously growing and intensifying problem. As the principal of Clay School maintained, "Affordable housing is necessary to stabilize the neighborhood and ultimately to improve test scores. Each year, up to 50 percent of my students move out of the neighborhood because they cannot afford housing."

Finally, decent, affordable housing was only one part of the equation to revitalizing historic Hyde Park. As one service provider asserted, "It's more than housing—it's about making a community." For a number of years, Hyde Park community members may have overly concentrated their efforts on the housing problem.

The following chapter explains the various levels of interagency cooperation that have been implemented to solve Hyde Park's numerous and varied problems, including housing. In addition to problem solving efforts in terms of crime, economic development, and adequate housing, Hyde Park community members were integrating community and outside entities to focus on educational, political, health, and additional social concerns. The collaboration of various systems and types of organizations was essential in order to solve multi-level and multi-systemic problems exhibited in the Hyde Park community.

Chapter 16

Interagency Cooperation

INTRODUCTION

Interagency cooperation is essential for effective community problem-solving to take place, especially in neighborhoods similar to Hyde Park where problems are multiple, intense, and varied. This cooperation involves not only public organizations such as the public school, but not-for-profit, private, and religious institutions as well.

Agreeing with this premise, Minzey and LeTarte (1994) maintain that community education is not limited to the community school—the community school is only one institution in the process. Parson and Halperin (1983) concur, maintaining that there may be too much emphasis placed on the school in community education. They express that community education should be a collaborative effort directed toward the process of various agencies coming together to serve the community. The Wood (1977) model discussed in the "Community Education Models" chapter speaks to the use of many community institutions for community education purposes—a multi-systems operation.

Minzey and LeTarte (1994) also write that, of all American communities, approximately 90 percent have a K-12 educational program, 50 percent make use of school facilities beyond regular school hours, 45 percent have activities for school-age children and youth, 40 percent have activities for adults, but only 10 percent have delivery and coordination of community services, and only 10 percent have substantial community involvement. The authors state that the first blockage to the desired community education model, of all previously mentioned stages, occurs after a K-12 educational program has been established; however, a major second blockage occurs beyond the activities for adults stage, because of funding, control, relationship, and functional problems.

Kliminski and Keyes (1983) assert that bringing services to people rather than having people get to the services will increase service usage by approximately 25 percent. This implies a role for the community educator as a processor—matching community needs with resources.   Emphasizing the impediments to effective service delivery and interagency cooperation, a St. Louis organization, Conference on Education, recently reported:

The discontinuity of jurisdictions presents a huge obstacle to interagency cooperation. . . Within the City of St. Louis there are aldermanic wards, police districts, school attendance areas, neighborhood boundaries, library service parameters, juvenile court divisions, health clinic boundaries, and social service delivery areas none of which shares the same delineation's. This confusing maze of jurisdiction presents a nightmare to the citizen needing assistance, and it also makes it very difficult for agencies which serve different populations to work together. (1993: 27)

Joseph Ringers (1976) writes about interagency cooperation by describing seven models of management to ease this maze of jurisdiction: (1) service contracting, (2) space sharing, (3) budget combining, (4) community education, (5) joint venturing, (6) the new unit model, and (7) the super size model. However, many community educators would claim that the "community education" model *encompasses* space sharing, budget combining, service contracting, and joint venturing. This held true in the Hyde Park community at the time of my study.

LEVELS OF INTERAGENCY COOPERATION

Interagency cooperation in Hyde Park may be evaluated by assessing various levels of establishing linkages. Arthur Himmelman (1992) writes about a hierarchical model of establishing linkages for interagency cooperation. He maintains that it is sometimes a developmental process that involves distinct steps. The levels of linkages are from bottom to top: (1) networking, (2) coordination, (3) cooperation, and (4) collaboration.

Networking

Networking involves little risk and allows a few individuals to establish informal contacts with others. The focus is usually narrow and specific, meeting an immediate need. Himmelman defines networking as exchanging information for mutual benefit. In line with this, Minzey and LeTarte (1979) advocate that the community educator serve as a broker, only providing the needed service if no other agency is available to fulfill the need.

Examples of this kind of networking, as Arthur Himmelman (1992) describes it, abounded in the Hyde Park Alliance and Friedens Haus organizations. The former director of Hyde Park Alliance related the networking function of her organization this way, "That's another thing, we're a traffic cop here to some extent—helping people find the right people in this community that they need to address their needs, organize their problems, or whatever. And if we can't do that well, or if we set it up so they fail, whatever we do, that really stops a lot of the energy from moving through the community."

Networking and communication were major functions of the Friedens Haus coalition. The director spent approximately 60 percent of her time connecting families and individuals to resources, whether it was for financial, health, housing, counseling, legal, or other needs. As Minzey and LeTarte advocate, the director felt that there sometimes needed to be a broker to mediate between family and agencies. For example, the director served as a link between landlords, realtors, and those who were in need of affordable housing or desired to upgrade their housing. Serving as initiator and facilitator of the Northside All Combined (NAC) organization, the director was also very involved with keeping communication channels open among numerous community and city service providers.

Coordination

Coordination is defined by Himmelman as "exchanging information and altering activities for mutual benefit and to achieve a common purpose" (Himmelman, 1992: 7). One example of coordination among NAC organizations was exchanging names of those receiving Thanksgiving and Christmas food baskets in order to reduce duplication of services while benefiting the needy in the Hyde Park area. There were numerous additional examples of coordination such as the disbursement of fliers that informed citizens of NAC member services. Finally, both Hyde Park Alliance (HPA) and Friedens Haus attempted to coordinate meetings and activities in order to reduce duplication and enhance each other's activities.

Cooperation

Cooperation is defined as "exchanging information, altering activities, and sharing resources for mutual benefit and to achieve a common purpose" (Himmelman, 1992: 8). Cooperation was exemplified in Hyde Park via several relationships that existed between Hyde Park Alliance and the Friedens Haus coalition until 1994–95. Several of the committees that were coordinated under the umbrella of Hyde Park Alliance convened their meetings in the Friedens Haus or Clay School facilities (Safety Committee and Landlord's Task Force at Friedens and some HPA community meetings at Clay School).

Hyde Park Alliance staff volunteered for various Friedens Haus endeavors, and HPA furnished information about Friedens Haus activities in its monthly newsletter. Equipment and materials were shared at various times, and many Friedens advisory board members and HPA board of director members served dual memberships. The reasons for the discontinuation of this high level of cooperation between the two organizations had much to do with a change in the

HPA directorship. Insights into this issue was provided in the chapter entitled "Citizen Councils." Nevertheless, there were numerous positive results realized from cooperative efforts in Hyde Park concerning short-term projects such as the beautification and transformation of the vacant lot adjacent to Clay School using staff of Clay, HPA, and Friedens Haus; Clay School students; the SLPSS; and The Assembly of God Church. The property is now used as a playground and outdoor learning center for Clay students and neighborhood children.

Collaboration

Collaboration is defined as "exchanging information, altering activities, sharing resources, and enhancing the capacity of another for mutual benefit and to achieve a common purpose" (Himmelman, 1992: 8). More specifically, collaboration includes the sharing of risks, resources, responsibilities, and rewards. "Those engaging in collaborative relationships view others as partners, not competitors, and seek to enhance their partner's capacity to achieve their own definition of excellence to help accomplish a common purpose" (Himmelman, 1992: 8).

Himmelman warns that collaboration is best used when other inter-organizational strategies cannot achieve mutual goals. This is true because collaboration often challenges traditional values, collaborative processes are complex, and the time requirements may be considerable. Himmelman recommends that collaborative processes be chosen only after conducting "careful, strategic assessments of its viability and appropriateness for addressing specific issues or circumstances" (Himmelman, 1992: 8).

Himmelman also writes about multi-sector collaborations—when public, private, and nonprofit organizations collaborate in support of a community, with the setting of priorities and control of resources remaining with community members. He views this type of collaboration as superior to one-level processes, because the strengths of one type of organization may be the weaknesses of another type. Thus, the combination of all three organizational types (public, private, and nonprofit) form a strong web of support—a synergistic approach that community educators espouse.

A good example of a multi-sector collaboration was the Bike Shop project that had been ongoing for five years. The idea, design, and a good part of the planning for the Bike Shop originated with a community resident and business owner. Since then, the idea had become a reality to the extent that a building had been refurbished, HPA relocated to this site, and the second floor residential space was rented. The Bike Shop had yet to move in.

It was envisioned that the Bike Shop would be the first entrepreneurial business in the neighborhood in four years. The shop would provide for a youth program involving Friedens Haus that would include training for bicycle repair and safety, community service projects, business development, and incentive for youth to stay in school. During the time of my study, the Bike Shop project was a collaboration of Friedens Haus, Hyde Park Alliance, the Hyde Park Housing Corporation, one alderperson, Operation Impact, Operation ConServ, the Safety Committee, and the Hyde Park Business Association. The public entities were the city agencies (ConServ and Impact) and the alderperson working through the Hyde Park Housing Corporation, HPA and Friedens Haus represented nonprofit 501(C)3 organizations, and the Business Association represented the private sector.

Hyde Park Alliance and the Housing Corporation co-owned the Bike Shop building. With the aid of Operation Impact, Operation ConServ, the alderperson, Friedens Haus, and the Business Association, funding was secured for renovation. One grant was received by the Business Association for inside renovation, a grant was received by Friedens Haus for initiation of the Bicycle Works program, Operation Impact provided $90,000 and a ten-year tax abatement, the Housing Corporation expended $17,000 of its funds, and a bank loan for $32,000 was secured. Friedens Haus recruited students to take part in a summer training program, aided in providing bicycles and other equipment, and planned to take responsibility for the educational part of the program.

The Bike Shop project meets Himmelman's definition of a multi-sector collaboration with the exception (more or less) of his more specific criterion—collaborative members viewing the other members as partners and not competitors: "No single organization can take credit for accomplishments because publicity about the collaborative's work acknowledges all partners" (Himmelman, 1992: 9). Several residents as well as other community members felt that the Housing Corporation and Hyde Park Alliance were overlooking or forgetting contributions and the roles to be played by other involved entities.

There was a lack of contracts or formal agreements between the neighborhood organizations—nothing in black and white to delineate roles, contributions, and responsibilities other than for Operation Impact and the Housing Corporation. Such formality may have aided in clearing up misunderstandings about ownership. Consequently, this collaborative project was an ongoing struggle to achieve full partnership (in lieu of a "who's in control" mentality) for the common community purpose of economic development, housing, and education. Himmelman's warning concerning collaborations challenging traditional values, often becoming complex, and requiring considerable time was certainly validated by the Hyde Park Bike Shop collaborative effort.

One example of a formal contractual arrangement was an agreement between The Deaconess Health Systems and Friedens Haus for provision of a community nurse. Funding was procured through a grant, and Deaconess staff in conjunction with the Friedens Haus Board of Directors served as the nurse's supervisors. Details of the nurse's responsibilities, duties, and chain of command were carefully worked out by Deaconess representatives and members of the Friedens Haus Board of Directors. Even with this formal contractual arrangement, there were misunderstandings because of oversights in providing comprehensive factual information.

Another example of a multi-sector collaboration among various neighborhood and outside organizations was the Energizing Youth for Employment (EYE) program (explained in the chapter entitled, "Assessing Needs, Planning, and Evaluating"). The idea was first presented by the Safety Committee to HPA for the purpose of using that organization's 501(C)3 status for fund-raising. Connection was then made with Friedens Haus since this organization had the educational and youth expertise. Finally, the Business Association was again brought in for financial support, technical assistance, and to provide job opportunities. The program eventually provided leadership training and summer employment for Hyde Park youth. The Bike Shop was to be the entrepreneurial component.

IMPEDIMENTS TO PROGRESS

Interagency cooperation witnessed in the Hyde Park community until 1994–95 evolved over several years. The director of Friedens Haus served on the Executive Board of HPA as a representative of the NAC organization that she facilitated. Chairs of the Safety Committee, Landlord's Task Force, and the Business Association were also represented on that board. Conversely, HPA was represented on the Friedens Haus Board of Directors until 1995, and the director of HPA cochaired the Friedens Haus subcommittee concerning community development.

In spite of several dual memberships, there remained tension among the major neighborhood organizations, especially between Hyde Park Alliance and Friedens Haus. Some Friedens Haus Advisory Board members felt that Hyde Park Alliance staff attended Friedens Haus Board meetings and then began to take credit for Frieden's accomplishments. Some Hyde Park Alliance former staff felt that some members of the Friedens Haus board spread rumors about Alliance staff and tried to sabotage HPA progress. This controversy remained a great concern for all community leaders in Hyde Park and for many neighborhood residents. One former community leader expressed it this way,

Everybody should be working together. It seems like there's a lot of territoriality among all the groups, and the territories all overlap. Just from a logistical and efficiency stand point, there ought to be a collaboration that divides stuff up by task rather than by territory.

I think Himmelman's model for multi-sector collaborations is a really good one and could work. It would really require a more formalized structure between the different organizations and even within the organizations.

One long-time Hyde Park resident and business owner had this to say about getting all parts of the community working together:

Communication—open your ears, open your eyes, and get away from this control kind of maneuvering. Realize what the bottom line is and get the personal crap out. People need to be honest with themselves. Everybody should be working for a common goal and that goal should be to get the community progressing as quickly as it can in a financially feasible way.

They have to know if their involvement is actually for themselves and their own egos, or do they truly want the community to progress? Maybe if they were honest, they might step aside or be open-minded to others. There is a prejudice problem regarding economic level here and maybe a little racism. A person's sexual orientation also seems to be a big issue.

Another resident's view substantiates Himmelman's advocacy of nonprofit, public, and private collaborations as being superior to one-type organizational collaborations:

One problem is the rhetoric of saying, "Let's work together, let's not be competitive, let's make this a collaborative effort"—but what I've learned is that's very common among nonprofits. They are all scratching for the same dollar. If you're all broke and poor, why fight each other?—or they end up working together, and one takes the glory.

Another thing that probably gets in the way is a lack of a cohesive goal for the neighborhood among all the different agencies. One agency may say housing is the solution here, and then you can't even agree on what kind of housing—another one says education is the solution here to the exclusion of maybe housing.

THE ROLES PLAYED BY CHURCHES

Three churches in Hyde Park maintained more influence than the others. These three included Friedens United Church of Christ, New Holy Trinity Catholic Church, and Bethlehem Lutheran. Friedens and Holy Trinity are located in the eastern half of the neighborhood while Bethlehem Lutheran is located in the western half. One community resident asserted that Hyde Park churches contributed to neighborhood segregation, because they had previously ended their offerings of social services while trying to preserve and protect what they had (congregations). Instead, they wound up destroying their congregations. Nevertheless, the philosophies of the respective church leaders differed concerning cooperation, community involvement, and who should be included in church programs and social services.

Views of Holy Trinity's priest and Bethlehem Lutheran's pastor follow. Friedens Church had only recently filled a one-year pastoral vacancy. First, the parish priest speaks:

It's OK what's happening—I think every church does their little thing in the neighborhood, and every church sponsor-group like Friedens Haus are all doing their little things. I really don't feel competition as far as social services. . . . We can work together and address the issues, the problems, and the needs of our neighborhood and its people.

Describe your church's relationships with the other churches and neighborhood organizations in the community.

Well, when I first came here, I tried to get to know people from other churches—ministers from other churches—and I didn't pick up that any of them wanted to work together except for the former pastor and his wife from Friedens Church. They lived in the rectory and were very involved in the community. We worked together on things, but I haven't worked with Friedens Church since there has been an interim pastor. I have never met the pastor [there seven months].

The pastor of Bethlehem Lutheran (located in the other side of the neighborhood) offered his view of the church's ideal function in the community:

The church's first function is to know its own identity. The church can be the catalyst and stabilizing force in a neighborhood. In our neighborhood, especially, it must be—there is so little else. The function of the church is, first, spiritual for people to know Jesus as savior. That's what the church does best is to bring the message of the gospel and the message of hope in God. The church has to have that identity very straight.

We have a food pantry, but we can't do what Feed My People or St. Louis Food Bank can do. We don't try to do that because we're not a food pantry. We help everyone, but those who we help on a regular basis are those who allow us to do ministry with them. That doesn't have to mean Sunday morning worship—it could be their kids come to our children's program. The key word is identity. Our food pantry is just an opportunity for us to tell people about the *real* bread of life, and that's Jesus.

Anybody in the community can come to any of our programs. There is a community gym program on Saturday which is really just a "hang out." I'm not into it totally because it doesn't bring about any accountability. I'm not there—most of the guys who come in for that have no care about the church—they just want to play basketball. I'm not really sold on the program. I think the job of us being a church is that every part, every spoke in the wheel of church life should have some spiritual component. When a program doesn't have this, the church is walking the line of being something we're not. We're not a YMCA. . . .

This is sort of our long-range vision of the community. If the majority of the community goes to Bethlehem Lutheran Church, Bethlehem Lutheran Church sets the agenda for the community. If 90 percent of the people on the street are Christians, the 10 percent who are drug dealers get kicked out. That's the only way you can take back the streets.

Do you think that these 90% have to be Christians in order to do that?

I think the church in the community is the place to rally around—yeah. I think Christian—yes in the sense that—especially with the voice that society has today—irresponsibility and lack of accountability are acceptable—drugs are acceptable—the church can stand up and say "no." I think there are people that know right from wrong who are not Christians, but the church is the majority. The minority cannot beat the problem. These people who want to do right and are not Christians are definitely in the minority—definitely.

I think non-Christians *could* work with the Christians, but I still think the church is going to be the major player. The church has a deeper level of commitment. We're living in a society where people are not committed to very much—they're committed to themselves. It's going to take a deeper level of commitment for people to evoke a change.

Describe your church's relationship with the other churches in the community.

There is very little relationship—mostly because we don't have enough time to get done what we're trying to get done here. I think there is some benefit in working together. I don't sense the same call to accountability in other ministries in the community. The goals maybe aren't the same.

. . . Our relationship with neighborhood organizations has also been very little. We have a booth at the Street Fair which is kind of nice. What are the goals of the neighborhood organizations? What is it that they want?

. . . I've seen too many Lutheran churches go down in inner cities because they went to so many meetings. They tried to do so much stuff instead of doing what they were supposed to be doing and that's telling people about Jesus.

Members of the Friedens United Church of Christ viewed the Friedens Haus program as a mission. Several church members volunteered as tutors, mentors, and served on the Friedens Haus Advisory Board and Board of Directors. One member offered free eye examinations and glasses to needy Clay students and performed maintenance work in the Friedens Haus facility. The church acquired a new pastor (black) after approximately one year without one. There was optimism that he would encourage local residents to become church members. The forty-five membership was then comprised of 98 percent white nonresidents.

THE ROLES PLAYED BY COLLEGES AND UNIVERSITIES

Area colleges and universities were also involved with the Hyde Park neighborhood at different levels of establishing linkages. An example of *coordination* was Washington University's former link to Friedens Haus. (The same university subsequently became collaboratively involved.) In connection with the YMCA, the university initiated a program entitled "Sunday in the Park for Kids" and provided this program in the Hyde Park neighborhood for approximately eleven years. Volunteers offered fun and recreational activities for community children during the school year, and the university contracted with Friedens church to use their fellowship hall during inclement weather. The volunteers also took the children on one or two field trips a year, and the Friedens Haus director arranged for transportation.

Harris-Stowe State College (located in St. Louis) was somewhat involved with the community and served as another example of coordination. Education students at the college were required to volunteer somewhere in the city before they did their student teaching. During the 1993–94 year, one student assisted with computer technology at Clay School and at Friedens Haus. Another student helped by surveying area businesses to find out how to attract additional businesses to the area and why the area businesses were not more involved with the community.

One example of *cooperation* with the Hyde Park community was the University of Missouri-St. Louis, which received a five-year federal grant through Center for Substance Abuse Prevention (CSAP). This program was designed to look at substance abuse within inner-city neighborhoods and evaluate specially developed curricula aimed at pre-teens who were considered to be "high risk." The university's involvement allowed for the hiring of a full-time employee for Friedens Haus while the university oversaw the CSAP research evaluation and procedures with the children's after-school club groups. Friedens Church facilities and Friedens Haus staff were involved in the research process.

St. Louis University also entered into a cooperative relationship with the Friedens Haus program by furnishing staff time and expertise through their departments of social work and sociology. Two members of Friedens' Board of Directors and Advisory Board were professors in the university's sociology and social work departments. The university and Friedens Haus also benefited by the arrangement of student practicums (BSW and MSW programs) in the Hyde Park neighborhood with the Friedens Haus director serving as supervisor. The practicum arrangements could be classified as *collaborative* linkages.

During the 1994–95 year, another collaboration was initiated (by means of a grant) between Washington University and Friedens Haus/Clay Elementary. Seven students from the university's department of education and school of social work also performed practicums with Friedens Haus and Clay School. Social work students helped with student follow-up, home visits, club group activities, and special projects; and education students assisted with teacher workshops and action research in collaboration with Clay School teachers. There were also thirty-eight additional education students who fulfilled field experience requirements at Clay. This collaboration, which included the Professional Development School concept, is more fully explained in the chapter about lifelong learning.

An interview with the director (MSW) of the Friedens Haus program gives one view, and probably the most knowledgeable view in the community, of higher education's involvement with the Hyde Park neighborhood, listing both positive and negative factors.

What are the most positive factors about their involvement?

Our chance to interact with students. Students bring freshness, a lot of interest, and new spark. Plus they bring in theories that are interesting to compare, and they update us to what is going on. They also want to learn and question you, so it makes you think about why you are doing things. It is an incentive to break out of your mold. Somebody new adds something to the kids and the neighborhood, because they are contributing. It takes a lot of people for the tutoring and mentoring programs.

What do you see as the negative factors?

The universities in general are not that convinced that it's important to get involved with the communities. That has been changing I think during the last few years. I think they realize that it benefits them to be involved with different places if it's for publicity, PR, or whatever. You see that when you go to workshops and hear them talking. I think it will change more when there is more and more incentives like federal grants to get involved and to have volunteers for community action. There are even federal directives, and I think they'll want to jump on the band wagon and be a part of the whole picture. I think there is a change from the national perspective that will have an effect on universities.

Another negative factor is that students and volunteers disappear very quickly. Students have to go on to the next thing, so it can be kind of disappointing to a kid—their favorite tutor is leaving. "They didn't like us enough?" It is hard for them to understand.

What is an ideal model of higher education involvement with a community?

One college in the city has an emphasis on their students doing volunteer work before they do their student teaching. It makes perfect sense. Anyone involved in a university is going to be involved with working with people, and they need expectations of all students doing some kind of practicum or volunteer experience. Students need to relate whatever data they get in the classroom to the outside world. It would make students a lot stronger for any kind of job if they have some hands-on experience of different kinds.

University students could also help with grant writing. They have access to expertise for data and computers—keeping up with a lot of paper work. Universities and colleges could lend other kinds of expertise in helping communities structure different things in ways of efficiency without running it for them. The business and nursing schools [community nursing] could also help. Business students could actually help the community develop businesses. Professors in different fields could help communities learn what to do about economic development—even in areas like housing.

What are the blockages to this ideal model?

University people tend to want to sit in their ivory tower, and they are used to people coming to them. One university, for instance, thought they were away from the rest of the world. They tended to have this isolated kind of thing and felt they were a little bit above the normal population. It's going to take a while for them to change that—really feel like they're a part of the community—not isolated and above the people of the community.

Politics and religious connections are also blockages. One university which has a Catholic orientation tends to deal more with Catholic-connected projects. Another university has its background with a large Jewish population—there is still somewhat of a religious block.

A city college and another area university have governmental policies which they have to abide by. They receive money from the state and are governed by state and federal policies. That's what I would call politics. Will the city and state see the benefits of helping the universities to become involved with communities to prevent crime, for instance, and therefore save money? City and state governments may have to start thinking about funding things differently.

What would be the results of such an ideal involvement?

A closer trade off and cooperation rather than so much isolation and separation. You would have a better flow back and forth and cooperation between school and community. People would know more about colleges and universities, see them in a more positive light, and may see them as a model for them. You would have a flow of information where communities could teach the universities and the universities could teach the communities. Each side could learn and grow from the other.

SUMMARY

Interagency cooperation taking place in the Hyde Park community was an ongoing and evolving process of networking, cooperation, coordination, and collaboration, as Himmelman defines these terms, among and between community organizations; public, nonprofit, and private agencies; churches; and colleges and universities. As expected, the interagency cooperation efforts in Hyde Park diminished on this hierarchical scale with most of the inter-relatedness happening at the lowest level of networking; less, but a good amount taking place at the cooperation and coordination levels; and only a few examples of the highest level of multi-sector collaboration taking place or developing. As noted earlier, greater efforts were needed for the formation of partnerships to achieve the common goal of community improvement as required at the multi-sector, collaborative level, but the rewards were greater in terms of community development (in this case, economic, social, and educational development through the Bike Shop project, the EYE program, and university student practicums).

As one NAC service provider suggested, "Duplication of services is good as long as we're not tripping over one another and getting in each other's way, because the need is so great!" However, barriers such as the lack of formal agreements and structure, turf and ownership issues, detrimentally strong personalities in leadership positions, and narrowly defined organizational philosophies hindered the cooperations and collaborations necessary to meet this great need. Finally, one church leader expressed a somewhat exclusionary and separatist view in terms of interagency cooperation, implying that Christians possessed a "deeper level of commitment" than non-Christians, and that only Christians would be able to effect positive change in the community.

For the most part, the leadership of the Friedens Haus coalition (Board of Directors, Clay School principal, Friedens Haus director) served as the networking and collaborating initiators in Hyde Park. These leaders realized that in order to bring needed services to the people, linkages at all levels (networking, coordination, cooperation, collaboration) had to be attempted and implemented with other community organizations, service providers, businesses, universities, and political entities.

In short, this story told by one Hyde Park resident summarizes the sense of community and collaborative spirit necessary for effective interagency cooperation:

A man wanted to find out the difference between heaven and hell. St. Peter showed him two different rooms. In one room there were people sitting around a big round table with a pot of stew in the middle. Each person had a spoon with a *very* long handle; however, they were starving because they couldn't get the food to their mouths. They were sad and miserable. St. Peter said, "This is hell."

Then St. Peter took the man to the other room. It was the same situation—people sitting around a big table with a pot of stew in the center, each had a spoon with a *very* long handle. But all these people were happy and healthy because they were using their spoons to feed another person sitting on the other side of the table. St. Peter said, "This is heaven."

Chapter 17

Assessing Needs, Planning, and Evaluating

INTRODUCTION

Effective community problem-solving must also include needs assessments, strategic planning, and various methods of evaluation. When thinking about these factors, John Dewey's concept of decision-making using a scientific methods approach comes to mind. Dewey's steps in decision-making, found in his classic work *How We Think* (1933), call for:

(1) Stimulation to begin the process of thinking through experiencing a "felt need" for it (recognizing there is a problem)
(2) Location and clarification of the nature of the problem (assessing and analyzing the problem)
(3) Suggestions of possible solutions (identifying constraints and resources)
(4) Hypothesis formation, that is, development of a vehicle that can initiate and guide observation as well as the gathering of facts and ideas (may be the development of a planning guide)
(5) Mental elaboration, or reasoning to determine the consequences of the suggested hypothesis or solution
(6) Experimental corroboration of the hypothesis selected by overt or imaginative action (may be a pilot study)

Finally, there is the necessary element of evaluation in order to see if the problems are corrected or alleviated (Knezevich, 1984; Taylor, 1965).

ASSESSING NEEDS

When answering the questions, "Where are we now?" and "Where do we want to be?," one creates the initial motivation needed to implement necessary strategic planning efforts for successful programming. Answers to these questions also provide required information to service recipients and funding agencies. Finally, needs assessments facilitate needed actions to develop and maintain credible and useful programs (Knezevich, 1984).

All is for nought, however, if needs assessment procedures do not relate to the situation or are not legitimate. For instance, a potential source of funding may require grass-roots input concerning community needs. Discussions, focus groups, and/or surveys and questionnaires may be hurriedly and carelessly conducted, including input from only a few community members. The purpose is to fulfill grant writing requirements and not to assess needs. If the grant is awarded, it is likely that the grant writing institution will be the program's decision-maker and guide for program implementation processes rather than community members.

A long-time Hyde Park resident and business owner had this to say about needs assessment:

A lot of bureaucrats get so accustomed to doing these professional studies. I don't know of any better information you can get than from people who live here themselves. They [bureaucrats] tend not to want to do surveys. Usually these professional studies may ask one or two residents and that's it. Usually they go from what they see! Well there's a big difference between what somebody sees as the needs and what people who live there know what the needs are.

A former service provider in Hyde Park shared this opinion concerning needs assessment:

Surveys would help—door to door surveys would make a difference. Better follow through with families who come to the food pantries, who come to the Friedens program, who come to PTO. A lot of the problems are not identified or are identified superficially but are not addressed on a family by family basis.

During the 1993–94 year, information garnered from focus group sessions with parents, teachers, and Friedens Haus Advisory Board members (for purposes of this study) aided with assessing needs. Additionally, a student-volunteer from an area college (Business Administration and Urban Affairs) completed a needs assessment of area businesses concerning community involvement. Finally, gathering data concerning the needs of the Hyde Park community was an integral part of grant writing, which was an ongoing necessity for the Friedens Haus program. For example, the organization received a grant from the Health Care Forum by way of Deaconess Health Systems that required continuous health and safety needs assessments.

PLANNING

Along with the decision-making outline as delineated by John Dewey, there must also be the necessary "who does what, how, and when?" Winecoff and Powell (1977: 75) state that objectives are part of the action plan: "Objectives are simply action statements which make the goal much more specific and measurable." The authors list the following three steps needed to implement developed objectives: (1) Identify the tasks which must be completed in order to meet the objective; (2) decide on a person(s) responsible for the completion of each task; and (3) set a date by which the task should be completed (77).

This type of planning was implemented by the Friedens Haus program as well as the Hyde Park neighborhood. Besides the necessity of day to day, week to week, and month to month planning by the Friedens Haus Board of Directors and staff, a Long Range Planning subcommittee met on a regular basis. Also, Friedens Haus participated in the Hyde Park strategic planning efforts with the aid of the Neighborhood Stabilization Office (formerly Operation ConServ). The various proscribed categories of planning efforts were (1) housing, (2) marketing, (3) beautification, (4) safety, (5) education, and (6) recreation. The committees representing these categories met periodically to update results and planning efforts.

Several community organizations attempted to meet the various categorical objectives. The principal and staff of Clay School, the director and staff of Friedens Haus, Holy Trinity School staff, and Bethlehem Lutheran staff worked in the areas of education and recreation. The Housing Corporation and Hyde Park Alliance worked on some of the housing objectives. Hyde Park Alliance also made efforts in the areas of marketing and beautification as did Clay School and Friedens Haus. It must be noted that the Hyde Park Strategic Plan was recognized by the City of St. Louis as a model for St. Louis neighborhoods. Figure 17.1 gives an example of Hyde Park strategic planning efforts for the category of "Safety."

EVALUATING

Emil Posavac and Raymond Carey (1972: 11) write, "Human behavior is adaptive only when people obtain feedback from the environment. Program evaluation seeks to provide timely feed back in social systems." They go on to say that program evaluation provides direction and purpose so that organizations and institutions can change and determine why some changes are more important than others. Fenwick English and Roger Kaufman (1975: 60) recommend using needs assessment as part of evaluation. They write, "Needs assessment is a method for determining if the collective behavior of the institution is compatible with and producing the outcomes the community says it desires."

Finally, evaluations may be formative or summative. Formative evaluation necessitates constant observation and analyzing in order to improve programs

Figure 17.1
Hyde Park Neighborhood Operation ConServ Strategic Plan—Safety

MISSION: *Create and maintain a safe and secure environment for all residents.*

Goals and Objectives	Strategies and Tasks	Responsibilities	Constraints	Accomplishments
1. Create and maintain a group of informed residents and police who are proactive in reducing the number of crimes.				
Maintain and expand Safety Committee to coordinate various efforts in the neighborhood.	*1-A Create and sustain Safety Committee to increase participation, provide information and develop special programs to decrease crime and improve safety.*			
	Conduct ongoing monthly Safety Committee meetings.	CSO/SafeStreet/Police		Crime Prevention Committee now the Safety Committee-regular meetings are occurring.
	Review of monthly crime statistics and trends.	OSS/Police		
	Guest speaker/training	*SC/CSO/OSS*		
	Explore "walk around" as an alternative.	Mobile Patrol/Safety Committee		
	Involve area sergeant and officers in meetings.			
	Use neighborhood "Tele" (telephone) Bulletin Boards for safety issues (i.e., supplement to phone trees).	HPA/Safety Committee		

January 21, 1993

Source: Operation ConServ. (1992). *Hyde Park Neighborhood and Environs Urban Design and Strategic Plan.*

and practices. This type of evaluation was an integral part of the Friedens Haus coalition.

On the other hand, summative evaluations (the whole picture after the fact) require more forethought, planning, and administrative and clerical work. This type of evaluation was taking place in the Friedens Haus program although time, staffing, and financial constraints provided limitations in terms of thoroughness and accuracy. The grant from the Danforth Foundation for the purpose of needs assessment and evaluation (implemented by a university faculty consultant) and the contributions of university student research, assisted with these endeavors during the time period of 1993 through the 1994–95 year.

Also, research activities for the purpose of this study served as summative evaluations for the Friedens Haus program as well as the Hyde Park neighborhood. As previously explained, the use of triangulation in the study alleviated the problem of maintaining external and internal validity and reliability (Merriam, 1988). This type of analysis (participant-observation, direct response data, and document examination) was used to discover the various community education components present or not present in the Hyde Park community problem-solving process and to what degree these components were present. For instance, integration of the K-12 program with the community was evaluated through a multi-methods approach: (1) collection of quantitative data in terms of test scores and report card grades of those students participating in the after school activities, summer programs, and other activities offered by the community through its collaborative efforts; (2) collection of qualitative direct response data through focus group sessions and interviews involving parents and school staff in terms of activity and program effectiveness; and (3) participant observation and documentation of parent and community involvement with the K-12 program and the use of community resources in terms of people, facilities, and services.

FRIEDENS HAUS PROGRAM EVALUATION

The Energizing Youth Employment (EYE) program was evaluated during the 1993–94 year by a student volunteer from an area college via interviews and observation. She writes:

Youth who participated in the 1993 EYE program were exposed to various work environments. All jobs were in the service industry, and the majority of the participants had dealings with the public. The majority of the youth reported the most important skills learned were accountability, cooperating with others, organizing, patience, and responsibility. Some were exposed to office situations where they learned to file, answer the phone properly, and learned other office communication skills. Those participating in the Day Camp Program were exposed to teamwork and supervisory situations.

It was also learned that 100 percent of EYE participants remained in school and/or continued with their education after high school graduation. (The high school drop-out rate for St. Louis is approaching 50%).

Additional evaluation data were obtained during the 1993–94 year by three focus group sessions with Clay teachers, parents, and Friedens Haus Advisory Board members for purposes of this study. A report was made to the Friedens Haus Board of Directors. The results were used as a basis for restructuring the Board of Directors to be comprised of a majority of Hyde Park residents (as opposed to service providers) and for additional operational changes.

The Advisory Board Focus Group Session

This session was comprised of twenty-three participants of eight residents and fifteen service providers divided into three groups. Results indicated that respondent perceptions were very positive concerning the Friedens Haus program and Advisory Board. The greatest achievements were seen to be in terms of collaboration, diversity, team work, action, linkages to resources, a close partnership between school and community, meeting needs, inclusiveness, acceptance by the community, and dedication to children. One participant expressed it this way, "If anything gets done in the neighborhood, somehow it has to have a connection with Friedens Haus, because that's where ideas are exchanged and that's where resources are matched up to needs. . . . It seems like all the roads lead to Friedens Haus!"

One service provider offered the following description of the program:

A collaboration of real services and experiences in order to raise the community so it can help itself, so it will stabilize, so its residents can learn, so the community becomes organized, and so it can work towards a community vision. It takes a whole village to raise a child but the village needs to be raised before you can raise the child!

Another described it as "the way things need to go . . . it makes a real difference." Still another described it as the best example in the St. Louis area that fills the void caused by dysfunctional families: "This is hope for our city and hope for our society—this is very important work that we're doing here!"

Hyde Park residents offered this description of the Friedens Haus collaboration: A worthwhile program that is central to our lives, continues our education, and offers a safe environment. It is a program that revolves around love and wants to see the community built up to where it used to be. It is a teaching place, including social skills, and a fun place for community members, especially for children.

Comments from several participants in all three groups indicated that the collaboration between Clay School and Friedens Haus was very unusual. One participant described the relationship as a partnership and constant communication and exchange of resources and ideas: "They feed on each other. It is a very unusual situation . . . we don't see this very often." Another described the partnership this way, "You can't really distinguish where Friedens stops and Clay begins and then some. . . . I felt the school's presence in the community—it's catching—it rubs off!" Another described it as an example of a successful collaboration: "It works as a team—a very open relationship."

The most prevalent blockage to even greater achievements and benefits of the board and Friedens Haus coalition centered around inadequate funding and the required time and effort that was devoted to fund-raising. Another blockage mentioned by several participants was "bureaucracy" in terms of red tape and "political nonsense" from the city and public school system: "We just take the risks and do it!" Finally, it was the general perception that the majority of the work was done by a few people and that more volunteers and local resident participation were needed.

Although the board was addressing these issues, one blockage mentioned over and over needed additional and immediate attention. This blockage was the apparent shifting of the board's focus from community empowerment to attracting outside agencies to help with resources and meeting needs. Some felt that this may have been one reason for low levels of citizen participation.

One service provider expressed feeling a necessity to juggle "listening carefully to resident needs and getting things done locally" with "bringing in outside agencies to meet those needs." Another expressed this dilemma more bluntly and to the point: "If you just turned it over to people from the community, you wouldn't have the organization, you wouldn't have the structure, you wouldn't be able to train people to take over—it would be nice for the community to run this whole thing but before that can happen, the community needs to be healthy!" Another mentioned the time that it takes to educate local residents to be able to take care of all their own needs.

Although realizing that the connection to outside agencies for needed resources was "vital," the opinion of other service providers and a majority of community residents was different concerning the citizen empowerment issue. As one resident stated,

Maybe what actually appears to be is not true . . . maybe the people have not been able to show how intelligent and experienced they are in certain aspects—(their actions come from the heart). The residents now take a sit-back attitude. . . . Empower the people to help themselves instead of serving or directing them!

One service provider agreed when expressing his perception by indicating that the board needed to "strengthen the *community* part of the board which was its heart when it started, and you want to make sure that heart doesn't need triple bypass surgery at some point!" One local resident and parent expressed it this way, "If you don't feel like you're important, there is no sense of being there!"

Service providers and community residents made suggestions to remedy this problem. Restructuring the board was mentioned in two groups: "Even though the involvement of outside agencies is good, I think it has ended up creating a perception of intimidation to the local resident. . . . It is a structural problem that we have to overcome in the future." One participant foresaw that there may have to be several kinds of boards serving various functions such as providing resources, direction, advice, speaking for the community, and so on.

Other suggestions for improvement centered around making changes in meeting procedures. They included sending the agenda to members and community residents before the meeting, individual invitations and personal contact, greeting residents at the meetings and making them feel welcome, provision of a facilitator to make sure all views were heard, meetings that followed a consensus model of decision-making to ensure equal participation, and even a suggestion box for residents to voice their opinions if they did not feel comfortable doing so before board members.

Participants envisioned the future role of the Friedens Haus coalition as strengthening already existing programs and adding programs when additional needs arose. In short, they saw the program helping to stabilize the community through addressing concerns of safety, housing, jobs, economic development, education, health, social needs, and individual and family needs. They felt that added programs would depend on added funding and staff, the possibility of Clay becoming a community education center, and working cooperatively with other community organizations: "We can't take on all the things!" Some of the specific additional needs mentioned were programs for young males, the need for black male role models, GED classes and other adult education, and a latchkey program.

It was the general feeling of participants, especially community residents, that parents and community members should have a say concerning school policies, curriculum, and instruction. Service providers and community residents saw themselves as helping and enhancing the school in these areas. One participant described the present involvement in these areas as, "I think what we're already doing is embarrassing the establishment into coming around to our way of thinking. . . . We're already doing things at Clay School that are comparatively better than the community schools!" Finally, one participant envisioned Clay School becoming so good that people would be attracted to Hyde Park or want to stay in the neighborhood because they wanted their kids to go to Clay: "It's not a 'pie-in-the-sky' sort of thing—I think it's vision!"

The Teacher Focus Group Session

This session was comprised of seven participants. I was not expecting the overwhelming positive perceptions of the Friedens Haus program. As one participant expressed it after significant probing, "I can't think of anything negative—if I could, I would tell you!" The teachers only mentioned negative perceptions of the program in terms of blockages such as not enough staff and funding. The findings, however, had to be analyzed in the context of limited and only peripheral knowledge of the Friedens program on the part of participants.

This was one area of concern that the Friedens Haus Board of Directors and Clay School administrative staff have since addressed.

The many positive perceptions of the Friedens Haus coalition centered around the "high touch" quality of the program: "The one-to-one ratio helps students to deal with problems at home and school. Many of the children need some counseling." And, "There is a sincere effort to reach out and touch." Specific positive impacts had to do with home visits, help with personal physical needs, counseling for students and parents, connecting families with resources, improved student academic achievement and social/emotional growth through the tutoring and mentoring programs, personalized contracts to improve student achievement in all areas, personalized invitations to club events, and the visibility and "real caring" of the Friedens Haus staff. All of this was perceived to be done through cooperation rather than interference with the duties of teachers.

Teachers viewed the immediate community surrounding Clay as "resource rich." They wanted to see local business establishments become more involved with students as far as furnishing learning experiences and on-site visits: "Local business establishments should take more interest in the students here—they are *in* the community but not *part* of the community." Another specific concern was the small number of black male role models: "I would like to see more black male volunteers so they can help young black males on their way to manhood in a more positive way."

Overall, teachers expressed very broad views of education to include using the community as a classroom, addressing social needs of families, stabilizing the community, sharing materials and facilities with the community, and involving parent and community members in educational decision-making. The teachers expressed welcoming responsible involvement of parents and community members in curriculum development and school policy-making as well as other less decision-making contributions. They viewed this involvement as enhancing public relations, a help to the nonomnipresent teacher, an encouragement of more parental and citizen commitment to the school, and an educational opportunity for all involved.

Teachers envisioned the Friedens Haus and Clay School partnership reaching out even more in order to stabilize the community. They foresaw the program addressing housing, physical environmental rehabilitation, involving other schools and the business community, and even becoming involved with making use of federal and city grant monies. In short, teachers saw the program expanding to meet the needs of all community residents even to the point of being able to "help stop a lot of the violence in the community." One participant related, "When I attended the last Advisory Board meeting, I learned that the board is trying to build the community up and encourage people to come back to the city."

Although most of the participants cited "lack of time and other commitments" as reasons for not personally participating, they generally perceived the Friedens Haus coalition as a support system between the school and home. Overall, they desired even closer and more meaningful partnerships among school, home, and community in the context of "education" defined in its broadest terms.

The Parent Focus Group Session

This session was comprised of six participants. The respondents in the parent focus group were more knowledgeable about the Friedens Haus coalition than those in the teacher focus group. The overwhelming positive perceptions of the program ("There should be more places like this!") were comparable to teacher perceptions except for the way in which some teachers were perceived. These perceptions centered around poor attitudes toward parents, many teachers not wanting parents in the classroom, and one annotated instance of physical abuse. Parents expressed a desire for more participation in the classroom and decision-making responsibilities in terms of curriculum and school policy ("We should have a say!") They viewed their responsibilities as helping their children, the school, the teachers, the Friedens Haus program, and themselves.

The many positive perceptions of the Friedens Haus coalition focused on safety for their children ("When we send our children here we know they're safe, and that's a lot of relief!"); a genuine caring expressed by the Friedens staff for their children and themselves; and opportunities for fun, learning, and meaningful activity for all involved. As one parent stated, "The director helped me to be up to date with my bills, helped me to get in Section 8 housing, furnishes transportation—she is there for me and my child. The school principal has also been here for me when I ran out of money at the end of the month."

The principal factors that prohibited even more benefit from the program was headed by concern for personal safety in the neighborhood in terms of fear and problems of drug sales, gang activity, and harassment from kids on the street. Decent affordable housing and transportation were next on the list of blockages to increased program effectiveness. One parent expressed it this way, "My gas bill for one month was $818 and I pay $250 a month rent! I need relocation help!" Additionally, uncaring parents, parents who used the program as a babysitting service, and low levels of parent and community participation were seen as inhibitors. Finally, participants felt that the community needed to be better organized and function as one neighborhood instead of being factionalized.

Participants foresaw the Friedens Haus coalition growing even stronger. They anticipated that many of the children would turn out to be successful citizens (due in large part to the program) who would be able to "give back" to the community in the future. Like the teachers, the parents visualized the program doing even more to stabilize the neighborhood through additional assistance with housing, job training, day care, and adult educational opportunities, especially if Clay became a "community school." In short, because of the myriad problems of low incomes, safety, and transportation, parents desired the program to assist in bringing needed services to community residents.

Results from the Quantitative Part of the Study

Quantitative results indicated that a significant number of Clay students participating in the Friedens Haus program improved their basic skill report card grades from the first quarter to the last quarter during the year of program enrollment. Teachers interviewed revealed that usually basic skill report card grades remained the same or declined over the course of a school year unless there was some outside intervention such as tutoring. Also, the following data concerning Stanford Achievement Test (SAT) scores, student attendance, and discipline referrals provide some indication of the Friedens Haus program's positive impacts on Clay students in tandem with other variables such as teacher changeover, the addition of an instructional coordinator and a teacher's aid who focused on school attendance, some changes in instructional methods, and the Professional Development School partnership with Washington University.

Time-pd.	Event	% Att.	SAT %ile	Disc. Ref.
1989–90	Clay/FH partnership formed	87.5	31.73	51
	Use of Friedens UCC facilities			
	Church buys drug-free signs			
1990–91	Advisory Board forms	89.6	37.56	28
	Soc. wkr. hired through UCNH			
	After sch. tut./grth. dev. grps.			
	1st PTO/commun. Thksgvg. dnr.			
1991–92	Parent groups	89.1	33.56	26
	Summer Day Camp			
	Art Club with Holy Trinity			
	Saturday tutoring			
	Middle school linkage			
	Mallinckrodt science lab			
	Add. soc. wkr. (UW grant)			
1992–93	HPA involvement	89.4	36.25	9
	EYE program			
	Deaconess involvement			
	Teen program			
	SHARP program			
	Grp. wrkr. (UMSL/CSAP grant)			
	Clay Inst. Crd. hired via grant			
	Clay act. resch. & whl. lng. inst.			
	Mentoring program			

Time-pd.	Event	% Att.	SAT %ile	Disc. Ref.
1993–94	Vol. from Belgium	93.2	38.1	21
	Tchr. Aid (attend.)			
	International Club			
	Community nurse			
1994–95	WU collab. (PDS)	95.6	49.11	16
	Conflict res. prog.			
	Science Club			

Clay student attendance (yearly percentage increase) was either the highest or within the top three listed for 1993 through 1995 (SLPSS). Since 1990 St. Louis "integrated" schools experienced a decrease of 1 percent in student attendance, "magnet" and "nonintegrated" schools experienced an increase of 1 percent, while Clay experienced an increase of 6 percent. *Clay SAT scores* rose by 43 percent from 1990 to 1995 and 29 percent from 1994 to 1995, whereas there was a 14 percent increase city-wide for the same time period (1994–95). The average *National Cumulative Evaluation points* (NCEs) city-wide for 1995 was 45.6—for Clay School the average was 49.11. *Discipline referrals* were significantly lower for Clay than the average of a sample comprised of those from magnet, nonintegrated, and integrated elementary schools—900 percent and 800 percent lower during 1994 and 1995 respectively.

Although these data are correlational with Friedens Haus interventions and do not show cause and effect, the overall positive transitions indicate that multiple factors are coming together to impact student achievement, attendance, and social and emotional growth. The Friedens Haus coalition played a major role in coordinating these efforts.

Other Evaluations

Additional evaluations included those conducted by the University of Missouri-St. Louis (Departments of Sociology and Social Work) of the drug prevention, cultural awareness, and self-esteem enhancement curriculum that was initiated by the university for research purposes. Results indicated little or no difference between the control and noncontrol groups; however, areas were targeted for curriculum improvement.

The outside evaluation conducted by a consultant via a Danforth grant focused on the structure of the Friedens Haus coalition. Results indicated that lack of administrative structure was the major weakness of the organization. It was recommended that administrative functions be separated from programmatic functions so that the Friedens Haus program, which was deemed to be very effective, would not stagnate. Evaluation results were evidence to the Danforth Foundation that additional funding was needed to provide administrative personnel.

Finally, the most noticeable indications of program effectiveness were the recognitions and awards the Friedens Haus coalition received. Clay Elementary won the National Drug-Free Schools and Communities Award in 1992, the Friedens Haus coalition was honored by a resolution from the Missouri House of Representatives (1993), and Clay received the federally recognized Gold Star School award in 1996.

HYDE PARK ALLIANCE EVALUATIONS

The former HPA director gave this analysis of needs assessment, planning, and evaluations taking place within this organization:

Well, we don't have results oriented abilities because we're so limited in resources. What I hear from people is that Hyde Park is really on the move, it's really doing things good, it's got some good community leaders, and it's tried some things that other neighborhoods haven't tried. On the north side, that's a plus.

If you had all the resources you wanted?

If we had the resources in place, what we would have are the programs in place, and what we would have with programs in place is a sense of who's taking the programs and how accurate and capable these program participants feel about having the program. That's obvious—we would have feedback. Any of the grants we have, we're asked to do formal evaluations anyway to get the money really accountable. In my opinion, we have formal just by virtue of success of the people who participate, and we follow them from the time they participated until they elected to stop participating.

SUMMARY

The problem-solving efforts of the Hyde Park neighborhood involved community organization (evidenced by its pluralistic power structure), assessing needs, planning, evaluating, and interagency cooperation. The neighborhood problems of housing and economic development required all of these problem-solving approaches that were taking place to a greater degree than in the former St. Louis community education program as survey, interview, and focus group results indicated (Community School Review Panel Report, 1993). As Minzey and LeTarte (1994) assert, very few community education programs have advanced beyond the adult programming plateau to include interagency cooperation and problem-solving/decision-making by community members.

Teacher, parent, and Friedens Haus advisory board focus group results indicated an overwhelming positive perception of the Friedens Haus program as meeting needs, exhibiting "real caring," being a safe haven for community residents, and collaborating with other agencies and organizations in order to garner resources for the community. Expressed problems concerned inadequate staffing and funding and a desire to maintain control among community residents so that there was an increased sense of ownership. Residents expressed a desire to contribute rather than being served by outside resources and service providers. There was concern that the organization was moving away from its purpose by being overly concerned with providing needed resources rather than developing leadership among Hyde Park residents to assume control in terms of ownership of their problems as well as solutions to these problems.

Nevertheless, compared to the pre-restructured St. Louis community education program, the Friedens Haus coalition exhibited superior needs assessment, planning, and evaluation efforts. This was due, in part, to grant-giving requirements and the efforts of university students performing practicums or completing research in the organization and/or community. However, as the organization expanded, there was a need for formal needs assessment, planning, and evaluation procedures to guide and ensure improvement along with growth. As stated in a Danforth Foundation grant proposal, "The rapid growth of Friedens Haus has made it difficult to pause and objectively reflect on our past and our future. Such an evaluation would be invaluable in identifying current strengths as well as areas of weakness in need of change." Evaluation results provided rationale to outside agencies for additional funding, spurred the restructuring of the Friedens Haus Board of Directors to include a majority of residents, improved communication between Clay School and Friedens Haus staff concerning Friedens Haus services and parent involvement in the classrooms, and emphasized the need for improved administrative functions.

Conversely, Hyde Park Alliance lacked evaluations and needs assessments because of needed resources, but then may have lacked adequate resources because of the lack of evaluations and needs assessments! Interview results indicated that this organization operated on the basis of "feel." As explained in the chapter entitled "Citizen Advisory Councils," this basis for evaluation and needs assessment proved to be unsuccessful. Large groups of community people were "left out," needs were not being met, and there were few programmatic successes. Perhaps with new direction and additional community participation, needs would be expressed, planning would be cooperatively and inclusively completed, programs would be implemented, and worthwhile evaluations would take place. These were a few of the structural and organizational elements found to be missing, elements that are essential for becoming a functional and viable neighborhood organization—accountable to the people.

In summation, the words of the former mayor of St. Louis express the necessity of community empowerment as well as comprehensive and cooperative efforts to solve inner-city neighborhood problems (Friedens Anniversary Celebration—November 3, 1993):

You are the fiber, fabric, and foundation of the city. All of us must become involved—there is a good example of racial interaction here today. We have to drive on *all* cylinders running to address all the problems.

Economics, crime, education, and health are all tied together. There is good health care in St. Louis if you can afford it. It's one of the worst cities to be sick in if you can't. The infant mortality rate in St. Louis is the same as in Sri Lanka and we have 5,000 doctors from the River to Skinker.

Friedens Haus has the concept of a comprehensive approach to all of these problems. We need to treat the problems on the front end. Education and crime go hand in hand—you can't talk about one without the other. It is not the big man who is able to solve these problems—it's people like you.

Chapter 18

Lifelong Learning

INTRODUCTION

The philosophy of community education embraces the theory of andragogy (Knowles, 1975) in that community education is about lifelong learning, self-directedness, and acknowledgment of individual life experiences. Additionally, community education is about community empowerment. Community empowerment thrives on the ideas of respecting all persons, and that the best learning takes place when there is a need to know, when learning is problem-centered, and when students of any age are internally rather than externally motivated.

This chapter will discuss the factors in Hyde Park that effected lifelong learning possibilities for neighborhood residents. These factors are the public school (Clay Elementary), the relationship between the school and community, parent involvement with the school and volunteerism, Clay as a Professional Development School, links between education and social work, the use of community resources and the community as a classroom, accessibility to services and facilities, and available and needed programs for Hyde Park residents.

CLAY ELEMENTARY SCHOOL

Youth involved in Friedens Haus' Energizing Youth for Employment (EYE) program and working in the Hyde Park Alliance office (summer, 1993) created and published a brochure about the Hyde Park neighborhood. Following is their narrative about Clay School's history:

Built before 1866 [established in 1859], Clay School was the first public school in St. Louis. The original Clay School was located on the corner of 14th and Farrar, opposite the present location of Clay School. William T. Harris, superintendent of Clay School, introduced educational theories which had a nationwide impact on the school system. Harris became superintendent of the St. Louis Public School system in 1868. His goal was the education and assimilation of immigrant students. Its purpose was teaching the children in their native language.

The school was named after the statesman, Henry Clay, and the language taught during Harris' tenure was German in hopes of persuading neighborhood Germans to support the school. William Harris later went on to serve as United States Commissioner of Education. Clay School now faces Interstate 70 and is easily identifiable by the white columns and its location next to the historical Divoll Library (owned by the St. Louis Public Schools and serving as a library service center).

Because of a desegregation Court mandate, all St. Louis Public schools were to be renovated. Clay Elementary was renovated in 1992, and a multi-purpose room/gymnasium and classrooms were added. In addition, a vacated truck repair lot adjacent to the north end of the school was purchased by the St. Louis Public School System (SLPSS) for gardening, science experiments, an additional play area, and an amphitheater. The gardening project had been ongoing for approximately one year, while the playground, soccer field, amphitheater, and gazebo were recently completed (July 1995) via a grant (made possible through the neighborhood organization) and by volunteer services of the Assembly of God Church. Clay teachers, students, the principal, and Friedens Haus staff also contributed many "roll-up-the-sleeves" and "let's-get-the-job-done" efforts. Seen from Interstate 70, the project is a testament and celebration of cooperative efforts by multiple neighborhood and outside organizations.

At the time of my study, Clay Elementary housed approximately 450 preschool through fifth grade students and fifty staff. The staff included seven special education teachers with one aide and four basic skills teachers with two aides. The student to teacher ratio averaged twenty-six to one; however, some classrooms comprised over thirty students.

Of the SLPSS's three school classifications (magnet, nonintegrated, and integrated), Clay was considered an integrated school even though the student population was 87 percent black. Children either walked to school or took public transportation from an adjacent neighborhood (Old North St. Louis). Conversely, Holy Trinity School just four blocks from Clay housed a 40 percent black and 60 percent white student population. Ninety-eight percent of Clay students were eligible for free and reduced-price lunches.

Student mobility was a constant challenge. During the first part of the 1993–94 school year, there were 176 students out of 430 transferred in and out of Clay from one and a half weeks after the beginning of the school year until December 9, representing 40 percent of the student population. Sixty percent of the student population transferred out during the 1992–93 school year. In one kindergarten there were ten original students left out of thirty-five enrolled throughout the school year as of May 1994. Due in part to this high mobility, the aforementioned social, economic, and health statistics for the Clay School area, and several additional factors beyond as well as within the school's control, many SAT scores of Clay Elementary students could be described as dismal. The majority were below the fiftieth percentile, and far too many were in single-digit percentiles.

Also, the social and emotional growth of Clay students proved to be a challenge for Clay and Friedens Haus staff. As the principal related,

One of our aldermen was a mentor, and he took his "mentee" and some of his friends out for pizza. He left a tip and found out that some of the boys took it off the table. He [the alderman] was ready to quit the program! I told him that this is what we deal with, and that's why the mentoring program is needed!

Let me give you an example of something that happened yesterday that I'm so proud of. A fifth grade boy—a tough kid—has some older brothers who are just really "bad" kids—one of our former students wanted to start a fight with him out here on the sidewalk. I walked over towards them, and they kept on moving up the street.

A whole gang of kids got around him and these two older brothers are there with them, and they're egging him on to "kick his ass, _____!" So I followed them up the street, and I finally said, "_____, walk away from it! You don't need to do this!" The brothers were saying, "Kick his ass, _____!" right when I was saying that. _____ looks at me and says, "Mr. _____, I'm not going to do anything." I said, "That's good enough for me," and I left. They went up, and they went around the corner.

_____ came in this morning and I asked him if he fought that kid. He said, "No, Mr. _____, I didn't do it." This is making a difference! This is one of the kids that plays football with us in the morning—big kid—tough kid—and he did it himself! I'm really proud of that kid for that!

THE SCHOOL'S PARTNERSHIP WITH THE COMMUNITY

Because Clay School is classified as an integrated school within the SLPSS and receives fewer desegregation funds and services than magnet and nonintegrated schools, the principal continuously sought needed resources outside the school system. He expressed it this way: "If you don't have the resources, you are forced to go elsewhere!" Additionally, the Parents as Teachers Program, highly regarded nationally as a Missouri initiative and very well implemented in many St. Louis county school districts, did not seem to be working in the St. Louis Public School System, at least for Clay School. The program involves educators making home visits in order to work with parents, encouraging them, and demonstrating how to teach their children in preparation for K-12 schooling. When asked about this program, the Clay School principal related, "We have it in the district but not at our school. They come out once in a while with the preschool kids and may do some workshops—five or six a year. Sometimes they bring several schools together [preschools] and have a program. Our preschool people make home visits, but I don't see the Parents as Teachers

Program doing much here."

Several agencies in and around the Hyde Park neighborhood became involved with Clay Elementary due in large part to the efforts of the principal and the Friedens Haus Advisory Board and staff. For example, until the 1994–95 school year, the U.S. Marshalls adopted Clay School and sponsored an annual fund-raising softball game.   During the 1993–94 school year the organization donated a substantial amount of money "to get the school year off to a good start." Friedens United Church of Christ and Friedens Haus Advisory Board members made additional gifts.

Mallinckrodt Chemical, located on the outskirts of Hyde Park, funded a fully equipped science lab housed in Clay, and volunteers from the corporation provided needed expertise to the science and classroom teachers. The teacher selected to become the science lab instructor during the 1995–96 year became very excited about the possibilities for Clay students and, consequently, spent a good part of the summer planning and writing a grant proposal for further funding. Her first attempt at grant writing was awarded by a $5,000 grant for field trips and other enriching experiences for Clay students. Impressed by her initiatives, the university involved with Clay as a Professional Development School provided funding for her and a colleague to enroll in a science course.

As previously described, Clay School's partnership with Friedens Haus provided a valuable community resource for students and staff. Connections to outside service agencies were substantial. As the principal expressed, "Friedens Haus is the best thing that's happened to Clay School since I've been here in nine years." Following is one teacher's view of Friedens Haus support, especially concerning students considered to be "at risk" (as presented at an educator's conference):

This is my first year of teaching. I currently am fortunate to have only twenty-one students. Seven of my students don't have phones. I do have emergency numbers, but am still unable to make direct contact when I use those numbers. When I have used the phone numbers of the other students, it's common to find that they have been disconnected.

Another problem I have had is low attendance. Often my kids return and tell me that they weren't absent because of illness They just didn't come. They don't see it as a big deal and, apparently, their parents don't either. Other times, there are specific reasons; for example, they didn't have clean or dry clothes to wear or a sibling was sick (or suspended), and mom didn't send *any* of the kids to school.

One student was causing major problems in my classroom. Since I was unable to contact the mother, I turned to the Friedens Haus director for assistance. She was able to give me some information on the home life of the family that definitely shed some light on the behaviors I was seeing. She also made contact with the mother by going to her house. Due to the extreme nature of this student's and her sister's problems, a counselor also works with each of them once a week at Friedens Haus. There has been a definite improvement in my student's attitude, behavior, performance and attendance since Christmas.

The Friedens Haus director also would see another one of my students running the streets during school hours, and she asked him why he wasn't at school. His reason was almost always that he didn't have any clean clothes to wear. The director would take him home and ask his mom for permission to give him clothes and get him to school. Mom always said it was "okay."

Another instance is when a new student enrolled in my classroom in the Spring. She was eight years old and had never, ever been to school. I learned that the mother had had problems and was finally being forced by the State to enroll her child. I quickly discovered that the student didn't know her last name, her alphabet, how to count, and did not seem as if she had ever written before.

The Friedens Haus director wanted to meet this student and her mother. The mother seemed receptive to this idea and allowed the director to pick them up and bring them to Friedens Haus for an initial tutoring session.

If I had not had the Friedens Haus program as a resource, my school year would have been a lot different. It would have been very difficult to help the students who really needed it. I should have gotten more of my kids involved in Friedens Haus, especially those with unstable home situations.

PARENT INVOLVEMENT AND VOLUNTEERISM

Many parents of children who are similar to the "at risk" students previously described by the Clay School teacher feel *estranged* from their child's school. Unfortunately, too many educators treat parents condescendingly or are leery of their involvement in the school instead of viewing parents as informed participants. For example, Litwak and Meyer (1974) recommend opening school systems to a smaller or larger degree depending on the type of community (balance theory). They maintain that a rational systems approach (a more closed systems approach) may be appropriate for some community situations. In my view, the balance theory smacks of parent and community manipulation, alienation of the same, and a "better than thou" aura surrounding the school. An open systems model of schooling that is inclusive of all parents desiring to become involved with the school and their children's education is consistent with the community education philosophy. The amount of parent involvement would vary according to parental desires, available time, and abilities.

William Wyson and colleagues (1988) provide a parent-school involvement model that depicts hierarchical levels of involvement:

- Observer level—choral concerts, school plays
- Interface level—parent conferences, phone calls, open houses, surveys
- Program level—troop leaders, program newsletters, school committees, PTO members
- Clerical level—parent office volunteers

- Instructional level—parent teacher aide, parent teaching own child
- Advisory level—parent advisory boards, PTO executive boards
- Administrative level—former practice in Chicago (community involved in hiring and firing principals, etc.)

The level of parent involvement with Clay Elementary during the time of my study was determined to be at the clerical level and somewhat at the instructional and advisory levels. Parents assisted in the school office and also in the library so that students could check out books every week (the school was assigned a part-time librarian who came to the school once a week). Parents were also involved with instruction in some classrooms. Primary grade teachers rather than intermediate grade teachers seemed to encourage this type of participation. Finally, PTO parent members served at the advisory level (office holders) and were substantially involved with special activity and fund-raising efforts.

For example, parents were responsible for the annual fund-raising Family Day carnival. They involved the teachers and arranged for carnival rides and games for the families of Clay children and the neighborhood. Finally, Clay School ranked either at the top or next to the top in terms of SLPSS parent volunteer hours for the years 1991 through 1994.

One parent and Hyde Park resident described parent involvement with Clay School:

Invitations from Clay School for parent involvement is great. The principal asks all parents to be involved, and all parents are welcome into the building. The parents can go into the school at any time and talk to the teachers—I've always liked that. Clay School is a place you can feel at home. The principal has been there for several years and that adds stability and some experience. Also, you can see the growth in the school, and you can at least attribute it to one person and to stability. It's a very open environment—the teachers have all been welcoming to me. I have a lot of great things to say about Clay School.

Why you might *not* get parental involvement is another thing. The principal explained to me that a lot of adults are not comfortable in an educational setting because of their experiences when they were going to school. That never dawned on me before, because all my school experiences have been good. That's your key right there—to make the school environment nonintimidating.

The principal related that some parents learned to read by sitting in some of the classrooms:

I would say four or five that I know of that were involved with the school as volunteers and PTO—people who were virtually illiterate have sat in on classes [to learn]. The beauty of this is that these people have sat in and have gotten involved in the school. They've either gotten GEDs and have gone on to bigger and better things—to get jobs for themselves—and they leave the school. It's almost like they've had success here working on projects. They take on these projects and they get satisfaction and success with them, and it's almost as if it carries over.

The principal desired to have parent and community involvement at the advisory level, believing this would happen when Clay Elementary became a "community center" within the SLPSS. He believed in bottom-up management and operating in an open-systems theoretical model. He also expressed a belief in parent and community groups having a say in school decisions concerning curriculum and policy-making.

Conversely, the problem of uncaring parents was mentioned by teachers, parents, and the school principal as an inhibiting factor to Friedens Haus program and schooling effectiveness. Parent participants in a focus group session lamented the fact that several parents used the Friedens Haus program as a babysitting service and that there was a need for increased parent participation. The teachers expressed welcoming *responsible* involvement of parents and the need for parental support in terms of science projects and homework assignments. One teacher shared that teachers have to "deal with too many parents who are alcoholic, drug dependent, irrational, abusive to their children, who curse, and have psychological problems."

One parent volunteer, who maintained a daily presence in the school, related that a parent came to school with a knife and threatened a student. She cited four or five incidents of parents using obscene language during the 1993–94 school year. One parent was arrested after robbing a local business owner at knife-point. The principal described the problem this way,

The teachers really have some significant problems with the behavior, with the discipline of [some of] these kids. These are the parents who don't show up for PTO meetings, who don't come to open houses, who don't work in any of our programs and committees—you never see them. And when you *do* send some kind of a disciplinary referral for them to come to the school, they're the first ones who will come in and rant and rave and tell you how bad the teachers are. We refer these kids to the Friedens Haus staff and they actually go out and make home visits.

One mother has come up and made a complete fool of herself at times. She's "gone off" on people and threatened to beat up teachers, and was just an obnoxious person. She really didn't care about her kids; she was more concerned that teachers were talking about her children's behavior than the behavior itself, and she would be on the defensive and just scream and holler. The kids now are involved in the Friedens Haus program. The director interacts with the mother all the time.

One lady came in here and she was controversial for a while, but I saw some really good in her. She has been through a lot in her life—lost some of her brothers to very violent kinds of acts. She uses the school now as therapy for her, for her family.

I'm trying to get her involved positively. She's doing a lot of neat things right now—as a matter of fact, every morning she plays football with the kids and she's one of the quarterbacks—I'm the other. She works in the cafeteria—she does the breakfast program, and about 7:45 she goes to the yard and we play football. We have a little competition there—her team against my team, and she thoroughly loves it!

Do you think teacher attitudes need to be changed as far as welcoming parents?

Yeah, to a certain extent, I believe that, yeah. A majority of our teachers work very well with our parents. I think there are some that are uncomfortable with parents. But let me say this—those teachers who are really sure about what they're doing—I mean, they're confident in themselves and their work and what they can do—normally those teachers enjoy having parents come in and getting involved.

In addition to parents, there were numerous volunteer hours expended by community members, college students and other outside participants in the Friedens Haus/Clay School partnership, especially through the mentoring and tutoring programs. During the 1993–94 year, a volunteer (CPA) from Belgium, who wanted to improve his English speaking skills, facilitated an "International Club" where Clay students learned the French language and about European culture. The program was deemed to be so beneficial that it was continued after the volunteer returned to Belgium. The International Club provided a program for "higher achievers" and thus diminished the possible stigma of Friedens Haus becoming a program for only low achieving and behaviorally difficult students.

In short, there were approximately 2,000 volunteer hours in direct program involvement during the 1993–94 year. As the principal expressed, "We're in it for the community. . . . We know the kids will change if we make a difference in the community."

SOCIAL WORK AND EDUCATION LINKAGES:
CLAY'S PROFESSIONAL DEVELOPMENT SCHOOL PARTNERSHIP

Teachers who *should* become familiar with the community from which their students come each morning and to which they must return each evening, can be assisted by social work services. This became a reality at Clay School via the social work services provided by Friedens Haus. (The SLPSS provided a social worker housed only part time in Clay.) The social workers at Friedens Haus made connections to families of Clay students; visited students' homes; made referrals; facilitated parent discussion groups; and developed structured educational, social, and recreational activities for Clay children. Most of Friedens Haus staff-time was spent at Clay School working directly with students and teachers.

In an urban setting similar to the Hyde Park neighborhood, social work contributions are essential. The home visitations, family and individual counseling, group work, and connection and individual guidance to and through the labyrinth of governmental and agency services proved to be invaluable for the improvement of Clay School student achievement and quality of life.

But even if school districts embrace outside assistance such as those provided by social work agencies and base their practices on a community education philosophy (viewing the school inseparable with its surrounding community), teachers and school administrators can serve as barriers to desired results if they are not exposed to a broader view of education. There may be turf battles and limited cooperation when it comes to sharing materials, supplies, and building use with community members and service providers. Also, there may be limited volunteerism, outreach to the community, and value of community resources, including those provided by social work agencies. Teachers and administrators attuned to the community education philosophy are better prepared to teach, reach, and value students from all types of backgrounds; maintain a broad range of knowledge; avail themselves to multiple resources; and serve as positive agents for school district public relations. In this venue, increased support, participation, and volunteerism may be garnered for the schools. Inclusion of the community education philosophy, process, and practice in teacher education courses would seem to be essential.

Supporting this view, the Holmes Group (1990) outlines many elements of the community education philosophy in *Tomorrow's Schools*: "Schools need to become organizers of community effort—to discover new ways of working with parents and community and government agencies responding to the needs of children" (32). The group goes on to say, "The school may be called upon to perform a number of tasks—child care, health screening, etc.—as conditions of families and the community change" (93).

In order to connect theory to practice, the Holmes Group advocates Professional Development Schools as "teaching" schools for college/university education students much as "teaching" hospitals are used for medical students. During the 1994–95 school year, Clay Elementary and Friedens Haus were introduced to this concept via a partnership with Washington University located in St. Louis that strengthened the already present education and social work connection. The university's department of education and school of social work combined their efforts in placing four social work and three education students who were committed to two-year practicums in the Clay School and Friedens Haus facilities. Action research (reflecting and then devising ways to improve one's own practices) was encouraged on the part of Clay teachers who worked with university education and social work professors and students, parents, and community residents and agencies. In addition, there were thirty-eight education students who carried out their field experience requirements in Clay, which enhanced the possibility of many Clay students receiving needed individual attention and instruction.

The foci of the Washington University collaboration with Clay as a Professional Development School and Friedens Haus were: (1) school-based services where all services are located in the school and/or school-linked services that use a networking approach within the community; (2) an integrated seminar where education and social work students meet with parents, teachers, community agency people, and education and social work professors in order to raise issues and design projects to address these issues; and (3) collaborative action research processes of studying new practices in teaching and social work in order to document the effects on children, families, and practitioners and to better understand how to meet the needs of children.

The Washington University/Clay School/Friedens Haus collaboration served as a catalyst to strengthen the already present link of social work and educational services provided by Clay School and Friedens Haus. The collaboration was an incentive for Friedens Haus social workers to increase their direct involvement with Clay teachers; teachers to increase their awareness of Friedens Haus services and how to use them (lack of this knowledge was expressed in a 1993 focus group comprised of Clay teachers); teachers to increase their inquiry into educational and social issues; teachers to become more involved in the community via home visits, tutoring after school hours, and attendance at various community events (parents participating in a 1993 focus group session expressed the need for greater understanding by Clay teachers of them and their children); and a greater number of parents to become involved with their children's education.

USING COMMUNITY RESOURCES AND THE COMMUNITY AS A CLASSROOM

One of the aforementioned foci of the Professional Development School partnership between Washington University and Clay/Friedens Haus was a networking approach that used community resources to provide school-linked services. Concerning the use of community resources and the community as a classroom, Mario Fantini (1983) describes four evolutionary models of community education in the United States: (1) The division of labor model united by common values of church, school, and farm prevalent in the eighteenth and nineteenth centuries; (2) the delegation of labor model in the nineteenth and twentieth centuries when industrialization led to a more comprehensive school; (3) the coordinative model when schools began delegating some responsibilities back to community organizations with flexible programming, expanded parental roles, individualization, development of alternatives such as magnet schools, and the "back to the basics" movement (the lighted schoolhouse concept was born out of this period, receiving much of its impetuous from the Mott Foundation in Flint, Michigan); and (4) the facilitative model where the learner puts together his own program working with the help of advisors, parents, and educators and using many community resources. Fantini believes there is a movement toward the last model. A philosophy that supports Fantini's facilitative educational model is expressed by John Gardner:

The ultimate goal of the educational system is to shift to the individual the burden of pursuing his own education. This will not be a widely shared pursuit until we get over our odd conviction that education is what goes on in school buildings and nowhere else. Not only does education continue when schooling ends, but it is not confined to what may be studied in adult education courses. The world is an incomparable classroom, and life is a memorable teacher for those who aren't afraid of her. (1990: 11 and 12)

Community resources, especially city-wide resources, were used to a great extent by Clay School staff. The instructional coordinator of the school (secured through a grant) arranged for many of the field trips and community activities. The immediate surrounding community was not used as much. One kindergarten teacher took her class to see several neighborhood interests such as barge traffic on the Mississippi, the McKinley Bridge, the two water towers, the park (Hyde Park), as well as other features of the community. In addition, a local business owner volunteered to teach classes about entrepreneurship, business skills and techniques, and business philosophies.

One community project involving Clay School and Holy Trinity students was artistically painting boards for the purpose of beautifying boarded-up buildings in the neighborhood. Students also designed posters for community meetings and as "thank yous" to outside agencies and personalities. The gardening project on the lot adjacent to the school was another way Clay students were involved with the community.

The poor perception of the neighborhood by several school staff may have been one reason for less than optimal use of immediate surrounding community resources and using the community as a classroom. Also, fourth and fifth grade teachers lamented the fact that local business owners and industry did not show more interest.

Nevertheless, for adult learners, the Hyde Park community *did* serve as a classroom. Community problem-solving became the greatest avenue for lifelong learning in the neighborhood. Residents learned about housing, economic, social, and educational issues by discussing, analyzing, planning, and implementing solutions. The Bike Shop project and Hyde Park's Mobile Patrol, Business Association, Safety Committee, Landlord's Task Force, Housing Corporation, Hyde Park Alliance, Friedens Haus and its various committees as well as a variety of additional programs and projects offered multiple opportunities, enabling Hyde Park residents to use their own community as a classroom.

ACCESSIBILITY AND USE OF SCHOOL FACILITIES

As Sumption and Engstrom (1966) remind us, the schools are the public's. Clay School was open for parents to come in any time during school hours. The involvement of the St. Louis Parks and Recreation Department allowed the school to remain open from 3:00 to 10:00 Monday through Friday for all ages to participate in gym activities, board games, and other recreational programs (1993–94). Security guards were present to ensure safety. Additionally, Clay

School facilities were often used for Friedens Haus committee meetings and Hyde Park community meetings. Finally, the Friedens Haus summer day camp program was housed in the school.

Friedens Haus was also very accessible to Clay school students, parents, and community organizations. One problem was that the doors had to remain locked because of safety concerns (offices were on the second floor). Nevertheless, the Friedens Haus facility, located two blocks from Clay, housed a community nurse, three social workers, and a pregnancy/new mother counselor. In short, attempts were being made to make needed services accessible to Hyde Park residents.

Finally, Clay School becoming a SLPSS community education center in 1995 enhanced the accessibility of services for the entire community. Previously, adults often had to travel to locations just outside the neighborhood for adult education classes; however, many residents lacked transportation and child care. As Kliminski and Keyes (1983) assert, services need to be brought to the people, and Clay School was a logical location for additional service coordination and delivery.

PROGRAMS FOR ALL

Learning objectives in terms of knowledge, understandings, skills, attitudes, and values (Knowles, 1986) are addressed in several ways through the variety of programs that a typical community education plan offers. Just a few examples are:

- Knowledge: GED and ESL classes and forums concerning political issues
- Understanding: Discussion groups for all ages
- Skills: "How to" classes ranging from vocational education, car repair, clowning, and parenting to filling out job application forms
- Attitudes: Activities that encourage self-esteem and a "can do" attitude in a comfortable and nonthreatening environment that offers a chance for success in at least one of the varied activities offered; this helps to change negative attitudes toward schooling to positive attitudes (Totten, 1970)
- Values: Activities that combine various ages, ethnicities, and abilities, promoting a realization of the worthiness of all people

Through the Friedens Haus coalition, there were programs that met the needs of all age groups and people from all types of backgrounds. The coalition continuously evolved. Friedens Haus advisory board focus group participants expressed that day care and added programs for adults were needs to be addressed. When Clay became one of the community centers within the SLPSS, the needed funding, staffing, connections, and technical assistance made additional adult programming possible. This allowed the opening of school doors beyond regular school hours for educational, cultural, enrichment, vocational, and recreational programming for community residents. A nominal fee was paid (if able) to cover instructional costs, and classes and activities were offered during evenings and weekends as well as year long. Examples of activities offered were General Education Development classes, computer classes, aerobics, gym-use, parenting skill classes, and conflict-resolution classes. Residents who served on the advisory council assisted in the planning of programs based on expressed community needs/desires and then took part in evaluating programs to determine if community needs were being met.

In other words, in addition to the aforementioned extended formal educational and enrichment opportunities for adult learners, the problem-solving and decision-making efforts that engaged Hyde Park residents provided "learning by doing" opportunities for leadership development and lifelong learning.

SUMMARY

Numerous behavioral scientists, educators, criminologists, sociologists, economists, and leaders in our government are talking about school and community linkages, interagency cooperation, and community development. The Clay School principal asserts, "A neighborhood elementary school reaches more people in the community than any other institution. The school should be a focal point of the community, especially when it is a neighborhood school as this is."

At the time of my study, the Friedens Haus coalition was the core of a community education multi-systems, multi-sector model. Cooperations and collaborations implemented with various community organizations and outside agencies were worthy of imitation by community education endeavors across the nation. Parent and community involvement as well as volunteerism were also at high levels and will improve when parents and community members become more involved with decision-making concerning school policies and curriculum.

There were high levels of community resource use; however, use of the immediate surrounding community as a classroom could improve. Perceptions of the community as an undesirable and unsafe place were definitely issues of concern. Assisting the community to become "healthy" as the principal desired would be a step toward encouraging increased use of the neighborhood for educational purposes.

This was being attempted through the link of social work and educational services by the Friedens Haus and Clay School partnership. The collaboration of these two entities with Washington University's department of education and school of social work strengthened this link and encouraged parent involvement with their children's education and teacher involvement with parents and the community.

Finally, community education as practiced in Hyde Park provides clues as to what a school that is involved in a successful community education program would look like. The school would exhibit most of the following characteristics:

- A governing body that is representative of the "school community," including the principal and representatives from central office administration, teachers, support staff (counselors, social workers, nurse, etc.), businesses, agencies, universities, parents, students, and community residents
- A problem-solving process that is focused on solving the school's and surrounding community's most pressing and pertinent problems with decision-making based on analyzing pertinent data and continuous evaluation
- A principal who is an instructional leader and who is perceived as a facilitator rather than a manager
- Parents/guardians who are involved with their children's education via participation on problem-solving committees, classroom assistance, involvement with school projects, and so forth
- Leadership development among teachers, parents, and other community members with the expertise of these individuals recognized and used by school staff and other service providers
- A climate of respect between and among administrators, teachers, support staff, parents, and students
- Time for professional development of teachers and other school staff in the way of seminars, study groups focused on pedagogical best practices, and planning groups that often include community members
- School staff knowledge about how to access services for students
- Teams comprised of teachers, health care providers, social workers, counselors, juvenile officers, and others planning and working to meet the needs of students
- High expectations for all students
- Decreased numbers of students assigned to special education classrooms
- Increased numbers of teachers who make home visits and are involved in community problem-solving and other community activities
- Use of the community as a classroom in terms of classroom/community projects; student community service; and frequent field trips to various businesses, agencies, and other community resources
- Parents, business people, and other community members who are often seen in the school and classrooms serving as resources for student learning
- Partnerships with universities and businesses providing Professional Development School partnerships, job shadowing, tutoring, mentoring activities, and so forth
- Services that are provided at the school site (health, family counseling, parent resource room, day care, preschool, tutoring, etc.) if space is available
- Maximum use of the school facility during evening, weekend, and summer hours for extended learning, enrichment, and recreational activities for students, their families, and other community members
- Extended student learning activities during evenings, weekends, and summers that have a direct connection to what is learned during the school day

- School data that reveal long-term improvement of student academic achievement, discipline problems, and student and teacher attendance
- A safe, orderly, and pleasant school environment that assists the school in maintaining the reputation of serving as the "hub" for community living and learning
- Broad community support demonstrable by increased availability of community resources and by passage of bond issues because the school is perceived as *belonging* to the community

At the time of my study, community problem-solving was the main avenue of self-directed and lifelong learning for many Hyde Park residents. Educational accessibility and programs for all were factors that were greatly enhanced when Clay Elementary became a "community center" within the St. Louis Public School System (Fall, 1995). This had become a reality due to political actions taken by Friedens Haus Advisory Board members that included publicizing, presentations to the Board of Education, and individual conversations and written communication with alderpersons, the mayor, faculty and administrators of area universities, and school district as well as community education lead administrators. This endeavor was an additional Hyde Park community problem-solving effort that realized positive results.

However, problem-solving efforts along with the presence of the aforementioned elements of community education, including   community empowerment and the involvement of all community members in the pursuit of lifelong learning, may falter because of inadequate and/or inappropriate leadership-styles. The following chapter gives some insight into the kind of leadership necessary for a viable and effective community education program in any type of community.

Chapter 19

Leadership for Community Education

INTRODUCTION

This chapter looks at leadership from three perspectives—orthodox, human relations, and critical theory. The issue of leadership personalities is addressed, and Hyde Park community members analyze their neighborhood's leadership and the conflicts witnessed among those in leadership roles. From this discussion, a conclusion is reached as to the leadership style that is most effective for the field of community education.

AN ORTHODOX PERSPECTIVE

An orthodox perspective of leadership (the rational managerial approach) looks to the development of rationalistic strategy programs as the way to meet organizational goals. This type of leadership style is necessary for the following change procedure developed by Havelock (cited by Foster, 1986: 151):

Stage 1: Enter into the organization: recognize its clients, leaders, and gatekeepers and its position in regard to its environment.

Stage 2: Make a diagnosis: identify the organization's problems and the opportunities; determine its goals and the amount of support behind them.

Stage 3: Discover the available resources: learn who are experts and who are innovators.

Stage 4: Choose a solution: after diagnosing the problem and identifying the resources, find a solution through research, brainstorming, and testing possible alternatives.

Stage 5: Build acceptance for the chosen solution: communicate the solution to other actors; identify and work around the resisters.

Stage 6: Stabilize the innovation and build in a capacity for self-renewal.

Unfortunately, the Hyde Park neighborhood was replete with service providers who exhibited orthodox leadership styles. If meetings were not conducted in a directive manner, the actions of community residents were often directed from behind the scenes. Many times, residents' creativity, ideas, and innovations were negated, or ownership was transferred to salaried community leaders and service providers. Finally, some of these leaders implemented their own well-worn plans for the "good" of the community and told about it afterwards.

The following interview results give credence to the above conclusion. As several service providers were attempting to describe effective leadership, they revealed much about their own leadership styles. Interview results coupled with observed and documented actions of these leaders revealed that the orthodox, directive, and "take control" type of leadership maintained a strong presence in the Hyde Park neighborhood.

A leader new to the community related the role she needed to play in a neighborhood with a pluralistic power structure. Her words and actions revealed that she was a strategist even though she talked of being a facilitator. Furthermore, her conversational language ("I want," "I want to see," "I will not tolerate," "I will not allow") indicated a more directive and power-oriented leadership style than the following words indicate. Observations by the author found that this leader vacillated concerning fundamental values of inclusiveness, community empowerment, and even honesty that a leader in her position should have espoused.

How does [the pluralistic] power structure affect the role you play in the community?

It would be a combination of facilitator and strategist. In order to survive, you probably must always be a strategist to some degree. I think the main role would be as a facilitator.

What do you find as blockages to being a facilitator and strategist?

There are some, because a lot of times when you're a facilitator, some people look at that role as being a director or a power position in some sense that is controlling. So you have to be extremely careful in how you approach issues and decisions. Most of the time, if most people would sit down and listen to what you're saying—all you're doing is repeating something they've already asked for, and *you're simply giving them a solution* to it. (emphasis added)

Another service provider had this to say when asked what he would do differently after reflecting upon his actions when first coming into the community. Interview results revealed a remaining directive, sometimes manipulative, and orthodox leadership style:

If I had to do it all over again, I would have taken a back seat a lot more often than I did. I was thrust into situations and issues that I thought I could handle. I would have talked more with those who work in the neighborhood, I would have had some more community consensus building meetings, I would have met and tried to identify and analyze the different goals that each agency had, I would have identified more thoroughly the point players and what their goals were, and how I could have effectively fit in a little bit better instead of being the lone rebel. . . .

I think that maybe my aggressiveness has been a part of my failure to be as positive—or more than positive—has made others stand-offish a little bit. I would have gotten to know those in the community better. There are people in Hyde Park who want to be the leaders. I'm not perfect, but I do care.

Now I'm stepping back and I'm watching and listening. I was thrust into a frying pan. It is difficult for me to sit back because of my oral presentation ability. . . . Because I'm so aggressive, I think I come off sometimes the wrong way.

What have you liked about your job?

I've liked . . . problem-solving as well as getting a general grasp of what's happening and learning the key players, and trying to learn how to facilitate without, you know, being dominant—but being dominant when necessary, passive when necessary, and being diligent and being available. I also like the ability to effectuate change. That's important to me—to be a catalyst for change.

What are the differences between the two neighborhoods that you serve?

There is very dynamic, aggressive, and energetic leadership in Hyde Park. There are a lot of smart people in Hyde Park, but I don't know if they're using their smarts effectively. . . . I'm able to teach them in O'Fallon how to build effective coalitions and it works very well. When I give instructions, when I try to help them, when I lead a meeting, when I give an assignment, they're pleased to do it. They don't feel that I sit there trying to run it, but they realize that I become less when they grow more.

Describe the most effective leadership style for your position in your opinion.

The [leader] needs to be a good listener, to have the ability to interpret and act upon what is heard, and to *be dominant without the perception of being dominant*. By that I mean the ability to build a good coalition by giving a plan and giving pieces of it to different entities, bringing them all together, and *giving them an idea and making them feel they are taking ownership of that idea.* That's something I think is effective. (emphasis added)

A HUMAN RELATIONS PERSPECTIVE

A human relations approach, included in the Natural Systems Perspective, sets out to change the person so that the organization will subsequently change. Schools of thought that have influenced this approach were explored by Mary Parker Follet who believed that the fundamental problem in all organizations was developing and maintaining dynamic and harmonious relationships. Also, the Hawthorne studies conducted in the Hawthorne plant of the Western Electric Company in Chicago supported this conclusion while stimulating further research in motivational, social, and leadership theories (Hoy and Miskel, 1987).

A human relations approach offers solutions to problems such as:

- Provide rewards and recognition for achievement
- Establish or re-institute organizational rituals, ceremonies, and slogans
- Encourage competition among organizational members
- Allow for membership participation in planning policies and action
- View all members as worthy individual

One former Hyde Park leader exhibited a human relations leadership style. This leader had a talent for making people feel good, promoted togetherness and getting along, and exuded enthusiasm for every project. One community member's description of this leader was "the cheerleader type." Conversely, behind the scenes, she was the sole decision-maker and implemented actions based on these decisions without informing community residents who performed leadership roles within the organization. This is what one community member had to say about this service provider's leadership style:

She was just real timely with the right mix. She did a good job of balancing—walking a tight rope between an open democratic approach and a strong executive role. She wasn't afraid to make decisions on her own, and she was pragmatic. Timing and her position made it possible for her to get away with that. I don't think I could do the same thing well; I have a different leadership style anyway.

What is the biggest difference between your two leadership styles?

I think I'm a little more open but at the same time structured.

What do you mean by open?

The board really didn't know what the [former director] did. I would have to share more what I did. This is somewhat gender related. People tend to trust women more than men. The board realized she did a lot on her own but didn't care. Being in this interim director position, I haven't felt comfortable with the same executive style, and when I have tried it, it drives the board a little nuts. . . . I think she was perfect for the time, but that leadership-style could have become problematic.

Asked about her own leadership style and how she wanted the Hyde Park community to remember her, the leader in question said she hoped community members viewed her as "someone who was progressive enough to know that she could make a difference in this community just through hard work and friendliness and a sense of commitment to this beautiful neighborhood. She was loved by all, and she loved everybody."

When talking about the necessity to train a local resident to fill her position, she had this to say:

It wouldn't take very long to train a person from the community, because we have the model right here now. It wasn't like that when I walked in; there wasn't anything. I had to start from scratch; it's really well on its way to being available for somebody for training. They would need to be trained in grant development, not just grant writing, and the method in which one makes friends in the grant-giving world.

Grant development is the area most would need training in because that's professionalism, that takes the highest level of professionalism in my view for this office to function. . . . The consistency has got to be the kind of personality it takes; the ability to be a sales person, and I'm a good sales person because I know my neighborhood, I know what makes it tick, I know how to make it credible to a grant funder.

The first person they promote is themselves; that's the number one key in grant making is having a person who people want to give money to—not just the neighborhood—but the person who's in charge, the one they have to have lunch with, the one they have to go seek, the one that calls them back and is a nice person—somebody they like to talk to.

Also, someone who can paint pictures with words about what's possible. That means they can come into a room and hear a few thoughts of peoples' ideas and then they can paint this picture for people that brings everybody in that room into "wow," that's a picture I really like or I really want to get involved in. They have to be able to bring people along.

That's where I think we're fortunate in that I have some of that background, but you get somebody in here who didn't, and you know it would have been impossible to get this amount of money, you know, going for the big bucks. And there's people in the community who don't even know how we spend it; they can't justify the time I spend on it. There needs to be a lot of education in the community about why you want a professional person doing community grant work because that's what those dollars are going to come to is somebody they think is professionally able to do it right. [It must be noted that none of the "big bucks" were granted.]

THE CHARISMATIC LEADER

The charismatic leader may possess human relations leadership qualities, but the relationship between this leader and his/her subordinates is the most salient feature. For instance, charismatic leaders often develop dependencies on their followers to support their extraordinary needs for attention. Hitler may be described as a charismatic leader who fed off the support of his followers to bolster his narcissistic personality. Another, Mao Tse-tung, is described as having the ability to understand, evoke, and direct human emotions. He exhibited numerous ways to use his own persona to command the sentiments and passions of others.

One Hyde Park resident described a former community leader as charismatic:

There used to be a leader in Hyde Park who was a good consensus builder. He was a "snake-oil" salesman. That's the kind of person you need. He didn't mean any harm—he was very passionate about what he was doing. It was make one deal to keep the next deal going, and he made promises that maybe he couldn't keep to keep the whole thing going. It was always a juggling act. I look back to the days when things were looking up for Hyde Park, and those were the days. If he could have kept it going, it would have been good.

You always seem to need one strong person. This [former Hyde Park leader] was very charismatic. He gave people the allusion or the feeling that they were making decisions and were in control.

To a large extent this type of person is a manipulator who ultimately retains control. Their talent is their ability to let people think that they are making a decision, but they are actually steering people and are controlling. The real talent is to manipulate people, and they don't know it—to get them to do what your vision is, and let them think it was their idea.

Do you feel you were manipulated by him?

You could use another choice of words and say it was guidance or good leadership. Yeah, I felt like I was manipulated by him, or it could have been just steered or led.

(The leader in question is said to be living out of the country, no one knows of his whereabouts, and the housing organization he led is now defunct. Tens of thousands of dollars remain owed, and there are many broken dreams for some Hyde Park residents who now feel trapped by the devaluation of their properties.)

A CRITICAL THEORY PERSPECTIVE

A critical theory perspective imputes additional qualities to leadership and views most leaders as persons drowning in old methodologies, habits, and rituals who do not lead to transform but struggle to keep the status quo (Foster, 1986). The critical theory perspective sees these leaders as not taking advantage of the richest resource available to them—the community. Control is the prevailing method used, and to loosen the grip would be too risky.

The successful leader, from a critical theory perspective, is seen as a visionary, leading to transform the community for the better even though it involves struggles and risk taking. He or she wants to stop his/her subordinates, colleagues, superiors, and those in the community from going to sleep. This leader persuades people on various sides of an issue to open themselves to each other even though there are risks involved in such an opening. He or she knows that the community culture is ever changing, that unhealthy attitudes can be unfrozen and healthier attitudes introduced, and that every change will soon be reshaped by another.

The critical theorist, as a problem-solving leader, promotes procedures of reflection, participation, implementation, and analytical evaluation through group planning and supervision and by drawing on the rich cultural resources of the community. He or she develops a participatory and informative environment that makes the task of confronting and intervening unhealthy attitudes more palatable and a matter of personal growth. This person leads in reflectively formulating and clearly understanding the group's mission and evaluating how the present group climate and processes are helping or hindering the mission goals. Finally, the human-relations values of inclusion and viewing each individual as worthy are included within the critical theorist's perspective of leadership.

The philosophy of community education calls for leaders who are facilitators in line with the critical theory perspective of leadership and as advocated by the educator, Malcolm Knowles. Knowles has written extensively concerning a facilitative style of teaching adult learners (andragogy) that can readily be transferred to effective leadership. He views the teacher as a facilitator who focuses on what is happening with students rather than him/herself, is able to expose him/herself emotionally, is a colearner with the students, and is a procedural guide (1975). He cites Carl Rogers' (1969) three characteristics of a facilitator:

(1) The facilitator has unqualified positive regard for the helpee
(2) The facilitator has a deep level of ability to empathize
(3) The facilitator has absolute authenticity as a person

LEADERSHIP CONFLICTS

Even when effective leaders are found, however, turf battles among them may weaken the goals and objectives they share. For example, turf battles between black leaders weakened the Civil Rights movement. Leaders of the NAACP wanted to work within the law while those of SNCC, CORE, and the SCLC promoted tactics that were not necessarily within the law but proved to be very effective. Roy Wilkins of the NAACP did not like Martin Luther King, and Thurgood Marshall said King was an opportunist and a rabble rouser (Rosenberg 1991).

Dolbeare (1974) suggests that groups such as the previously mentioned Civil Rights organizations need to have their collective purposes in mind and not compete with each other. He warns of letting the maintenance of organizations, internal ideology and loyalties, and people competing for status and control take over while the purposes fall by the wayside.

Unresolved conflicts among Hyde Park leaders proved to be a leading reason for the lack of more demonstrable community progress. One service provider complained about the ineffective leadership in Hyde Park:

Another blockage [to my effectiveness] has been ineffective community leadership in the neighborhood because it was nonexistent. Those leaders who had been put in place were ineffective, inactive, indifferent, and they had a private agenda! They'll never admit it!

What have you disliked about your job?

Well, the factions that exist in neighborhoods, the backbiting, and the back-stabbing. . . . Until we get these agencies, until they stop having so much of their private agendas and work for the good of the community, I think that [my agency] as well as the police officers are doing the best jobs they can. . . . I don't think that the people are being well represented. No sour grapes on my part, but when you look at the attendance at the community meetings, do you have a lot of residents there? No!

If you were to take a poll of the residents of the area and you asked them what were the good points and the bad points, the good points would be the Friedens Haus program for the kids in the evening times, the Safety Committee and the revitalization of the Mobile Patrol, the police meetings, and probably Holy Trinity and their involvement in the community of the Catholic parishioners. The bad part would be Hyde Park Alliance and the factionalism and the ineffective board!

One community resident described the factionalism among community organizations and leaders as a blockage to her participation:

What have been the blockages?

Territorialism and codependency. That sounds strange. I think what's really blocked me a lot are the way the leaders in the community relate to each other—I see it as codependency. I've been telling them for quite a while—we all need to go to the Housing Center for one of those half-day codependency seminars that are free—sit through it and understand our behaviors.

I equate the behaviors to codependency with not being able to break the cycle of abuse from generation to generation. I think there is that kind of neglect and abuse among people trying to do different things in the community. That's where we are codependent in that we need to learn to break the cycle of not appreciating each other, the territorialism, belittling each other, not including each other, and things like that.

. . . If you're doing something that's avant-garde or something new, somebody else might want it and want to call it their own. I have a big problem with that. So to me—where to someone else resolving personality differences and problems is not important—it's kind of important to me. That has blocked me from wanting to do other things in the community because of the denial of existing personality problems and refusing to address them.

There are a lot of intelligent people and leaders in the community, so I couldn't figure out for a while—if these people are such good friends and aware of normal abuse situations and things like that, why aren't they seeing their neglect and abuse of each other? For example, if you have a board that doesn't appreciate the person who directs the program, after a period of time that person will act from that lack of appreciation and will fail to appreciate others working on projects with other agencies and on and on.

So I'm not one to get caught up in that cycle and become a victim, and I almost was. That personality issue has a lot to do with it, because I can work with almost anybody. If I get to the point where I can't work with someone, then I won't do it.

Another community resident and leader had this to say about the issue:

What mistakes do you see being made by community leaders in Hyde Park?

I just wish community leaders could work better together and put the personalities aside. There are a lot of qualified, bright, and educated people in Hyde Park. I wish some of those people would come out and work with us, because with all those people together and all the knowledge, and all the information we could pull together, Hyde Park could be a really good neighborhood.

You can't change a person's personality. People need to learn how to control their emotions. I've learned to control my bad temper, because it's not about fighting with each other—it's about pulling together with each other. . . . There are some leaders in Hyde Park that need to work out their personality problems between each other.

SUMMARY

I did not find any Hyde Park community leaders who could be described as leading from a critical theory perspective. I found a few leaders with charismatic attributes and numerous authoritative leaders who were comfortable leading from an orthodox perspective. Several leaders in the Hyde Park community did not give evidence of truly believing that community residents were just as knowledgeable and/or exhibited more knowledge concerning certain issues than themselves. Instead of facilitating, supporting, and coordinating, many Hyde Park leaders felt a need to be the ones to make things happen, to be the catalysts for change, and to serve and/or direct the residents.

Effective community procedures and projects should be added to and built upon—not changed or turned around. Community leaders and residents are insulted and put off, and rightly so, by the directive and "all knowing" leadership styles that are too often exhibited by strong and/or manipulative personality types who come in to "better" the neighborhood. Perhaps unconsciously, these leaders are trying to enhance their own personas rather than assisting community residents to better themselves and their environment.

Moreover, there is the issue of controlling emotions, which one Hyde Park resident addressed in her interview. Another resident cited abusive relationships between and among community leaders. I witnessed verbal and emotional abuse toward staff and volunteers—two ingredients for stunted growth no matter "good intentions," creativeness, and vision of the leader/director. A pinch of the human relations leadership style would do nicely at times; however, the critical theory perspective requires truly respecting all persons as worthy human beings who possess various kinds of abilities and deserve opportunities to reach their varied potentials.

Perhaps a combination of three perspectives—orthodox, human relations, and critical theory—(minus the authoritative feature of the first and the manipulative features of the first two) would need to be present in an effective leader who leads to reform and facilitates leadership development as well as lifelong learning. A certain amount of structure (as delineated in the orthodox perspective) is necessary for viable learning organizations (community, school). The human relations perspective adds celebration, developing optimal interpersonal relationships, and viewing all persons as worthy. But most importantly, an awareness and new consciousness that the critical theory perspective encourages must not be lacking for leadership development and lifelong learning to take place and thus effect reform through genuine community problem-solving. Finally, although not a necessity, a "pinch" of charisma could add spice to the mix if this quality is not used for manipulative purposes. Charismatic leaders have too often offered "fool's gold" to community residents. In short, an effective community education leader could view his/her role and the processes he/she uses to fulfill that role as an *art* rather than a specific managerial or administrative technique. Each situation and each community demands an added or subtracted nuance with the backdrop of personal qualities that include honesty; trustworthiness; and continuous self-analyzation, reflection, and learning.

Finally, a status quo, entrenched "leadership" within the field of community education itself may be the greatest obstacle to the discipline's possibility to effect true reform for PreK–12 students, parents, and the wider community. A "community of learners" that community educators advocate necessarily *includes* leaders as learners and learners as leaders. Do community education leaders really see themselves as continuously learning and even learning from community residents in distressed communities as are most inner-city neighborhoods? Do community education leaders endeavor to discover the expertise that is present in these communities and encourage leadership development among neighborhood residents as they are encouraging this development within themselves? Do they even recognize potential, talent, creativity, and leadership qualities within others; and if so, do community educators then "block" potential leaders within communities and within the field of community education, especially if these learners may "out shine" the community educator? Is self-recognition deemed more important than for all types of communities to become "self-actualized" as Jack Minzey and Clyde LeTarte (1994) hope for? Effective leadership for community educators is giving this leadership away by assisting and encouraging the development of leadership skills in others and experiencing "joy" rather than fear in doing so.

Writing for the *Community Education Journal,* David Mathews, President and Chief Executive Officer of the Kettering Foundation provides a succinct summation about leadership concerning community educators:

The most serious obstacles to making communities leaderful come from conventional notions of leadership. The "leaders-followers" paradigm, which dominates much of the thinking about leadership, implies that there are some people who are leaders and others who are not. It makes "the leaders" responsible for "the followers"—as in the business maxim "managers have to create an environment where workers can be productive." If that is good business advice (which is doubtful), it is terrible advice for community leaders. (1996: 13)

Chapter 20

Summary

The Hyde Park neighborhood typifies many inner-city communities across the nation exhibiting economic, social, educational, housing, and health deteriorations. Hyde Park may be atypical, however, in that there remains a substantial white population. Elements of racism and economic stratification may be the major blockages to neighborhood improvement in addition to federal, state, and local governmental policies, and entities from without (via strong directive leadership personalities) coming in to "better" the community.

The Friedens Haus coalition was found to be the core of a community education multi-systems, multi-sector approach to addressing the many needs of the Hyde Park community. It was the neighborhood entity that substantially demonstrated the community education principles of community empowerment/locus of control in terms of political awareness and action, inclusiveness, citizen councils, and leadership development; community problem-solving in terms of community organization, interagency cooperation, and needs assessments, strategic planning, and evaluations; and the effort to involve everyone in the pursuit of lifelong learning in terms of linkages between school and community, parent involvement and volunteerism, using community resources and the community as a classroom, accessibility, and programs for all. The numerous networking, cooperative, and collaborative efforts of the Friedens' staff and advisory board members with community (HPA, Housing Corporation, area churches, businesses, smaller organizations and committees) and outside organizations and agencies could serve as a model for community education endeavors across the nation and as a means to address foreground and background causes of criminal behavior.

There is cause for looking to new answers for crime prevention. The Justice Department reports (1994) that our prison population is soaring—for several years the United States has been locking up a larger portion of its population than any other nation. In 1992, 455 out of every 100,000 Americans were in prison or jail; South Africa under its old government was next at 311 for each 100,000. Finally, we are considered the most violent of all western industrialized nations.

The most disturbing fact is that criminals and murder victims are becoming younger. According to the Children's Defense Fund in 1994, homicide is now the third leading cause of death for children in elementary and middle school. One revealing statement was made by a friend of a St. Louis high school student who was fatally shot in school. "I'm tired of it," she said, "You expect this to happen in your own backyard but not in your school" (Bryan and Little, 1993: 1A). Finally, some feel that we have lost an entire generation of black males.

Geri Redden, executive director of the Educational Center of Family Violence in St. Louis, asserts that many children are not resilient. "Some non-resilient kids grow up to be violent criminals. Eighty-nine percent of violent criminals come from violent homes" (1993: 7B). A *St. Louis Post-Dispatch* series (Shirk, 1994), entitled, "Juvenile Injustice," describes the almost hopeless task of the juvenile justice system and the deplorable family backgrounds of some juvenile "clients." The following quote supports these views: "The road to Attica begins with families uprooted, with bad housing, racial prejudices, drug profiteering; with schools and social agencies unresponsive; with kids growing up feeling left out. Improving the quality of life for these persons would result in fewer setting foot in jail or prison" (Sturz, 1971: 175).

Many criminologists, educators, politicians, and workers with the juvenile justice system talk and write about prevention efforts at the front end of young lives through comprehensive approaches. Scott Decker, criminologist and professor at the University of Missouri-St. Louis, and Dietrich Smith write about comprehensive prevention efforts concerning gangs:

Clearly, strengthening families and their ability to function should be a key priority in any program designed to respond to gang activity. . . . No single group holds the key in responding to gangs. Effective responses will be forthcoming only when a broad coalition is involved. Though law enforcement and the courts are essential to this response, they will be unsuccessful unless schools, neighborhood groups and all levels of government participate. We must keep in mind that gangs cause many problems, but that a larger number of problems cause gangs themselves. (Decker and Smith, 1992: 3C) (Figure 20.1)

CONFRONTING FOREGROUND CAUSES OF CRIMINAL BEHAVIOR

It was found that the crime problem in Hyde Park was the result of the same causes of criminal behavior throughout the United States. There are multiple causes including genetics (nonresilient, complex, and comprehensive factors), deteriorating family conditions, American culture, frustration and alienation due to relative deprivation (economically, educationally, politically), institutionalized

Figure 20.1
Cartoon

'Good Thing We Voted Down Money For Education, Jobs And
Health Care Years Ago So We Can Spend It On Crime Now'

Source: St. Louis Post-Dispatch, November 7, 1993, C2.

racism, and rationalization of cost and benefit (foreground causes concerning opportunity). All of these indices were found in Hyde Park.

Through deductive reasoning, it was concluded that the underlying cause of criminal behavior, unique to the United States, is our American culture that, unfortunately, includes the festering sore of institutionalized racism. These two factors were also woven into the texture of Hyde Park community life. There were overt and many subtle indications of racism and the American cultural heritage of materialism, individualism, and "quick-fixes." The relatively lower socio-economic status of Hyde Park residents did not negate these factors. The correlates to crime deriving from these underlying causes of institutionalized racism and American culture—female headed households, population loss and transition, low socio-economic status, high unemployment—were present at high levels, demanding a multi-systems, comprehensive approach to alleviating criminal behavior. Consequently, besides the possible long-term effects of the Friedens Haus coalition alleviating background causes of crime, Hyde Park residents understandably turned to the police to help them address, at least a *foreground* cause of crime—opportunity.

However, residents did not view policing in the Hyde Park neighborhood as community oriented, much less adequately responding to criminal activity on Hyde Park streets and within business and residential establishments. Poor police response to calls in terms of time, attitudes, follow-ups, and "no-shows," and minimal police availability were frequent complaints voiced by residents. Moreover, residents did not want to be told that the crime problem was theirs because they chose to live in Hyde Park. Some efforts were made by police to address these issues of concern; however, residents noticed that these efforts soon abated. They expressed a desire that police officers exhibit the Community Oriented Problem Solving (COPS) style of policing in Hyde Park, as this philosophy encouraged officers and community residents to work cooperatively in order to alleviate criminal activity at the neighborhood level.

Nevertheless, the COPS philosophy was viewed by SLMPD rank-and-file and one sergeant as a community-oriented program that would be nice if there were the resources and manpower to effectively implement it. Overall, the understanding of the program supported a community-oriented philosophy (public relations and assisting city agency involvement) rather than a problem-solving philosophy as described by Herman Goldstein (1990). The limited training in the COPS program for SLMPD officers may have been a reason for these misunderstandings and limited views of the philosophy. The former captain of the 5th District did not think the COPS program would work—whatever the resources and manpower. Since it was the captain who determined if and how much the COPS philosophy was implemented in a St. Louis policing district, his view about the program was problematic for Hyde Park residents during his 5th District tenure.

Another hindrance to problem-oriented policing may have been the enticement of excitement, adventure, authority, and respect (expressed by rank-and-file officers) to the profession itself. The overall bent of policing philosophies expressed by the officers and captain was the "we-them," tough, almost militaristic style of policing. Moreover, there were elements of racial prejudice expressed by some focus group and interview participants.

Finally, through analyzing various community crime prevention approaches and programs, it was determined that a comprehensive approach, addressing both background and foreground causes of criminal behavior, provided the best chance for optimal results. The mobile patrol component of the Hyde Park Safety Committee, as well as attempting to make the police accountable to the community, addressed "opportunity" for criminal activity. During years of mobile patrol operation (1991 and 1992), reported incidents of crime in the categories of aggravated assault and burglary were down somewhat and down significantly in the category of robbery. These rates generally remained the same or went up in seven demographically similar neighborhoods. Hyde Park crime then went up for the categories of burglary and aggravated assault in 1993 (post mobile patrol operation). A combination of increased resident vigilance and thus keeping the police more accountable to the community assisted in significantly reducing incidents of robbery, a more overt crime than aggravated assault and burglary.

Addressing background causes of criminal behavior was the concern that we turned to in Part II. Together with problem-solving efforts to address the situational factors of criminal behavior, the Friedens Haus coalition assisted in completing a comprehensive approach to crime prevention in the Hyde Park neighborhood.

CONFRONTING BACKGROUND CAUSES OF CRIMINAL BEHAVIOR

To address the background causes of criminal behavior, it was suggested that a community education philosophical approach would yield the best results because social malaise requires multiple, systemic, and comprehensive solutions. Elements of a community education approach include:

Community empowerment
    Political awareness and action
    Inclusiveness
    Citizen councils
    Leadership development
Community problem-solving
    Community organization
    Interagency cooperation
    Assessing, planning, and evaluating
    Volunteerism
The effort to involve everyone in the pursuit of lifelong learning
    Use of community resources and the community as a classroom
    Maximum use of school facilities
    Accessibility (facilities, programs, and services)
    Programs for all
    Parent and community involvement in school and community governance

The Friedens Haus model of community education was found to operate at the highest level on Nance and Dixon's chart of Process and Program Dimensions (1980). It excelled in community organization and development, community problem-solving, and community-based decision making. The program served as an example of:

a multi-system operation—the teaching-learning which occurs through the actions of a community's systems,—institutions, organizations, and other formalized groups, which are the community's instruments for developing and administering the formal classes, apprenticeships, problem-solving efforts, formal advising, and planned human interactions which constitute much of the educational experience of people. (Wood, 1977 as cited in Nance and Dixon, 1980)

The designation of Clay School as the next community education center in October 1994 was a proactive move on the part of the city and the SLPSS because of the already superior community education program working in Hyde Park and the great educational, social, and health needs of the neighborhood. Because Clay subsequently became an "official" community education center in 1995, services were expanded and added, especially adult education programming, to make the Friedens Haus coalition an even more relevant and outstanding model of community education.

A report published by Conference on Education states,

We recommend that all local groups find ways to be more actively involved in school issues, both with their neighborhood schools and at a system-wide level. In the few neighborhoods where such active involvement is already happening, it is amazing to see how much can be accomplished when the wall between school and community comes down. These examples, as their stories become known, will do much to ease the way for other neighborhoods as they work to become true partners with the schools. (1994: 36)

The Professional Development School partnership with Washington University's department of education and school of social work enhanced the education and social work linkage already present through the Friedens Haus coalition. As the backers of the Professional Development School concept (Holmes Group) recognize, the schools alone will not effect the changes we desire in our society. Agreeing, Harold Howe (1993), an educator, emphasizes the need to look at educational reform as a much broader issue than just the improvement of schooling. He addresses the role of families, social agencies, and communities as well as the impact of poverty and discrimination. Like Vasil Kerensky (1989), he warns that children cannot be thought of as having two separate lives, a school life and an out-of-school life, and points out the ways in which families are not supported by our society. Donna Shalala, secretary of Health and Human Services, writes, "Schools must turn themselves into community centers open after school and on weekends where young people can study, play ball, make new friends, and spend time with caring adults" (1993: 11B).

In line with this thinking, Friedens Haus focused on addressing social, health, and educational needs of preschool through fifth grade children year round and had more recently included programming for teens. Friedens Haus programming was continuously expanding with the view that "it takes a healthy village to raise a healthy child."

In fact, the Children's Charter of Metropolitan St. Louis (Shirk, 1993), which drew pledges of support from 250 participants at a children's summit held in St. Louis, outlines strategies that could be described as those adopted by the Friedens Haus coalition. They are:

- Invest in children as the highest priority.
- Empower families so that they are able to access needed services.
- Provide comprehensive services in a coordinated manner.
- Deliver necessary services at the neighborhood level.
- Promote school and agency partnerships so that schools can function as community resource centers [this improved when Clay became a community education center within the SLPSS—Fall, 1995].
- Use partnerships between and among agencies and groups serving children and families.
- Evaluate and monitor the effectiveness of services designed to meet the needs of children and families.
- Involve parents in the decisions which affect the lives of their children.

Parent involvement in Clay School was determined to be at high levels including the fulfillment of clerical, instructional, and some advisory roles. The principal expressed joy in seeing parents and teachers take charge of projects and letting them "run with it." For many parents, involvement with the school was a way of feeling useful and beneficial. Clay School ranked at the top or next to the top in "volunteer hours" within the SLPSS for many years. However, the advisory role of parents and community members will be enhanced when they maintain a voice in school policy and curriculum decision-making. This type of participation by parents and community members would strengthen teacher, parent, and community relationships.

There was good use of the wider St. Louis community by Clay School and Friedens Haus by way of field trips and guest speakers. Use of the immediate surrounding community was somewhat limited, except for the gardening project and Energizing Youth for Employment (EYE) program, because of the belief that Hyde Park needed to become a "healthy" community. The EYE program was one collaborative endeavor (Safety Committee, Friedens Haus, Business Association, HPA) that provided learning and job opportunities within the neighborhood through leadership training, job training, and summer employment. Moreover, it was foreseen that the Bike Shop would extend the partnership between community and school as well as serving as an incentive for neighborhood economic development. If the Bike Shop project is renewed, connections of this project with the potential completion of the River Front Bike Trail could provide Hyde Park children and teens additional learning and job opportunities in their immediate surrounding community.

The successful collaborations formed with the Housing Corporation, Hyde Park Business Association, Hyde Park Safety Committee, and HPA concerning the development of the Bike Shop project and with the Safety Committee, HPA, and Hyde Park Business Association concerning the EYE program had much to do with Friedens Haus participation and ongoing efforts. Although initiated by the Safety Committee, the leadership for the EYE program was provided by Friedens Haus. Friedens Haus did not lead in the Bike Shop endeavor, and that project was unnecessarily prolonged and truncated.

As of 1994 the Friedens Haus coalition served as a good example of a multi-sector (private, public, nonprofit, and religious) collaboration. The Friedens Haus entity itself served as a unique multi-systems, multi-sector coalition of church (Friedens United Church of Christ), private social service agency (Neighborhood Houses), public school (Clay Elementary), and community members and organizations. Several area businesses were included, but the coalition would have benefited by increased business and river front industry involvement. The latter will take a concentrated effort and focus.

A unique and "out of the box" feature of the Friedens Haus coalition was the important role of churches. The Friedens United Church of Christ viewed its role as its "mission" in the Hyde Park neighborhood and attempted to fulfill that mission by in-kind contributions of facility use. Additionally, the Assembly of God church contributed by furnishing materials and labor for the construction of a gazebo and playground for Clay School students and neighborhood children. Nevertheless, the separation between church and state as outlined by the courts was adhered to. Perhaps the fear of encroaching on this separation has blocked many schools from the use of church facilities and other resources that are sorely needed, especially when school facilities are not available to community residents beyond school hours.

It must be noted, however, that involving multiple systems and institutions to effect positive change will be for naught if communities relinquish locus of control, and locus of control demands inclusiveness. Hyde Park may have been more inclusive than many neighborhoods. At least one part of the community exemplified a pluralistic power structure with four entities sharing leading community roles—the Friedens Haus coalition, Hyde Park Alliance (HPA), the Housing Corporation (city involvement), and Holy Trinity Church. Bethlehem Lutheran on the "other side of town" was "off on its own." There was demonstrated separatism both racially and economically between the two halves of the neighborhood. Besides the exclusion of the western half of the neighborhood, Hyde Park exhibited signs of moving toward a bi-factional power structure comprised of HPA and Friedens Haus factions and perhaps even to a more authoritative structure controlled by one powerful alderperson.

The recent history of the Hyde Park community indicates a great amount of exclusiveness and separation even among residents living in the eastern half of the community. This recently evolved through various Hyde Park organizations such as Hyde Park Historical, Inc., HYPRE, and the Trinity Square Association. Only within the last seven years has separatism begun to significantly break down. Evidence of increased inclusiveness was seen with the neighborhood organization's change of name from Trinity Square Association to HPA, the restructuring of the HPA Board of Directors to include blacks and renters, and the emergence of the Friedens Haus coalition.

Friedens Haus moved even further toward inclusiveness by the restructuring of its decision-making body, the Board of Directors, to include a majority of community residents and new officers. Conversely, HPA, which was the "designated" neighborhood organization resisted restructuring that would have allowed for new board officers and increased community involvement. On the one hand, the city may have been too directive and on the other, too lax, in assuring that community members were not abused by the neighborhood organization, especially concerning inclusion and decision-making processes. Additionally, maintaining effective structural and meeting procedures would have assisted both HPA and the Friedens Haus coalition in ensuring that all community-member voices were heard and alleviating issues of "control." Finally, racism, which maintained a strong presence in Hyde Park, will best be addressed through continuing efforts of black and white residents and service providers collaboratively solving neighborhood problems.

Collaborative problem-solving also serves as an avenue for leadership development and maintaining locus of control within communities. Leadership was developed in Hyde Park by community members accepting leadership roles within various neighborhood organizations and committees (Mobile Patrol, Safety Committee, Landlords' Task Force, and the Business Association) and by parent involvement in Clay School. Community-wide problems of most concern and involving the majority of Hyde Park organizations in problem-solving efforts were housing, economic development, and safety. There may have been too much effort expended on the housing problem, when Hyde Park problems were multiple and varied. Nevertheless, a majority of community leadership was developed through "learning by doing," a Deweyan concept.

Because of the importance of maintaining locus of control, leadership development was determined to be inseparable from the leadership styles of those who were responsible for and/or allowed leadership development to take place. The orthodox style of leadership (directive, strategic) fights to maintain control and basks in the glory of bringing about change. This leadership style was all too prevelant in the Hyde Park community. Many qualified and potential resident leaders had been put off, frustrated, and demoralized by such directiveness. Several had "given up" and were no longer involved with community activities and community problem-solving efforts. Those who remained in the struggle were often "shut out" by several leaders, service providers, and organizational officers who welcomed passive participation but not necessarily "thinking" participation.

Most of the "designated" community leaders and service providers in Hyde Park were determined to be strategists as opposed to facilitators. Other well-intentioned leaders talked instead of really listening to what community residents had to say about solutions to community problems. Most importantly, several Hyde Park leaders did not deem the core values of truth, honesty, inclusiveness, and respect for all individuals as sacrosanct. It was determined that an effective community education leader would possess leadership attributes as seen from a critical theory perspective, leading to transform while facilitating community involvement in decision-making processes and problem-solving efforts.

Problem-solving efforts and noticeable results of these efforts in the Hyde Park neighborhood centered around the Friedens Haus coalition. Holy Trinity and Bethlehem Lutheran were fulfilling social and educational needs of the community; however, the Friedens Haus coalition remained more inclusive and continuously expanded its issues of concern. The coalition experienced greater success with networking, coordination, cooperation, and collaboration.

Additionally, assessing, planning, and evaluating were determined to be at high levels in the Friedens Haus coalition. In addition to grant requirements for these procedures, the leadership and staff felt a need to assess, plan, and evaluate in order to continually improve and expand community services. Friedens Haus improved these procedures during the period of 1993 to 1995 through a grant providing for an outside evaluation. Evaluation results indicated that this effective organization needed to separate administrative from programmatic functions in order to continuously grow.

Assessments and evaluations of the Friedens Haus coalition for the year 1993–94 included focus group sessions conducted for this study with teachers, parents, and the Friedens Haus Advisory board. Results indicated overwhelmingly positive perceptions focused on the "high touch" and "real caring" qualities of the program. Areas for improvement centered around providing more information about the program to teachers, increased parent involvement with the education of their children, added social services for parents, additional resident participation on decision-making bodies, and, most importantly, increased funding and staffing in order to expand the program. Quantitative data indicated improvements in student test scores, report card grades, attendance, and social and emotional growth.

Finally, the theme of citizen/community empowerment/locus of control runs throughout this book whether it be empowerment of community members in toto or individual citizens. Several Hyde Park community members were articulate in expressing that locus of control must remain with communities and individual residents for effective problem-solving to take place. Outside agencies, service providers, and officials coming in to "better" communities diminishes the ability of communities and residents to maintain control.

In Hyde Park, the control issue was a continuous struggle. There were community residents who exhibited strong abilities to lead their neighbors in improving community life with the *support* and *assistance* of service providers. Viable community programs and efforts should have been added to and built upon instead of "change agents" coming in to "reinvent the wheel." As William Raspberry writes, "Treat people primarily as clients, as consumers of social services, and they become better, more-demanding consumers. Devise ways to involve them and their neighbors in solving their own problems and they become more expert problem solvers and better neighbors" (1992: 4B). However, to effect positive social change, it was concluded that it takes a citizenry who is aware, organized, willing to act, and believes in its inherent collective power.

Although there remained the issue of relinquishing control on the part of church members, funding agencies, and the private social service agency, the Friedens Haus coalition was found to be the core of a community education program that could also serve as a model for St. Louis and the nation as a comprehensive approach to addressing both background and foreground causes of criminal behavior. As one community resident expressed, "We can't just keep painting it [graffiti] out without getting at the cancer. We'll keep painting—we'll keep painting—we'll keep painting."

The author acknowledges that this type of comprehensive community education program cannot have a *direct* impact on American institutions that reflect our culture and embody institutionalized racism except at the margins by encouraging political awareness and action, critical thinking in educational endeavors, and inclusion of all community members in problem-solving efforts. Conversely, this model of community education *can* directly address other background causes of criminal behavior by focusing on deteriorating family conditions associated with correlates to crime such as unemployment, female-headed households, inadequate education, health issues, inadequate housing, lack of economic development, and so on. At the same time, this community education model is able to address the foreground causes of criminal behavior through problem-solving efforts resulting in activities such as citizen mobile patrols, "block watch," and other coordinated efforts with local agencies, organizations, and the police. (See Figure 20.2.)

The Hyde Park Mobile Patrol, with residents patrolling and working closely with policing efforts, addressed foreground causes of criminal behavior such as opportunity and rationalization of cost and benefit. It, therefore, had the possibility of effecting immediate crime deterrence. Conversely, the Friedens Haus coalition focused on addressing the background causes of criminal behavior such as educational, social, and health needs of the community. The citizen patrol may have had more immediate effects at the macro-level (neighborhood) while the Friedens Haus program may have long-term effects at this same level while having immediate effects at the micro-level (individual participants and their families) as shown by student report card and test data; increased student attendance and lower number of discipline referrals; interview generated data; teacher, parent, and advisory board focus group results; program evaluations; and anecdotal accounts. It must be noted that results of proactive problem-solving policing and community efforts to address background causes of criminal behavior could prove a disappointment to several Hyde Park police officers—there may be a reduction of excitement and adventure in the neighborhood.

In summation, the Pulitzer Prize-winning historian, Daniel J. Boorstin, offers

Figure 20.2
Community Education: Confronting Background
and Foreground Causes of Criminal Behavior

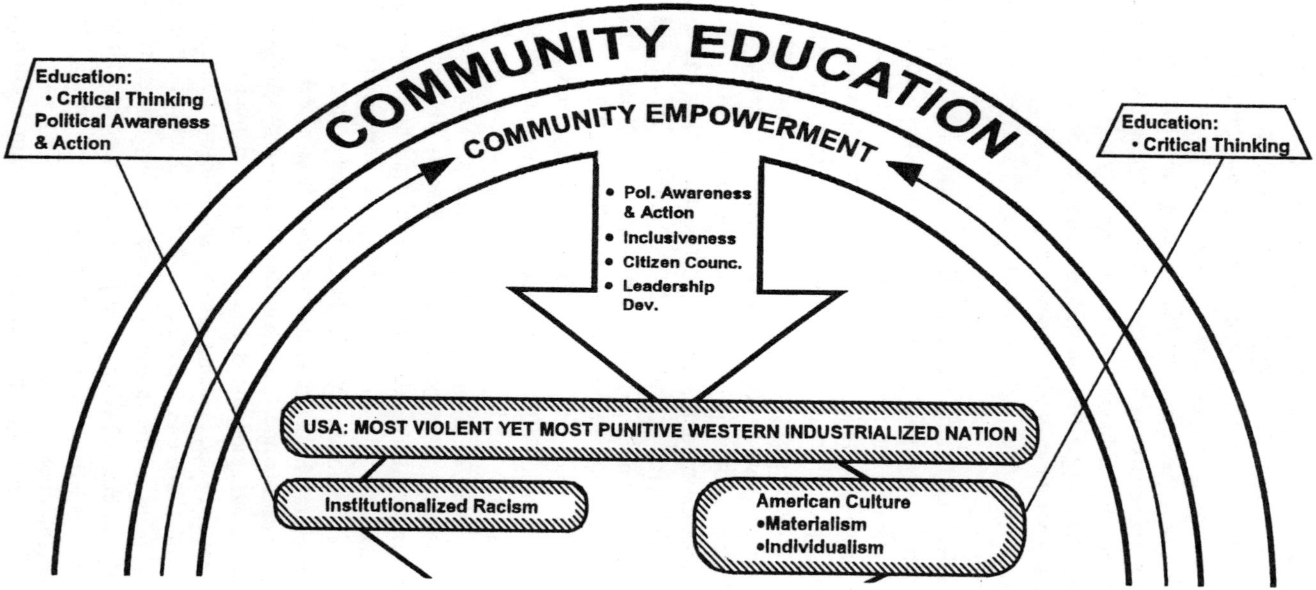

COMMUNITY EDUCATION

COMMUNITY EMPOWERMENT

- Pol. Awareness
  & Action
- Inclusiveness
- Citizen Counc.
- Leadership
  Dev.

USA: MOST VIOLENT YET MOST PUNITIVE WESTERN INDUSTRIALIZED NATION

Institutionalized Racism

American Culture
- Materialism
- Individualism

Education:
- Critical Thinking

Education:
- Critical Thinking
  Political Awareness
  & Action

254

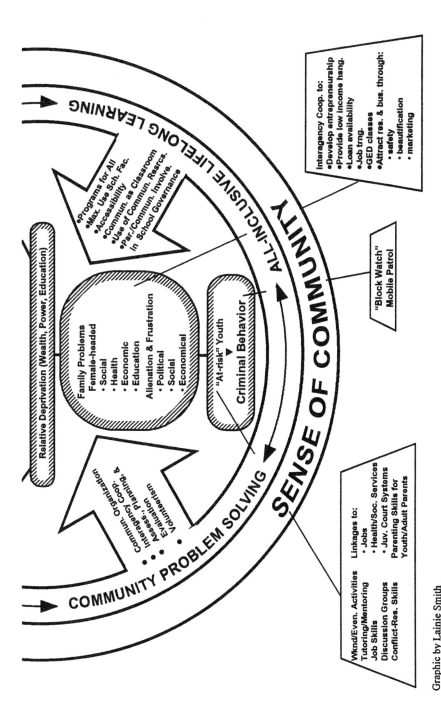

Relative Deprivation (Wealth, Power, Education)

ALL-INCLUSIVE LIFELONG LEARNING

- Programs for All
- Max. Use Sch. Fac.
- Accessibility
- Commun. as Classroom
- Use of Commun. Resrcs.
- Par./Commun. Involve.
  In School Governance

Family Problems
Female-headed
- Social
- Health
- Economic
- Education

Alienation & Frustration
- Political
- Social
- Economical

"At-risk" Youth

Criminal Behavior

Interagency Coop. to:
- Develop entrepreneurship
- Provide low income hsng.
- Loan availability
- Job trng.
- GED classes
- Attract res. & bus. through:
  - safety
  - beautification
  - marketing

"Block Watch"
Mobile Patrol

SENSE OF COMMUNITY

- Commun. Organization
- Interagency Coop. &
  Planning
- Assessment
- Evaluation
- Volunteerism

COMMUNITY PROBLEM SOLVING

Wknd/Even. Activities   Linkages to:
Tutoring/Mentoring   • Jobs
Job Skills   • Health/Soc. Services
Discussion Groups   • Juv. Court Systems
Conflict-Res. Skills   Parenting Skills for
                              Youth/Adult Parents

Graphic by Lainie Smith

these words of wisdom: "I think it's time that we reaffirmed the fact that what has built our country is community and that community is not dependent on government. It's dependent on the willingness of people to build together" (Zulc, 1993: 4). Perhaps in a community rife with social, educational, economic, and health problems similar to the Hyde Park neighborhood, the need to build together is deemed essential. For example, community residents must come together to effectively fight crime, help neighbors, and provide for their children. Also, the process portion of community education may be seen as more important in a neighborhood where residents must solve their own problems when governmental policies have failed.

Community education and similar educational philosophies can provide some answers to these perplexing problems. Added to this, the fact that the community education philosophy, processes, and programs are already practiced across the nation, many linked to the National Community Education Association, indicates that there is reason to expand community education models like that found in Hyde Park. Comprehensive community crime prevention initiatives do not have to begin from "ground zero."

Bibliography

Acree, S. (1997). Tax credit could revive neighborhoods. *St. Louis Post-Dispatch.* June 17, 7B.

Associated Press. (1992). *St. Louis Post-Dispatch,* March 23, 9A.

Associated Press. (1997a). Public gets message: economy booming and outlook bright. *St. Louis Post-Dispatch,* May 23, 16A.

Associated Press. (1997b). U.S. lowers barriers to homeownership. *St. Louis Post-Dispatch.* June 13, 5B.

Baldwin, J. (1971). A talk to teachers. *Democratic Legacy in Transition: Perspectives on American Education.* Sturm, J. E. and Palmer, J. A., eds. New York: Van Nostrand Reinhold Co., 284–91.

Barber, B. (1993). America skips school: Why we talk so much about education and do so little. *Harper's Magazine, 287*(1722), 39–46.

Bennett, T. (1987). *An Evaluation of Two Neighbourhood Watch Schemes in London, Executive Summary,* Final Report to the Home Office Research and Planning Unit, London.

Bernard, B. (1987). Protective factor research: What we can learn from resilient children. *Prevention Forum, 8,* 3–10.

Bowles, S., Gorden, D., and Weisskopf, T. (1983). *Beyond the Waste Land: A Democratic Alternative to Economic Decline.* New York: Anchor Press/Doubleday.

Bradley, B. (1992). The real lesson of LA. *Harper's Magazine,* July, 7–8.

Brink, W. and Harris, L. (1967). *Black and White.* New York: Simon and Schuster.

Bryan, B. (1991). Shootings here by police top 10-city study, *St. Louis Post-Dispatch,* October 24, 1C.

Bryan, B. (1995). Leader of officers group says race important in chief choice, *St. Louis Post-Dispatch,* December 5, 4A.

Bryan, B. and Little, J. (1993). Student, 17, fatally shot at Sumner. *St. Louis Post-Dispatch,* March 25, 1A.

Caroll, S., Donaldson, T., Kiesling, H., and Pincus, J. (1974). *How Effective is Schooling? A Critical Review of Research.* Englewood Cliffs, N. J.: Educational Technology Publications: The Rand Corporation.

Castleman, M. (1984). *Crime Free.* New York: Simon and Schuster.

Centers for Disease Control and Prevention. (1994). *Morbidity and Mortality Weekly Report:* 726.

Chrislip, D. and Larsen, C. (1994). *Collaborative Leadership: How Citizens and Civic Leaders Can Make a Difference.* San Francisco: Jossey-Bass.

Christenson, R. (1990). Rich-poor gap has become a canyon. *St. Louis Post-Dispatch,* January 30, 3C.

Cirel, P., Evans, P., McGillis, D., and Whitcomb, D. (1977). *Community Crime Prevention Programme in Seattle: An Exemplary Project.* Washington, D.C.: U.S. Government Printing Office.

Clapp, E. (1939). *Community Schools in Action.* New York: Viking Press.

Clark, K. (1970). The interests of the privileged are at stake. In *Social Science and National Policy,* ed. F. Harris. New York: Aldine Publishing, 21–24.

Coates R. (1987). Social service and citizen involvement. In *Handbook on Crime and Delinquency Prevention,* ed. E. Johnson. Westport, CT: Greenwood Press.

Cohen, A. (1962). The bottom of the heap: Problems of the working class boy. In *Man Alone: Alienation in Modern Society,* eds. E. and M. Josephson. New York: Dell Publishing, 373–87.

Community Development Agency (1993). *Neighborhood Demographic Profiles: City of St. Louis, 1990.*

Community Schools Review Panel Report. (1993). *St. Louis Public Schools Community Education Needs Assessment,* March–April.

Conference on Education. (1993). *Conference on Education's Community Involvement Project 1990–1993.* Unpublished Report and Recommendations. St. Louis.

Congressional Quarterly. (1997). Focus on crime control, *St. Louis Post-Dispatch,* May 1, 3A.

ConServ, Operation; St. Louis Development Corporation; Community Development Agency; Hyde Park Residents and Committees (1992). *Hyde Park Neighborhood and Environs Urban Design and Strategic Plan,* October.

Cromwell, P., Olson, J., and Avary, D. (1991). *Breaking and Entering: An Ethnographic Analysis of Burglary.* Newbury Park, CA: Sage.

Cross, T. (1987). *The Black Power Imperative: Racial Inequality and the Politics of Nonviolence.* New York: Faulkner Books.

Currie, E. (1985). *Confronting Crime: An American Challenge.* New York: Pantheon Books.

Currie, E. (1988). Two visions of community crime prevention. In *Communities and Crime Reduction,* eds. T. Hope and M. Shaw. London: Home Office Research and Planning Unit.

Davidson, L. (1989). Observing a Yang Ch'in lesson: Learning by modeling and metaphor. *Journal of Aesthetic Education, 23*(1), 85–99.

Decker, L. (1980). *Foundations of Community Education*. Charlottesville, VA: Community Collaborators.

Decker, L. and Schoeny, D. (1983). *Community, Educational and Social Impact Perspectives*. Charlottesville, VA: University of Virginia Press.

Decker, S. and Smith, D. (1992). No single solution for gang problem. *St. Louis Post-Dispatch*, October 9, 3C.

Decker, S., Kohfeld, C., Rosenfeld, R., and Sprague, J. (1991). *St. Louis Homicide Project: Local Responses to a National Problem*. A report made to the community on March 22–23, Kiel Auditorium, St. Louis, MO: University of Missouri-St. Louis.

DeJong, W. and Goolkasian, G. (1982). *The Neighborhood Fight Against Crime: The Midwood Kings Highway Development Corporation*. New York: Office of Development, Testing and Dissemination, National Institute of Justice.

Dewey, J. (1933). *How We Think* (revised edition). Boston: Heath Publishers.

Dolbeare, K. (1974). *Political Change in the United States: A Framework for Analysis*. New York: McGraw-Hill.

Doleschal, E. (1984). *Prevention of Crime and Delinquency*. Davis, CA: International Dialogue Press.

Edelman, P. and Radin, B. (1991). *Saving Children and Families Effectively*, monograph. Washington, D.C.: Institute for Educational Leadership.

English, F. and Kaufman, R. (1975). *Needs Assessment: A Focus for Curriculum Development*. Washington, D.C.: Association for Supervision and Curriculum Development.

Fantini, M. (1983). Changing concepts of education: From school system to educational system. In *Community, Educational, and Social Impact Perspectives*, eds. Schoeny and Decker. Charlottesville, VA: University of Virginia Press, 25–46.

Federal Bureau of Investigation. (1990). *Uniform Crime Reports*. Washington, D.C.: U.S. Government Printing Office.

Federal Bureau of Investigation. (1994). *The Sentencing Project*. Washington, D.C.: Bureau of Justice Statistics.

Federal Bureau of Investigation. (1995). *Uniform Crime Reports*. Washington, D.C.: U.S. Government Printing Office.

Foster, W. (1986). *Paradigms and Promises: New Approaches to Educational Administration*. New York: Prometheus Books.

Fowles, R. (1996). Harpers index, *Harper's Magazine, 299*(1761), 13.

Freeman, G. (1993). Racism column ruffled feathers, *St. Louis Post-Dispatch*, December 10, 9D.

Gardner, J. (1990). *On Leadership*. New York: The Free Press.

Garrow, D. (1986). *Bearing the Cross: Martin Luther King, Jr. and the Southern Christian Leadership Conference*. New York: Morrow.

Geason, S. and Wilson, P. (1989). *Designing Out Crime: Crime Prevention Through Environmental Design*. Canberra, Australia: Australian Institute of Criminology.

Gillham, J. (1992). *Preventing Residential Burglary: Toward More Effective Community Programs*. New York: Springer-Verlag.

Glasser, I. (1992). Talking liberties. *Civil Liberties, 375*, Winter. New York.

Glickman, C. (1985). *Supervision of Instruction: A Developmental Approach*. Boston: Allyn and Bacon.

Glidden, D. (1990). Feeling good about self-esteem. *Los Angeles Times* as cited in the *St. Louis Post-Dispatch*, March 4, 3B.

Goldstein, H. (1990). *Problem-Oriented Policing*. Philadelphia: Temple University Press.

Goodman, E. (1997). Kids at risk after school, *St. Louis Post-Dispatch*, April 10, 7B.

Grier, W. and Cobbs, P. (1968). *Black Rage*. New York: Basic Books.

Hamburg, D. (1997). Inside the money chase, *The Nation*, May 5, 1997, reprinted in *Harper's Magazine*, July, 1997.

Harper's Magazine. (1996). Does America still work? On the turbulent energies of the new capitalism. *292*(1752), 35–48.

Harper's Index (1991). *Harper's Magazine, 284*(893), 2.

Harper's Index (1992). *Harper's Magazine, 285*(1709), 2.

Hart, J. (1924). *The Discovery of Intelligence*. New York: The Century Company.

Herzberg, F. (1968). One more time: How do you motivate employees? *Harvard Business Review*, January-February, 53–62.

Herzberg, F., Mausner, B., and Snyderman, B. (1959). *The Motivation to Work*. New York: Wiley Press.

Himmelman, A. (1992). *Communities Working Collaboratively for a Change*. Minneapolis, MN: The HIMMELMAN Consulting Group.

Holleman, J. (1994). Study urges city to shift emphasis, *St. Louis Post-Dispatch*, January 22, 4B.

Holmes Group. (1990). *Tomorrow's Schools: Principles for the Design of Professional Development Schools*. East Lansing, MI: Author.

Hope, T. and Shaw, M. (1988). *Community Approaches to Reducing Crime: Communities and Crime Reduction*. London: Home Office Research and Planning Unit.

Howe, H. (1993). *Thinking About Our Kids*. New York: Free Press.

Hoy, W. and Miskel, C. (1987). *Educational Administration: Theory, Research, and Practice*, 3rd ed. New York: Random House.

Hutchinson, E. (1990). *The Mugging of Black America*. Chicago: African American Images.

Johns, R. and Kimbrough, R. (1968). *The Relationship of Socio-economic Factors, Educational Leadership Patterns, and Elements of Community Power Structure to Local School Fiscal Policy*. Washington, D.C.: Bureau of Research, Office of Education, HEW.

Johnson, E. (1987). *Handbook on Crime and Delinquency Prevention*. Westport, CT: Greenwood Press.

Jones, E. and Horn, J. (1985). *The Hyde Park Partnership: Summary of Activities and Research*, unpublished manuscript, St. Louis, MO: University of Missouri-St. Louis.

Josephson, E. and Josephson, M. (1962). *Man Alone: Alienation in Modern Society*. New York: Dell.

Kant, I. (1963). *Lectures on Ethics*. New York: Harper & Row.

Katz, J. (1988). *Seductions of Crime: Moral   and Sensual Attractions in Doing Evil*. New York: Basic Books.

Kennedy, R. (1997). *Race, Crime, and the Law*. New York: Pantheon Books.

Kerensky, V. M. (1989). *The Sovereign: New Perspectives on People, Power and Public Education*. Dubuque, IA: Kendall/Hunt.

Kerensky, V. and Melby, E. (1971). *Education II—The Social Imperative*. Midland, MI: Pendell.

King, M. (1968). A new kind of power. In *Man Against Poverty: World War III*, eds. A. Blaustein and R. Woock. New York: Random House, 192–203.

Kliminski, G. and Keyes, S. (1983).   Reactions to the DeJong and Gardner Paper. In *Community, Educational, and Social Impact Perspectives*, eds. Schoeny and Decker. Charlottesville, VA: University of Virginia Printing Office.

Knezevich, S. (1984). *Administration of Public Education: A Sourcebook for the Leadership and Management of Educational Institutions* (4th ed.).   New York: Harper & Row.

Knowles, M. (1975). *Self Directed Learning*. Chicago: Follett Publishing.

Knowles, M. (1986). *Using Learning Contracts*. San Francisco: Jossey-Bass.

Lapham, L. (1992). City lights. *Harper's Magazine, 285*(1706), 6–9.

Ledewitz, B. (1992).   Why family values faltered: Capitalism. *St. Louis Post-Dispatch*, October 8, 3C.

Linsalata, P. and Novak, T. (1991).   Spent effort: City, HUD at loggerheads over charges of misuse of federal block grant funds. *St. Louis Post-Dispatch*, December 9, 1A.

Litonjua, B. and Hacker, A. (1992).   Two nations: One white, one black. *St. Louis Post-Dispatch*, April 20, 5C.

Litwak, E. and Meyer, H. (1974). *School, Family, and Neighborhood: The Theory and Practice of School-Community Relations*. New York: Columbia University Press.

Lurigio, A. and Rosenbaum, D. (1986). Community crime prevention: A critical look at programme evaluation in the field, In *Community Crime Prevention: Does it Work?* ed. D. Rosenbaum. Beverly Hills, CA: Sage.

Manley, C., Reed, J., Bernard, W., and Burns, R. (1961). *The Community School in Action: The Flint Program*. Chicago: The University of Chicago Press.

Maslow, A. (1954). *Motivation and Personality*. New York: Harper & Row.

Mathews, D. (1996).   Why we need to change our concept of community leadership. *Community Education Journal, XXIII*(1/2), 9–18.

McCall, N. (1994). *Makes Me Wanna Holler: A Young Black Man in America*. New York: Random House.

McCarty, D. and Ramsey, C. (1971). *The School Managers*. Westport, CT: Greenwood Press.

McClellan, W. (1995a). The smart money wasn't very smart, *St Louis Post-Dispatch*, December 6, 1E.

McClellan, W. (1995b). Mea culpa, '95: Trying to get it right, this time, *St. Louis Post-Dispatch*, December 31, 1E.

Merriam, S. (1988). *Case Study Research in Education: A Qualitative Approach.* San Francisco: Jossey-Bass.

Messner, S. and Rosenfeld, R. (1993). *Crime and the American Dream.* Belmont, CA: Wadsworth Publishing.

Metz, N. (1983). Sources of constructive social relationships in an urban magnet school. *American Journal of Education, 91*, 202–42.

Meyers, D. (1992). Don't overlook the social recession. *St. Louis Post-Dispatch*, June 3, 3B.

Michener, J. (1992). We can create a decent society. *Parade Magazine*, November 24.

Minzey, J. (1974). It takes people to make it happen, *Community Education Journal*, January–February.

Minzey, J. (1978). Community education: An overview, *The Journal of Alternative Human Services*, Spring.

Minzey, J. and LeTarte, C. (1979). *Community Education: From Program To Process To Practice: The School's Role in a New Educational Society.* Midland, MI: Pendell.

Minzey, J. and LeTarte, C. (1994). *Reforming Public Schools Through Community Education.* Dubuque, IA: Kendall/Hunt.

Miringoff, M. (1992). *Index of Social Health.* Fordham Institute for Innovation in Social Policy.

Moe, R. (1996). Progress without sprawl: Planning can maximize land use, prevent waste, *St. Louis Post-Dispatch,* December 12, 3B.

Monti, D. (1985). *A Semblance of Justice: St. Louis School Desegregation and Order in Urban America.* Columbia, MO: University of Missouri Press.

Moynihan, P. (1965). *The Negro Family: The Case for National Action.* Washington, D.C.: Office of Policy Planning and Research, U. S. Department of Labor.

NAACP sets advanced goals. (1954). *New York Times*, May 18, 16.

Nader, R. (1996). *The Monitor.* Washington, D.C.

Nance, E. (1996). Evaluating restructuring efforts: The St . Louis experience. *Community Education Journal, XXIII*(4), 4–11.

Nance, E. and Dixon, J. (1980). Community education and the urban dilemma. *Community Education Journal, VIII*(1), 13–17.

Nance, E. and Foggy, M. (1992). Economic imperatives for minority communities: A community education perspective. *Community Education Journal, XX*(1), 22–28.

O'Connor, C. (1997). Are we more than the sum of our genes? *Washington University Magazine and Alumni News, 67*(3), 10–15.

Office of Juvenile Justice and Delinquency Prevention. (1994). *Juvenile Court Statistics 1993.* Washington, D.C.: U.S. Government Printing Office.

Page, C. (1993). NAFTA supporters must protect blacks, *St. Louis Post-Dispatch,* November 8, 15B.

Pajak, E. and Seyfarth, J. (1983). Authentic supervision reconciles the irreconcilables, *Educational Leadership, 40*(8), 20–23.

Palmer, P. (1978). *Burglary Prevention: Inmate Interview Project.* Lakewood, CO: Lakewood Department of Public Safety.

Parish. (1997) Murphy Park: New complex offers public housing hope. *St. Louis Post-Dispatch.* June 1, 1A.

Parson, S. and Halperin, S. (1983). Reactions to the Iannaccone Paper. In *Community, Educational, and Social Impact Perspectives*, eds. Schoeny and Decker. Charlottesville, VA: University of Virginia Printing Office.

Peirce, N. and Johnson, C.. (1997). *The Peirce Report: A Call to Action.* A report submitted to the *St. Louis Post-Dispatch,* The Regional Commerce and Growth Association, and the William T. Kemper Foundation.

Piaget, J. (1962). *Play, Dreams and Imitation in Childhood.* New York: Norton.

Podolefsky, A. (1983). *Case Studies in Community Crime Prevention.* Springfield, IL: Charles C. Thomas.

Posavac, E. and Carey, R. (1972). *Program Methods and Case Studies.* Englewood Cliffs, CA: Prentice Hall.

Project Respond (1993). *The Children of Metropolitan St . Louis: A Report to the Community*, April.

Raspberry, W. (1992). Let neighborhoods tackle social issues. *St. Louis Post-Dispatch,* February 21, 4B.

Redden, G. (1993). Children are not resilient: A commentary. *St. Louis Post-Dispatch,* August 16, 7B.

Ringers, J. (1976). *Community/Schools and Interagency Programs: A Guide.* Midland, MI: Pendell.

Rogers, C. (1969). *Freedom to Learn.* Columbus, OH: Merrill Publishing.

Rosenbaum, D. (1988). A critical eye on neighbourhood watch; does it reduce crime and fear? In *Communities and Crime Reduction,* eds. T. Hope and M. Shaw. London: Home Office Research and Planning Unit.

Rosenberg, G. (1991). *The Hollow Hope: Can Courts Bring About Social Change?* Chicago: The University of Chicago Press.

Rosenfeld, R. (1989). Different levels, common causes: St. Louis homicide rates in national perspective. In *St. Louis Homicide Project: Local Responses to a National Problem.* St. Louis, MO: University of Missouri-St. Louis, 1–4.

Rusk, D. (1993). Focus on metropolitan reform. *Newsday*, reprinted in *St. Louis Post-Dispatch,* June 13, 3B.

Sawyer, J. (1997). Europe on the edge, *St. Louis Post-Dispatch.* June 22, 1B.

Schlinkmann, M. (1991). Report card: Region gets low grades compared with similar cities in interim study. *St. Louis Post-Dispatch,* October 23, 6A.

Seay, M. and Crawford, F. (1954). *The Community School and Community Self-Improvement: A Review of the Michigan Community School Service Program, July 1, 1945 to October 1, 1953 by Lansing, Michigan*; Clair L. Taylor, Superintendent of Public Instruction.

Shalala, D. (1993). Band together to fight violence. *St. Louis Post-Dispatch,* December 16, 11B.

Sherman, L. (1997). *Congressional Quarterly* as reported in the *St. Louis Post-Dispatch,* Focus on: Crime control, May 1, 3A.

Shirk, M. (1993). Bold vision for children in trouble. *St. Louis Post-Dispatch*, May 23, 1B.

Shirk, M. (1994). Juvenile injustice. *St. Louis Post-Dispatch*, May 1, 2, and 3, 1A.

Sixty Minutes. (1994). The Chief. January 9, CBS News.

Sklar, H. (1996). Dr. King's message of economic justice: Commentary. *St. Louis Post-Dispatch*. January 15, 1B.

Skogan, W. and Maxfield, M. (1981). *Coping with Crime: Individual and Neighborhood Reactions*. Beverly Hills, CA: Sage.

Smith, B. and Gillerman, M. (1992). Slain baby called gang-feud victim. *St. Louis Post-Dispatch*, September 20, 1A.

Sorkin, M. (1994). Aces got brawler on police force, *St. Louis Post-Dispatch*. June 5, 1A.

Sprinthall, N. and Thies-Sprinthall, L. (1983). The teacher as an adult learner: A cognitive-developmental view. In *Staff Development: Eighty-second Yearbook of the National Society for the Study of Education, Part II*, ed. G. Griffin. Chicago: The University of Chicago Press, 13–35.

Squires, G. D. (1992). Enterprise zones don't work. *St. Louis Post-Dispatch*, June 29, 3B.

St. Louis Metropolitan Police Department. (1991). *Information Service*. St. Louis, MO: St. Louis Metropolitan Police Department.

St. Louis Metropolitan Police Department. (1993). *Information Service*. St. Louis, MO: St. Louis Metropolitan Police Department.

St. Louis Post-Dispatch. (1990). Factionalized school board. October 17, 3A.

St. Louis Post-Dispatch. (1991). Slum landlord. January 13–17, 1A.

St. Louis Post-Dispatch. (1994a). Overall, Section 8 is good program, February 3, 6B.

St. Louis Post-Dispatch. (1994b). A first step toward affordable housing, March 23, 2B.

St. Louis Post-Dispatch. (1995). Conference Asks: Is Crime Genetic in Origin? September, 23, 13B.

Sturz, H. (1971). Interviewed for the *New York Times* in *Our Cities Burn While We Play Cops and Robbers* by Bernard Botein, 1972. New York: Simon and Schuster.

Sumption, M. and Engstrom, Y. (1966). *School-Community Relations: A New Approach*. New York: McGraw-Hill.

Taub, R. and Taylor, D. (1982). *Crime, Fear of Crime, and the Deterioration of Urban Neighborhoods*. Washington, D.C.: U.S. Government Printing Office.

Taylor, D. (1965). Decision-making and problem-solving. *Handbook of Organizations*, (J. G. March edition). Chicago: Rand McNally, 48–86.

Titus, R. (1984). Residential burglary and the community response. In *Coping with Burglary*, eds. R. Clarke and T. Hope. Boston: Kluwer-Nijhoff.

Todd, C. (1994a). Housing subsidies set off exodus: City homeowners want changes in U.S. program. *St. Louis Post-Dispatch*, March 18, 1A.

Todd, C. (1994b). City, county launch housing program. *St. Louis Post-Dispatch*, April 20, 1A.

Todd, C. and Holleman, J. (1993). Task force has ideas for housing. *St. Louis Post-Dispatch*, September 26, 1A.

Totten, F. (1970). *The Power of Community Education.* Midland, MI: Pendell.

Trojanowicz, J., Trojanowicz, R., and Moss, F. (1975). *Community Based Crime Prevention.* Pacific Palisades, CA: Goodyear.

United States Department of the Census. (1990). *Country and City Data Book.* Washington, D.C.: United States Department of the Census.

United States Department of the Census. (1995). *Country and City Data Book.* Washington, D.C.: United States Department of the Census.

United States Department of Justice, Bureau of Justice Statistics. (1994). *Sourcebook of Criminal Justice Statistics.* Washington D.C.: U.S. Government Printing Office.

Walker, J. (1968). A critique of the elitist theory of democracy. In *Public Opinion and Public Policy: Models of Political Linkage,* ed. N. Luttberg. Homewood, IL: The Dorsey Press, 454–67.

Warden, J. (1979). *Process Perspectives: Community Education as Process.* Charlottesville, VA.: Mid Atlantic Consortium for Community Education.

Weiss, R. (1987). The community and prevention, In *Handbook on Crime and Delinquency Prevention,* ed. E. Johnson, Westport, CT: Greenwood Press.

Werner, E. and Smith, R. (1982). *Vulnerable But Invincible: A Study of Resilient Children.* New York: McGraw Hill.

Wilson, J. (1985). *Thinking About Crime.* New York: Vintage Books.

Wilson, J. and Kelling, G. (1982). Broken windows. *Atlantic Monthly.* March, 19–38.

Wilson, W. (1987). *The Truly Disadvantaged: The Inner City, the Underclass, and Public Policy.* Chicago: The University of Chicago Press.

Winecoff, L. and Powell, C. (1977). Community involvement: A model for systematic planning. In *Planning and Assessment in Community Education,* eds. H. Burback and L. Decker. Midland, MI: Pendell.

Winright, T. (1995). The perpetrator as person: Theological reflections on the just war tradition and the use of force by police. *Criminal Justice Ethics, 14*(2), 37–56.

Wirt, F. and Kirst, M. (1989). *The Politics of Education: Schools in Conflict,* 2nd ed. Berkeley, CA: McCutchan.

Wood, G. (1977). Community Education as a Multi-System Operation, Unpublished. Muncie, IN: Ball State University, Institute for Community Education Development.

Wright, R. and Decker, S. (1994). *Burglars on the Job: Street Life and Residential Break-ins.* Boston: Northeastern University Press.

Wyson, W. et al. (1988). *Handbook for Developing Confidence in Schools.* Bloomington, IL: Phi Delta Kappa Educational Foundation.

Yaquib, R. (1996). Funeral procession circles city police station in protest, *St. Louis Post-Dispatch,* January 13, 1B.

Yeager, W. (1939). *Home - School in Community Relations.* Pittsburgh: University of Pittsburgh.

Young, D. (1983). *Where We Live: Hyde Park.* St. Louis, MO: Missouri Historical Society.

Zulc, T. (1993). The greatest danger we face. *Parade Magazine,* July 25, 4–7.

Index

About the Author

CAROLYN SIEMENS WARD is a member of the National Community Education Association and has taught graduate courses in the community education field. She has been a consultant for schools, school districts, colleges/universities, nonprofit organizations, and a desegregation monitoring committee.